Always
the Music

How a lifelong passion
framed a future for orchestras

Thomas W. Morris

"Tom Morris offers both inspiration and counsel — and sometimes a bracing but refreshing bucket of icy cold water — for arts presenters seeking to maintain vitality and relevance in our rapidly ever-changing world." – Ashley Capps, founder of
Big Ears Festival

"You hold in your hand a treasure trove of insights, reflections, predictions and even divinations — as well as a hearty dose of scintillating industry tales! Like the author himself, the book is full of grace and wisdom and exuberant optimism. Every musician and music lover must read it." – Claire Chase, flutist, founder of International Contemporary Ensemble, founder of Density Arts

"Across his lifelong adventure in music, Tom Morris partnered with some of the most inspired and inspiring personalities to bring forth exquisitely provocative programs that overwhelmed audiences with their beauty and power. If there is one book to read about music, one book that captures the human alchemy that makes a great orchestra or festival tick, this is it." – Jim Collins, author, Good to Great

"Tom Morris's fascinating, inspiring book is chock full of crucial life lessons and vivid anecdotes. Layered with rich insights and big-picture takeaways, this book feels like the education we need: an invaluable tour through the last several decades of the classical music business, and a helpful set of suggestions for its future."
– Vijay Iyer, pianist, composer, Harvard University faculty

"Morris is now the universally respected sage of the classical music world without having lost any of his mischievous and at times almost anarchic sense of humor. *Always the Music* shows us why we need provocateurs such as him in a business that so easily goes stale and tends to take itself too seriously way too often."
– Esa-Pekka Salonen, conductor, composer

"Chapter after captivating chapter, Morris opens the door to his deeply personal friendships with musical luminaries as well as the next generation's pioneers. In doing so, he reveals his undiminished curiosity, passion and optimism for classical music's future. Ultimately, his career is a roadmap for anyone wanting to understand what service leadership looks like in music and the arts." – Chad Smith, President and CEO of the Boston Symphony

To Bapop – for igniting the fuse

To Jane – for nurturing the burn

CONTENTS

Cover art:
The music manuscript on the front cover is from Oliver Knussen's 70th-birthday gift to the
author. It is reproduced in full on page 73.

FOREWORD

Tom Morris is a visionary in the classical music world, having managed two of the most successful American orchestras, The Cleveland and Boston Symphony Orchestras — only two of the many hats he has worn over more than half a century of service to classical music. I first met Tom in 2002 when he hired me as a young soprano soloist with The Cleveland Orchestra, but our friendship really got going in 2010, just as I was about to start my conducting career. 15 years later, we are on the phone at least once a week and meeting several times a year, talking repertoire, programming, always deeply connected by a shared love of music.

Whether in London, Hamburg, Paris or New York, enjoying a fantastic meal together was always very important at the end of long days of work. I remember one dinner in Chicago in the early days in our friendship, when I referred to him as a mentor. And Tom said, "Well, I'd rather you think of me as a friend." On the one hand, I can't help but think of him as a mentor because I admire and respect him so much, and I am so eager to learn from every moment I have with him. On the other hand, our friendship is paramount to me, and Tom has stood by me for difficult moments in life. I remember when he had his cat Basil "write" me a very touching letter of condolence when my beloved cat Monty was hit by a car. Indeed, our relationship is outside the box, and there is no one word to define it, so I invented a new one for him: "Friendtor."

Tom's boundless curiosity astounds me: he always wants to know about new composers and musicians, and to hear new pieces. Even this morning, he sent me a text about a unique singer-composer he'd just heard in Norway. He is incredibly generous in sharing his knowledge. And he celebrates the successful implementation of a great idea, wherever it came from. I particularly love how our having differing opinions usually leads to amazing solutions which have nothing to do with compromise and everything to do with creativity.

On top of his incredible drive and a lifetime of hard work, there is always room for a joke. We certainly have laughed, hard.

Tom invited me to be the guest curator of the 2019 Ojai Festival, where he held the position of artistic director for over 15 years. This incredible 4-day event, is, as the *New York Times* writes, "a utopia where open-minded audiences welcome adventurous works presented against a backdrop of green hills, bird song and Pixie tangerines." Every year a different artist is invited to work closely with the artistic director to put their own stamp on that year's festival. From top to tail, we worked for almost 5 years to put the 2019 edition together. We would meet in person, 2 to 4 times a year for several days of planning, working from overall structure to the most minute of details. Sometimes we'd just tweak the order of a program we knew was a winner, and other times, scrap a whole concert because we had an even better idea and couldn't let it go. Tom knows how to put things together and how to put people together, just like he loves to build extravagant and complex Lego-like structures with his grand-kids.

On a constant learning curve working with Tom in this way, I learned about what could be achieved collectively. He was so free-thinking and yet so organized! He was in his element, sparkling with ideas as we dug into research, repertoire, flexibility, all the while trying to keep in mind the preparations and demands on myself as singer and conductor, and on everyone involved once the festival would actually get underway. We tried to stay realistic but dream big at the same time, a state of being you'll read about a lot in this book. Keep an eye out for the acronym BHAG! A meeting with Tom was always a masterclass: exhausting and invigorating in equal measure, and our resulting 2019 Ojai Festival embodied those same two adjectives, which was more or less what we were going for.

Tom and I continue to talk as much as we always did. Even more, actually. It was only a few weeks into March 2020, when he started writing *Always the Music* and sent me the first draft of the introduction and a detailed layout of the chapters which were to become this book. Why was I not completely surprised? I found the email he had written me back then, wanting feedback because he was concerned as to whether the book really had promise. I responded: "This is already a compelling read — it's got a beautiful combination of attitude, authority and emotion — it's your personality plus the unbelievable wealth of expertise you have acquired and helped to create in others, and I can't wait to read more, because what reads is YOU — the curiosity and gratitude, also the vast experience/wisdom/knowledge. You've got this. Keep writing."

And keep writing he did, for four years, and the result is this book. The introduction credits Tom's grandfather with recognizing and nurturing little Tommy's love for music, and the final chapters reveal a vision and concrete suggestions for how classical music can not only survive but flourish in the 21st century. Each chapter centres on trust and relationship, be it with an individual, a group of musicians, management teams, or audiences. From the chapter on renowned film composer and conductor John Williams, taking over the Boston Pops when he was barely known as a conductor, to a riveting portrait of timpanist Vic Firth, who played nearly half a century with the Boston Symphony and whose focus and drive translate easily to any trajectory of a celebrated high achiever.

The chapter on Jim Collins is worth the price of admission. Tom is not just one of the many people who read and implemented ideas from Collins' best-selling books, including my favourite *Good to Great*. He recognized the need to know and work directly one-on-one with Collins. So, he made the connection, and the result of their ensuing friendship and work together creates powerful resonances for the classical music industry.

When thinking about whom this book is for, I know musicians and orchestra managements will eat it up. But it is not just for them and has much wider reach: it's for anyone who hungrily cross-references all manner of thinking related to management, leadership, developing ideas, working with teams and achieving audacious goals. Readers don't need to be working in the music industry to enjoy, learn and be inspired from what they'll read on these pages.

It has been infinitely clear from the outset as to why Tom has had the energy to do everything he did and in the way he did it – passion. Passion for music has been the driving force behind all his choices, including the enormous undertaking of writing this book! I can't imagine how he distilled his experiences in music into one volume, with all the memories, friendships and anecdotes he must have had to choose from. That said, Tom has followed his own advice (which he repeats to me frequently): "Keep it simple." With the laser focus for which he is renowned, Tom has managed to bring everything together — his life's work and vision for the future — around his love for music, a singular focus that is always at the heart of the book.

Barbara Hannigan, Nova Scotia, Canada, August 2024

ALWAYS THE MUSIC

INTRODUCTION

"Writing a book is an adventure. To begin with it is a toy and an amusement. And then it becomes a mistress, and then it becomes a master, and then it becomes a tyrant. And the last phase is that just as you are about to be reconciled to your servitude, you kill the monster and fling him about to the public."

—Winston Churchill

On Sunday morning, June 11, 2017, I attended a concert that spoke to me with such singular power that it stands out from all the others I have attended. The music was improvised in a style often called "free jazz," in which performers break down the conventions of regular meters and predictable chord changes. The result was an otherworldly mix of what could seem like bewildering sounds and disjointed musical threads. The performance featured three artists long associated with the Association for the Advancement of Creative Musicians, an organization founded in Chicago in 1965 by a progressive group of African-American musicians grounded in an adventurous mix of avant-garde, jazz, classical and world music. The trio spanned generations — pianist Muhal Richard Abrams, one of AACM's founders, was 87; multi-instrumentalist Roscoe Mitchell, a founding member, was 77; and composer-trombonist George Lewis, who chronicled its history,[1] was 65. The event was one of the many I programmed that year as part of the California's Ojai Music Festival.

What transpired that morning was unexpected and transformative, an event that spoke to me with blinding coherence and impact. It was music at once most experimental and most familiar, most jar-

---

1 Lewis, George, *A Power Stronger Than Itself: The AACM and American Experimental Music*, The University of Chicago Press, 2008.

ring and most calming, most unrestrained and most disciplined. It had an elemental purity, with nothing extraneous to three seasoned artists bringing to bear all of their experience and artistry to make music that was both timeless and immediate, intimately creating sonic magic in real time. It proved that the new is not the exclusive province of the young, as creative innovation is anchored in the traditions of past yet molded in the vitality of the present. It was an occasion of total unity between performer, music, audience, setting and context — the concert toward which my entire life had led me.[2]

This event seems an improbable apex of a long career steeped in traditional classical music. Why did this concert and those artists so hypnotize an orchestra junkie like me? What opened my mind to these surprising new musical sounds, why and how? Was it just evolving taste and experience or were there underlying societal changes occurring that affected how I perceived and viewed music? How did this different sphere of creativity inform my views today?

The search for answers to these questions lies at the heart of this book. Looking today at the ways my ambitions evolved in the positions I held and work I did, I see logic in how following my instincts created the path that dramatically opened my ears and expanded my tastes. Living that journey through multiple musical worlds provided experiential understanding of the gulf that exists today between the rigid, institutionalized culture of orchestras and the fragmented world of creativity around them, giving me perspectives on how the two might be reconciled.

I am a musical omnivore with broad tastes and insatiable curiosity. I have had a fulfilling lifetime of first-hand participation in the magical experience of live music through attending performances, performing in concerts, collaborating with great artists and running world-class organizations. At the center of my journey has always been an obsession with music, a passion instilled in me as a child growing up in Rochester, New York, under the primary influence of my grandfather.

M. Herbert Eisenhart was an immensely successful businessman, having been a top executive in the early days of the Eastman Kodak Company and then CEO of the Bausch & Lomb Optical Company. He was an elegant presence, soft-spoken, patient, kind and

---

2 The concert can be viewed in the 2017 video archives section of the Ojai Music Festival website, ojaifestival.org.

always genuinely interested in whomever he was with. Called Bapop by the family (a name coined by my older cousin's first attempts to say "grandpop"), he drank his daily scotch, smoked, never did an ounce of exercise and lived a full life to age 91. He was a respected community leader, serving as chair of both the University of Rochester board and the Eastman School of Music governing board, and was a major force behind the Rochester Philharmonic. Though not a musician himself, he appreciated music greatly. My grandmother was the more musical of the couple, but it was Bapop who was the quiet-yet-dominant influence on me.

They lived in a grand house that contained an Aeolian-Skinner pipe-organ. It had a mechanical device much like a player piano

M. Herbert Eisenhart, aka "Bapop"

that would "play" music, triggered by moving rolls of paper on which the notes were punched. To me it was exotic and magical. At a very young age, I found the intricate machinery hypnotic and spent hours

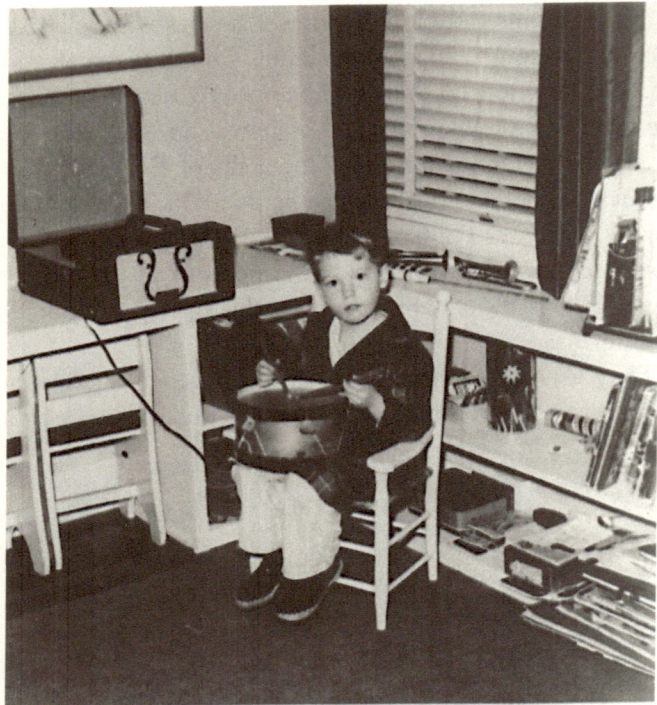

At age 3, when it all started

watching the patterns on the paper as they went by. I learned to climb on a chair to reach the rolls placed on a high shelf and to recognize a few by name. I would play them in endless repetition, transfixed by the majestic sonority of the organ and the sheer magnificence of Bach in particular. And it was there, on that bench in front of the organ, that my intoxication with music began.

I soon started listening to classical recordings — at first those belonging to my grandfather but soon starting my own collection, which included many gifts from him. I became mesmerized by the sonic splendor of an orchestra. Favorite discs were Elgar's *Pomp and Circumstance* March No. 1, the Grand March from Verdi's *Aïda* and Waldteufel's *Skaters' Waltz*, all performed by Arthur Fiedler and the Boston Pops. I got hooked on the glories of band music, John Philip Sousa in particular, and was fixated on *The Stars and Stripes Forever*.

My grandparents bought the seat next to theirs in the front row of the Eastman Theater mezzanine so I could join them at weekly Philharmonic concerts, where I first became seduced by the glories of a live symphonic performance. They later took me to Tanglewood, summer home of the Boston Symphony, introducing to me a world of music-making that far exceeded anything I had experienced in Rochester.

It was because of Sousa marches that I began playing percussion. I spent hours beating on a small drum along with those scratchy 78s, pretending to be one of the performers. My grandfather introduced me to William Street, percussion teacher at the Eastman School and the Philharmonic's timpanist, from whom I started taking private lessons at age eight.

And it was my grandfather who, when I was fourteen, gave me my first pair of Avedis Zildjian cymbals, instruments I was drawn to early and which continue to fascinate me today. A year later and at his urging, I attended Interlochen's National Music Camp — a summer that fundamentally changed my life, immersing me in real orchestras

Performing Milhaud's Percussion Concerto in 1961

and bands performing major pieces that I would never have thought possible. I was totally hooked.

My grandfather was always there as my passion continued to blossom, encouraging and nurturing me. So many fundamental building blocks that would later prove critical were initiated through him in those early years — percussion, concerts, orchestras, band music, Bach, Sousa, Tanglewood, the Boston Symphony and Boston Pops, Fiedler, recordings, and cymbals.

Performing was my initial calling, but I feared early on it would not provide enough stimulation as my life's central thread, particularly within the narrow confines of playing the orchestral repertoire. Thank goodness for this insight. Although I continued to do some performing on the side throughout my career, working in management, while keeping me immersed in classical music, seemed to provide a far broader canvas of challenges as well as opportunities for having greater impact.

To my wonderment, I landed my first job in the business office of my dream orchestra, the Boston Symphony, at age 25. After a dizzying series of unexpected promotions, I suddenly found myself — enthusiastic and driven but woefully ill-prepared — running the organization less than ten years later. While heady and all-consuming, that position's pre-supposed glories waned and, after seven years, I left. Two years working as a consultant deepened my management skills, sharpened my perspectives and reawakened my enthusiasm, so I changed course to run The Cleveland Orchestra, a post I happily held for 17 years. Through it all, I was increasingly preoccupied with artistic planning and became fixated on collaborating with artists and keeping the programming fresh.

These three-and-a-half decades were satisfying, but only up to a point, as I confronted the inherent rigidity of the American orchestral machine — the limitations on being able to experiment and the unchanging monotony of constantly-repeating cycles of planning and execution. After all, how many labor agreements can you negotiate? How many more European tours can you book? How interesting is it to ponder yet again what to perform before Mahler's Symphony No. 5?

At the ripe age of 60, I began a completely new direction, anchored as artistic director of the Ojai Music Festival and focused exclusively on planning programs without the burdens of administration.

INTRODUCTION

Since Ojai was not full-time, I diversified by consulting, teaching and joining boards, along with creating a start-up festival at Carnegie Hall.

Ojai proved revelatory, as I was freed from the confines of the orchestral model and thrust into the free-form milieu of contemporary music and the concentrated span of a four-day festival. My imagination was unleashed as I experimented with music beyond the orchestral repertoire, planned programs each year with different creative partners of my choice, and was liberated from the inflexibility of a rigid performance schedule. I realized my true calling was sharing my own intense response to music with others — a fervor for planning performances featuring the varied pieces I loved, with the specific artists I admired and under the conditions I needed.

This was where I had been heading over the course of a 50-year career, with three remarkably equal periods in Boston, Cleveland and Ojai. I had never imagined pursuing so many different avenues through a somewhat non-standard path — certainly the opposite of the traditional starting small and getting ever bigger. It was never planned. Experiencing it felt not like a linear progression, with each element leading logically to the next, but more like opportunities and circumstances magically materializing. With the perspective of time and distance, my journey shows a strangely cumulative logic and feels now like a gradual gathering-together of various strands, motivated by a single underlying focus — that intense love of music.

This story, however, is about more than just my own musical journey, and appreciating it is impossible without understanding how institutions and the environment around them were simultaneously evolving.

The orchestra model I entered in 1969 was established in the early 20th century: one hundred mostly-white-male musicians under a seasonal contract; yearly concerts constructed in a weekly subscription format; educational programs, occasional tours and recordings; led by a larger-than-life music director conducting repertoire concentrated on the so-called "canon" of 19th-century masterworks; and all of this supported by a combination of ticket revenues and philanthropy.

These defining pillars have remained remarkably unchanged, despite increasing complexity in orchestras' breadth of activity, scale of operation, competitive environment in both selling tickets and raising money, financial planning and accounting, along with a new world of human resource management. At the same time, music education in schools was in decline, audience habits in purchasing tickets were changing, and that central repertoire of 19th-century masterpieces was receding into the past — even the perceived astringencies of Schoenberg and Webern are now 100 years old.

The first of two earth-shattering disruptions to the model emerged in the early 2000s: the digital revolution. Music became instantaneously obtainable by anyone anywhere at any time for little cost. Boundaries between genres evaporated. Distribution gatekeepers — record companies, broadcasters, producers — no longer controlled what gets consumed, how and when. Creators became able to generate content that was immediately and directly available to anyone. One result was an explosion of niche activity — performances, works of art, digital dissemination — that is ubiquitous, continuous and borderless.

By the time online consumption became prevalent, I had left managing orchestras and was deeply immersed in an alternative universe of contemporary composers and performers at Ojai. My growing embrace of a wide range of artists and music was stimulated by my expanding curiosity and a desire to embed such voices at the very core of artistic thinking for the festival. I did not anticipate the magnitude of disruption caused by the Internet, and I bear responsibility for preserving the status quo far too long. I now recognize that the very inflexibility that I helped perpetuate in orchestras was at the root of my own disillusionment and subsequent flight to the much more alluring creativity beyond them.

The second disruption was the pandemic shutdown in 2020, which eliminated live events for over a year, escalating the speed of change in audience consumption habits and forever altering how people interact with each other. It was heartening to see so many organizations quickly adapt to new ways of staying in touch with constituents, only to watch them revert to the more comfortable business-as-usual as the shutdown ended. The basic model doggedly persists.

Today's real crisis in classical music is most institutions' inability to adapt in lasting ways to these elemental disruptions, magnified by stubborn resistance to the opportunities for change by doubling down on the status quo. This is a crisis not of circumstance but of inaction. The old model that I grew up with is simply no longer viable. As then-President of Lincoln Center Henry Timms said, "Any organization that behaves in 2022 exactly as they did in 2018 and expects the same results is going to be disappointed."[3] And it is not as if there were no looming challenges to their viability before the shutdown— quite the opposite, as has been well documented.

My journey cannot be viewed in isolation from the changing social environment around it, influencing how very differently music and institutions now function, and are viewed, from when I started. In the context of today's swirling volatility, much of my experience seems in retrospect one-dimensional, as it coincided with a period of fairly sustained economic growth, creating a one-way culture of always more and bigger.

This is all to admit to the realities that informed my journey. I accept that I started my career in an era when I had the benefit of privilege, giving me opportunities not available to everyone. I was fully retired prior to the pandemic and the long-overdue emergence of racial equity as a critical priority.

Facing a deliciously quieter life in 2019, having retired from Ojai, followed by the unexpected stay at home due to the pandemic, I started looking back in order to make better sense of what I had experienced and to gain deeper understanding of how it happened, how it fit together, what surprised me, what disappointed me and what it all meant. My views today on the state of the music world are rooted in the sheer breadth of what I have done and the knowledge I have accumulated, all of which have given me the benefit of perspectives from both the inside and outside. I am fascinated by how musical institutions function or do not, and enraptured by the sheer variety of music and artists that attracts me. I have opinions and perspectives I want to share. While I do have strong ideas, the purpose of this book is not to be rigidly prescriptive in today's dynamic environment but to provoke discussion and enrich both current and future debate about these important issues.

The idea was always percolating of writing something based on what I had learned and come to believe, but how to do that proved elusive. Appreciating the early influence of my grandfather brought into focus the power key individuals had on me, not only in the sequence of my career but in shaping my thinking and beliefs. I realized my path has been built around seminal relationships which were critical to my

---

3 Davidson, Justin, "The New Geffen Hall is Here. How Does It Sound?," *Vulture*, October 8, 2022.

journey, all overlapping in their influences and cumulatively informing what I did, how I did it and what I believed. It was a career that provided the ultimate post-doctoral education with a world-class faculty.

While I acknowledge that I and the individuals featured in the first eight chapters are all white males, I cannot change that, as it was reflective of the music business over the first 35 years of my career. My artistic partnerships during the subsequent Ojai years were considerably broader as my perspectives widened and the world of music changed.

The centrality of these incredible individuals to the varied paths I followed created a structure for this book — to frame my beliefs about music and musical organizations in the context of how they evolved through my interactions with people and projects.

Beating the Drums (Chapter 1) sets the stage for my love of orchestras as I became a friend and then colleague of Vic Firth, longtime timpanist of the Boston Symphony. I came under the spell of his mesmerizing musicianship at age 13. He almost motivated me to become a professional percussionist. I switched gears and entered management, but I never lost my love of performing, thanks to him.

The Dream Job (Chapter 2), the first of three chapters about my time at the Boston Symphony, focuses on Arthur Fiedler, legendary conductor of the Boston Pops. Having admired him from afar, I unexpectedly found us working closely together as I began my career. Over ten years, he taught me about programming and the importance of clear musical vision to guide decision-making. I came to understand how the power of such principles can permeate and define an organization.

Adventures in Repertoire (Chapter 3) centers on Oliver Knussen, the eminent composer-conductor, whom I met at Tanglewood. He opened my eyes to the vast wonders of contemporary music as well as the creative processes of composers, lessons that would impact my entire life. Our forty-five-year friendship and collaboration were packed with musical adventure, good food and uproarious fun.

Succession and Reality (Chapter 4) tells the story of my courting and then hiring film composer and conductor John Williams to succeed Fiedler at the Boston Pops. While already well-known for his scores to *Jaws*, *Star Wars*, *Close Encounters of the Third Kind*, and *Superman*, he was a surprise choice to the orchestra world. We shared five years collaborating as he successfully transformed himself from a studio musician into a public performer. It was during this period that I learned sobering lessons about managing the BSO, resulting in my eventual departure, disillusioned with both myself and the field.

Being Fearless (Chapter 5) describes the pivot point of meeting composer-conductor Pierre Boulez, an unrelenting advocate of 20th-century music. We collaborated on a project that served as a powerful wakeup call on the significance of unambiguous artistic principles and showed what working with a great artist with idealist fervor could be like. It was an event that dramatically altered my trajectory, and it cemented a friendship and collaboration that lasted almost thirty-five years.

Clarity from the Top (Chapter 6), the first of two chapters that frame my years running The Cleveland Orchestra, centers on Ward Smith, the organization's board president. His persuasive clarity drew me back into running a large institution —for all the right reasons and at the right time. He demonstrated how the structural ambiguities of having co-equal leaders, a music director and an executive director, can be made to work productively. In the process, he gave me a graduate degree in how boards can and must be effective.

Not Number Two (Chapter 7) describes my 15-year partnership with Christoph von Dohnányi, Cleveland's music director. The longest ongoing collaboration of my career, it was extraordinarily productive and rewarding, thanks primarily to our shared embrace of goals and purpose. Together we fundamentally reshaped the institution's image in a textbook case of creative partnership in all its strengths but also, in the final years, its fragilities.

A Wider Perspective (Chapter 8) is about my meeting Jim Collins, best-selling business author of *Built to Last* and *Good to Great*. He opened my eyes to the broader principles underlying organizational and individual success at just the moment I was yearning for such understanding. His encouragement and perspective helped guide my decision to leave what was becoming an unfulfilling executive vocation for a more flexible life of multiple endeavors and creative outlets.

An Idealized Laboratory (Chapter 9) focuses on the first of two key projects in which my creative energies flourished. Having left orchestras, I still fretted about their boring programming. So, two partners and I created Spring for Music at Carnegie Hall to showcase creative programming with a broad spectrum of North American ensembles. The only requirement for participation was submitting an artistically creative program. The experience reinforced my belief that orchestras can be imaginative and innovative when motivated, and just as significantly, that there are new and younger audiences for adventurous concerts. But, after four years, the project laid bare the challenges of getting such organizations to permanently change practices and beliefs from the outside.

The Power of Twos (Chapter 10) tells of my sixteen years as artistic director of the Ojai Music Festival. In reality, this was a series of annual creative partnerships with extraordinary and varied artists serving successively as music directors — from conductor Robert Spano, to contemporary music ensemble Eighth Blackbird, to soprano Dawn Upshaw, to choreographer Mark Morris, to director Peter Sellars, to violinist Patricia Kopatchinskaja. I was surprised and continually stimulated by the ever-wider range of music and artists that were opened up to me, completely altering how I thought about the world of music. Without the pressures of administration, I was able to reach what I felt was my true calling, working purely creatively and with unfettered imagination.

Orchestras Redux (Chapter 11) draws on everything I have learned and reflects on the current state of orchestras and musical creativity. And that state today is a paradox, both perilous and hopeful, with a serious disconnect between the calcified world of institutions and the lively and messy cauldron of creativity around them. To my mind, this presents opportunities. While daunting and difficult, a constructive way forward is possible, and exhilarating in its necessary reorientation of such organizations back to their core purpose of serving music.

I am continually astonished at and energized by how divergent my own tastes and beliefs have become from where I started. The key has been always following the music. This opening of my ears and mind is the very basis of my lifelong fight to rescue the classical music business from its own impulses to be artistically routine. Throughout my journey, the incredible joy and thrill of live performance have driven everything I have done, and they continue to do so to this day. That is the basis for my steadfast optimism, and it explains my rapturous reaction to that Sunday morning concert in June 2017 of music and artists so completely distant from where I began.

CHAPTER 1
BEATING THE DRUMS: VIC FIRTH

I became passionate about percussion at an early age. In classical music, you play "percussion," not "drums," admittedly a snobbish-sounding distinction. But there are critical differences between the terms in the degree of detailed musical notation and the broader outlines for improvisation. What's more, percussionists must master a broad array of instruments — timpani, snare drum, cymbals, xylophone and other mallet instruments, and multitudinous accessories, like tambourine, triangle, gong and sound effects. The multiple challenges appealed to me, as did the theatrical aspects of playing them on stage. I was fascinated by that huge arsenal of toys and felt a visceral thrill watching the pure theater of a percussionist calmly sitting and counting rests, then standing up and unleashing an explosion of sound. I could not escape the adrenalin rush of knowing that this is the only musician in the orchestra playing that sound and the stomach-wrenching realization that any slight miscalculation — coming in early or late, playing too loud or too soft, producing an ugly sound or missing the entry altogether — will be noticed by everyone. And to be honest, it just seemed like fun. Who doesn't like hitting things?

I started taking private lessons at age eight from the Eastman School's master teacher, William Street. Originally a vaudeville drummer, he had endless stories and a persistent manner that inflamed my fascination. Percussion study is not glamorous: it begins with the rudiments of stick control and rhythmic patterns, learned by practicing on a rubber pad, which feels like playing on a real drum but is a lot quieter. Over time I moved to melodic mallet instruments, learning more stick patterns, control and accuracy, and subsequently to timpani, with more work on patterns, tone projection and tuning. Practicing can have all the allure of endless calisthenics.

In Rochester, the school I attended was not large enough to have a band or orchestra, so my performing experience was limited to the occasional all-state or all-city ensembles. I learned repertoire by attending live performances and by playing along with favorite recordings in my room, a far cry from actually performing with others. I would hand-copy percussion parts from scores in the public library as a way of learning the pieces. How my parents put up with the banging and loud music I will never know.

A summer at Interlochen's National Music Camp between my sophomore and junior years of high school was life-changing. It gave me a concentrated eight-week period of performing — I was at last in the very middle of the music. While I had gone there thinking I played well, I discovered, in the intensely competitive atmosphere, that I was not as good as I thought, a serious life lesson that motivated me to practice harder.

Playing percussion in an ensemble is much more complicated than it looks and involves myriad considerations beyond technique — the context of the notes in the musical score, choosing exactly what instruments and sticks to use in order to achieve the desired effect, where to place the actual notes in the rhythmic patterns, how to accentuate or support those rhythms and how to color the instruments' sounds. All of this comes only with actual performing, not by repeating technical exercises alone in a practice room. The conductor Frederick Fennell, a percussionist himself, distributed to every percussion section he conducted a typed sheet called "Percussion Procedures" in which he outlined his expectations: "Your only concerns are: 1. When? 2. With what? 3. How? and 4. How much? — and usually in that order." To which I would add "5. Why?" He was merciless in correcting players on their choices of beaters or instruments in order to get the musical effect he wanted. I once heard him admonish a player with the question, "Why are you using that triangle beater?," to which the player replied, "It's the only one I have." Fennell's pungent retort, "Wrong answer."

THE BOSTON SYMPHONY ORCHESTRA

As a wide-eyed 13-year-old, I attended my first concert by the Boston Symphony at its summer home, Tanglewood, in the Berkshire Mountains of western Massachusetts. I was taken by my grandparents, who wanted me to experience that magical place. I knew something of the BSO from recordings, but nothing prepared me for the sheer polish, stunning presence and aural glory of that orchestra. It changed my life.

Tanglewood sits outside the small town of Lenox on a country road, its entrance unobtrusively marked only by small signs directing you to the unpaved parking areas nestled in the woods. My first impression was of the verdant beauty of its manicured lawns and stately pines. Contrasting with this was the stark simplicity of the huge 5,000-seat Shed, where the concerts are performed, with room on the surrounding lawns for another 10,000. I was overwhelmed by the pristine and serene beauty of the place: it exuded class and excellence.

But the setting was more than matched by the impact of the concerts. At 8:30 on that Friday night, with the Shed packed and the BSO on stage elegant in white dinner jackets, the conductor Charles Munch walked through the door, a tall and imposing presence with silver hair. He conducted with a long baton in wide sweeping gestures while standing erect and still, far from the distracting gyrations of others I had seen in Rochester. In the opening piece, Beethoven's Leonore Overture No. 3, the orchestra's smooth sonority surprised me, as did the theatricality of the off-stage trumpet solo, performed distantly from the edge of the Shed's surrounding woods. Next came a completely new composer and piece for me, Arthur Honegger's Symphony No. 3, strikingly direct in its musical language, bracing in its power and deeply moving in the contemplative stillness of its ending. At the weekend's final concert on Sunday afternoon, the orchestra, now in full dress whites, performed Beethoven's Ninth Symphony, my first live experience of that masterpiece. Hearing it performed by such an immaculate orchestra and chorus under a great conductor in this magical setting was an overwhelming sensory experience.

Since 1919, the BSO had remarkable consistency in its musical leadership, by the Frenchman Pierre Monteux, the Russian Serge Koussevitzky and now the Alsatian Munch, all of whom honed the orchestra's inherent French-Russian style. Over his tenure, Munch sharpened the playing with brilliant rhythmic precision, an explosive dynamic range, a lightness of touch, gossamer transparency and an extraordinarily wide palette of color. Primarily a performer and often bored with rehearsing, Munch would dismiss the players early from rehearsals, saying, "pas nécessaire."1 What resulted was an electricity of the unexpected in concerts of sheer visceral excitement, musical experiences truly made of the moment.

While Munch's repertoire was in reality quite broad, it was through his numerous recordings of music by Berlioz, Ravel and Debussy that the Munch-BSO reputation spread as the quintessential French partnership. One of my first LPs was their 1953 recording of Berlioz's *Symphonie fantastique*, a true Munch specialty that, to my ears, no one has ever bettered. It was drenched in excitement and intensity. I played it over and over in my room on a small record player that my parents had given me. Munch's recordings of Berlioz's *Damnation of Faust* and Requiem, Debussy's *La Mer* and showpieces by Ravel — *Bolero, Rapsodie espagnole, La Valse* and *Daphnis and Chloe* — became favorites.

THE TIMPANIST

This repertoire and the BSO's dynamic style of playing perfectly suited a young man who loved percussion, so naturally I paid a lot of attention to the orchestra's magnificent section. From those first concerts, one musician I could not keep my eyes off was the timpanist, Everett Firth. He was young and handsome, had slicked-back black hair and stood ramrod straight at the timpani when playing (most players sit on a stool behind the drums). He exuded total command.

Timpani, unlike other drums, are tuned to specific pitches that can be changed with a pedal mechanism. The player must be not only rhythmically exact but also in tune with the rest of the orchestra. As the only player on the instrument, and given its dynamic range, there is no place to hide. Firth's musicianship was mesmerizing — those explosive timpani outbursts in the scherzo of Beethoven's Ninth had shattering impact.

I began collecting all the BSO's recordings, devouring each new one as it was released and hearing Boston Symphony and Boston Pops (for which Firth was also the timpanist) concerts whenever I could. I heard the orchestra in Symphony Hall for the first time in 1960 on a college visit to Boston. Starting in 1961 I revisited Tanglewood fre-

---

1 This was reported to me by countless BSO members who played under Munch.

Vic Firth in the Boston Pops in 1957

quently, eager to show off the place to my friends. I attended Munch's final weekend as music director in 1962, an extravaganza that featured in one concert Berlioz's *Symphonie fantastique*, Debussy's *La Mer* and Ravel's *Daphnis and Chloe* Suite No. 2, a colorful feast of French music if ever there was one. The BSO played with complete abandon and unfettered emotion as it said *au revoir* to its maestro. On the last glorious note of the Berlioz, I specifically recall Firth playing a loud timpani roll through the held chord, even though the score specifies playing only on the downbeat while the rest of the orchestra blares through that final triumphant sonority. The effect seemed appropriate to the organic tumult of the occasion, setting off a spontaneous eruption of cheers. Years later, I heard a tape of the performance, and to my surprise, there was no roll, but there was tumult. Clearly I had embellished the excitement of the occasion in my imagination!

In all those recordings and performances, I intently studied every note Firth played, deeply absorbing his impeccable technique, exquisite mastery of sound and color, watching his precise body language mirror the rhythmic verve of his playing. He could play loudly, overpoweringly some thought, but only when the music demanded it.

How orchestras play together is somewhat of a mystery, far more complicated than just following the conductor's beat. Different players have their own tricks for whom to listen to or watch in order to precisely gauge their own entrances. Firth's secret, he later admitted in a Tanglewood master class, was to place his notes imperceptibly ahead of the beat, thereby driving the rhythms forward. To do this, he followed not the conductor's beat but the concertmaster's bow arm. He found timing his notes to the violinist's landing his bow on a string a far more precise guide than the conductor's vaguer beats in the air.

Firth was the kind of percussionist I aspired to be. I loved his sound, his style and his presence, and I vowed to hear him play as often as I could. In 1961, I finally screwed up the courage to meet him backstage during an intermission. For such a commanding figure, I was surprised to find him approachable, affable and funny. Most important, I learned that nobody ever called him Everett — he was known as "Vic."

While getting to know Firth, I became familiar with the rest of the BSO percussion section, which included another musical giant, Harold J. "Tommy" Thompson, the acknowledged master of cymbals. He was an imposing figure on stage, his sheer physical size and strength allowing him to crash together the largest cymbals with little visible effort other than flicks of his wrists and lower arms. He was a specialist on Avedis Zildjian cymbals, each one of which sounds unique because of being handmade. From the considerable arsenal at his disposal, Thompson selected exactly the right one to perfectly color and support each sound in the orchestra, amplifying its effect. Nothing was tentative about his playing. You heard every note, and it was always tasteful and fully appropriate to the music. He was a character and peppered his speech with the casual jive of a jazz musician — his every other word was "man," and he referred to his cymbals as "pies." My fascination with him ignited a life-long love affair with playing and collecting cymbals.

BSO percussionists Charlie Smith, Tommy Thompson and Vic Firth in
Bruckner's Symphony No. 8 in 1962

Through all of this, I became obsessed with the Boston Symphony — its playing, its sound, its aura, and its history. Starting in 1965, I even built a scale model of the Symphony Hall stage, complete with miniature musicians and instruments. I worked on it for well over 10 years but it remains unfinished. Little did I know then how large the place would loom in my future.

PRINCETON

After high school, my parents insisted I get a proper college education rather than just study music, so I went to Princeton. I joined the marching band, concert band and orchestra, and I played freelance percussion all over New Jersey, thanks to having access to the band's 1953 Cadillac hearse for carting around all the instruments. My constant performing was somewhat manic, as if to make up for not being able to play much while in high school. I hardly had time to study, much to my parents' and teachers' dismay.

I found myself suddenly playing a lot of timpani, instruments I studied only fleetingly. I thought I understood them well through my continual observation of Firth, but a major drawback was not owning adequate sticks. A percussionist needs not only good technique and the right instruments but exactly the right sticks to bring out the desired sound.

On that visit to Tanglewood in 1962, I explained my need to Firth. Because of careless manufacturing at the time, most commercially available drumsticks neither weighed the same nor were perfectly straight, so each one felt unbalanced in your hands and sounded different on a drum. An exacting artist, Firth found this unacceptable. Fixated on ensuring that his were utterly straight and balanced in weight and density, he started making his own and developed a technique to measure each one and match it with a precisely identical one to make a pair.

During the visit, he showed me his new creations, and, to my total surprise and delight, he gave me pairs of his early timpani and snare drum sticks. With those sticks (which I still have) I accumulated an incredible amount of playing experience while at college, performing repertoire as varied and daunting as Bernstein's *West Side Story*, Bartók's Sonata for Two Pianos and Percussion, Stravinsky's *Les Noces*, Ravel's *Bolero* and, with the Princeton University Orchestra, Milhaud's Percussion Concerto. It seemed I was on an ever-clearer track to be a professional percussionist — until August 1964, when the humbling glare of reality intervened.

TURNING POINT

That summer, between my junior and senior years, New Jersey celebrated its 300th anniversary. The state's political powers decided to highlight the occasion with a two-week music festival on the campus of Westminster Choir College in Princeton, for which they would assemble a pickup orchestra. Most of the musicians came from The Philadelphia Orchestra, and I was hired as principal percussionist. Conducting the final concert was Eugene Ormandy, longtime Philadelphia music director, leading Verdi's Requiem with the Westminster Choir. Other than timpani, the piece has only one percussion part, for bass drum — and what a part it is, including the repertoire's loudest and most thunderous thwacks during the Dies Irae. To perform this with an orchestra of such quality under Ormandy seemed the opportunity of a lifetime, the stepping stone toward a glorious career. I felt as though I had made the big time.

The first problem was that the rehearsals and performance took place in the humid heat of summer under a canvas tent. The acoustics provided no natural resonance and soaked up any low frequencies that might exist, difficult conditions for the bass drum. What resulted was a dry, inert sound. No matter what I did, Ormandy was completely dissatisfied. As the young kid amid the august Philadelphians, I became his foil. He wanted more bass resonance, he wanted the sound of thunder, and wanted to feel the booming quality of the drum at all dynamic levels. Nothing I did satisfied him. It didn't help when I tried to explain that the cause was not me but the acoustic muffling of the tent in the hot, humid air. He didn't buy it and made my life miserable. Orchestra members, particularly the Philadelphia horn players seated in front of me, were constantly encouraging, explaining that conductors were simply "jerks" and to pay no attention.

On the night of the performance, I went on stage to set up and found, glued to the middle of the large bass drum head, a small cut-out photo from the program book of Ormandy's face and a small sign saying, "Hit Here," a gift from the horn section. While amusing, it gave me an unsettling glimpse into the world of professional orchestras and conductors I had not seen before. Ormandy's boorish behavior and the cynical attitudes of some of the musicians disturbed me. While the performance went off without incident, the stark reality of what day-to-day orchestral life might be like suddenly became less attractive. I decided then and there that being a percussionist in a big orchestra was not the career for me.

ORCHESTRA MANAGEMENT

The urgent question then became what to do after graduation in a year. My Princeton adviser was Robert Freeman, who later became director of the Eastman School of Music (and incidentally lived in my grandparents' house in Rochester, which they had donated to the school on their deaths) and whose father was a longtime bass player in the BSO. Freeman knew all about life in orchestras and totally understood my change of heart. He suggested a path that had never occurred to me — going into management. He advised I look into a Ford Foundation program called Administrative Interns in the Arts, under which young professionals were placed in organizations to start careers and gain early experience. The idea appealed as a way to capitalize on my love of music and orchestras without the routine that playing all the time can become. I applied, was accepted and went to the Cincinnati Symphony upon graduation in 1965.

Given the relatively small size of the staff in Cincinnati, I found myself doing every conceivable job — concert production, scheduling, budgeting, labor negotiations, marketing and tour management — so the learning experience was extraordinary. Creating performances of great music gave purpose to all the hard work and provided strong motivation to succeed. To my surprise, I discovered that I really loved the varied tasks of planning, organizing and producing, although I did miss the playing.

In the middle of my two years there, the U.S. State Department, as part of its international cultural exchange program, sent the orchestra on a 10-week tour that literally went around the world, with concerts in Athens, Istanbul, Beirut, Tel Aviv, Lucerne, Bombay, Singapore, Kuala Lumpur, Manila, Tokyo, Okinawa and Seoul.[2] My job, in addition to organizing the logistics, was to be the advance man to double-check concert, housing and travel arrangements, always staying two days ahead of the orchestra. The adventures and challenges were many, from dealing with State Department handlers who didn't know Beethoven from the Beatles to transporting a concert grand piano, a promotional gift from Cincinnati's Baldwin Piano Company. It was a crash course in running a tour, and taught me the lasting lesson that under no circumstances was a 10-week tour a good idea!

As the grant ended, much as I enjoyed my experience in Cincinnati, I was not convinced management was the right path. From what I had observed, good organizational and leadership skills were in high demand, but I felt the need for additional training in business, finance and marketing. Knowing that a graduate degree would provide those and a stronger resume, I decided to attend the Wharton School in Philadelphia for an MBA. While there I resumed some modest freelance playing, but unlike at Princeton, I stayed focused on my studies. I found that business school existed in a theoretical bubble, where so many practical skills are taught by professors with no real experience running anything. Luckily, Cincinnati had provided me a

2 In those days before orchestras were employed year-round, tours like this by the State Department not only gave the orchestra exposure and furthered cultural exchange but provided extended employment for the musicians.

practical foundation on which to ground the learning. Two important skills I learned at Wharton, how to think critically and how to structure problem-solving, would end up serving me well.

On graduation, I decided definitively to pursue a career in orchestra management. Even with my self-inflated confidence that I possessed the ideal skills — a love of music, practical experience in Cincinnati and an MBA — finding a job proved challenging. Sending out resumes to a number of orchestras, I was shocked to hear responses from only a handful, of which only two were real possibilities: the Rochester Philharmonic and the Boston Symphony. No contest! I accepted a position in the BSO's finance department. It was an entry-level job, but I was convinced that being the smallest cog in this most inspiring musical enterprise was a worthwhile trade-off. My childhood infatuation had indeed led me to what I thought was the promised land, albeit in a different role than I had originally envisioned.

PLAYING PERCUSSION IN THE BSO

The job allowed me to hear the BSO regularly in concerts and rehearsals. I found Firth was indeed the musical heartbeat of the orchestra and recognized as one of the key drivers of its musical personality. At the same time, he was building a substantial drumstick business. While its creation had been driven by his own need for acceptable timpani mallets, he realized the real potential was in snare drum sticks, a market open to not only classical but rock, pop, jazz and school drummers. He befriended all of the greats, for whom he fashioned custom-designed sticks emblazoned with their names in exchange for endorsements. He made sticks with different lengths, weights, shapes, colors, and tips, each one perfectly matched.

For manufacturing, Firth leased lathes during the downtime of a wooden peppermill maker in Maine. As his business grew, he bought the company, ultimately relegating peppermill manufacturing to down-time from the stick business (and in the process becoming a prominent maker of peppermills). Firth's entrepreneurial endeavors went beyond drumsticks: for years he was a prominent dealer in American art and the American dealer of German-made Ringer timpani, his own instrument of choice.

INTERLUDE: THE GRATEFUL DEAD

Firth's sticks became associated with almost every famous percussionist and drummer: he got to know them personally and often attended their performances. In a 2002 profile in *The Boston Globe* on his retirement from the BSO,[3] Firth described an unexpected cameo appearance with the Grateful Dead in Providence, R.I.: "I was sitting on the stage, and they asked me to lead off the big drum solo. I was wearing a coat and tie, and I told them I'd look like a stuffed shirt. But they persuaded me to take them off, and I did start off the solo. Through an audience member, word of my escapade reached a member of the BSO's august board of directors, and before long, the orchestra's manager called me into the office. 'Tell me it isn't true that you played with the Grateful Dead,' the manager asked. So I told him it wasn't true. As I headed for the door, he said, 'Did you really do it?' And I said, 'Of course I did.' 'Just don't do it again,' he said, and I didn't."

He was impressive as a musician and a businessman, and we became friends. But over time, as my position at the BSO unexpectedly rose from finance department staff to general manager, the relationship became complex, with me ultimately becoming his boss, even negotiating contracts with him. Throughout, I found his artistry ever more compelling, and I watched with admiration as he built his drumstick business into a juggernaut.

Observing and listening to Firth stirred anew the allure of performing. In 1970, knowing I was a percussionist, he invited me to his teaching studio at Boston's New England Conservatory. For an artist of his stature, I found it a surprisingly junky room, tucked away in the building's basement and filled with an old marimba, a few snare drums and some perfectly dreadful timpani. His gracious and cheerful manner was welcoming, even as he scared me to death by saying he wanted to see what I could do, asking me to play various snare drum, marimba and timpani passages. It was over in a flash, but somehow I passed his considerable muster, as shortly thereafter I was asked to play in the Boston Pops, filling in for one of the regular players who had called in sick. I was totally surprised — and petrified: I was about to play under Arthur Fiedler in the orchestra of my dreams. And it went well! Maybe, I thought, I could balance a life of management as a vocation with performing as an avocation.

---

3 Dyer, Richard. "Vic Firth is the Ultimate Stick Figure," *The Boston Globe*, June 16, 2002.

Soon thereafter, I was engaged as an extra percussionist in the Boston Symphony when additional players were needed or a regular was out. It meant I performed beside Firth and rest of the legendary percussion section of the time — Charlie Smith, Arthur Press, Tom Gauger and Frank Epstein (another great cymbals player, he replaced Thompson after his tragic death in a 1968 car accident). Even as I rose in the management ranks to CEO, I spent my entire Boston tenure playing as an extra percussionist in the BSO and Pops, and I became a regular member of the Boston Pops Esplanade Orchestra, the freelance ensemble put together for the portion of the Pops season the regular performers could not cover because of BSO commitments.

My artistic high points were no doubt playing cymbals (using Thompson's own incredible instruments, which remained with the orchestra) in Ravel's *La Valse* under Seiji Ozawa in 1978; playing Berlioz's *Symphonie fantastique* under Ozawa on tour in Japan in 1979 and performing one of the four timpani parts in the third movement, standing next to Firth; and playing Ravel's *Rapsodie espagnole* under Leonard Bernstein in concert and on film as part of his Charles Eliot Norton Lectures at Harvard. During those years, I performed frequently with the Boston Pops, so often that I no doubt played *The Stars and Stripes*

Playing with the BSO in Lou Harrison's Canticle No. 3
with Arthur Press and Charlie Smith

Forever well over 200 times, excessive fulfillment of my early fascination with the piece. I even "soloed" in the Pops' unique version of Leroy Anderson's *The Typewriter.* The production, perfected by Charlie Smith, has the "soloist" typing on an antique Remington placed in front of the orchestra like the piano for a concerto. It is full of shameless schtick: the soloist wearing an accountant's green eyeshade and puffing on a fake cigar, a sight gag with a gigantic eraser, plus incessant mugging back and forth with two other percussionists playing the typewriter bell and carriage return. It never failed to bring down the house.

Performing Leroy Anderson's The Typewriter *at the Pops in 1979*

I always insisted, with both Firth and the personnel manager, that I play only if everyone agreed I was up to the task. The lone objection I ever heard about was years later: Ozawa, then the BSO music director, reportedly felt that it somehow upset his traditional view of a proper and respectful hierarchy of roles. But it didn't stop my continued playing. In all cases I asked to be paid the appropriate extra player fees so there could never be a cynical accusation that I was hired as a cost-saving move. At the end of each year, I quietly donated the amounts earned back to the orchestra.

Experiencing the life of an orchestral musician and under-standing what playing inside the BSO was like gave me perspectives that informed my work in management, particularly when it came to negotiating individual contracts or with the union. It helped establish a level of trust with the musicians, who not only saw firsthand my ability to perform but learned of my deep love of music. Those early experi-ences in Boston formed the seeds of my lifelong ability to form close and easy working relationships with creative individuals.

I was so fortunate in being able to play regularly with the BSO and Pops without having to earn a living at it and to perform with Firth, not just emulate him from afar. And all of this while I established myself in management. It seemed the best of all possible worlds.

INTERLUDE: PERCUSSION SCHTICK

Boston Pops concerts were always full of hilarious high jinks we called "schtick," usually originating in the percussion section, a tradition that started with the Sousa Band. As some of the Pops arrangements called for various sound effects, the percussionists always had a large collection of such toys on hand. A favorite sight gag was a rubber chicken flying through the air after a blank gunshot. As a percussionist, I always felt this is a tradition to be nurtured, and I introduced many such pranks to Blossom Festival Band concerts, where there is never a performance without an appearance by the rubber chicken. Wielding props and donning funny hats became standard practice for our percussion section. We wore Darth Vader masks for the "Imperial March" from *Star Wars*, Viking helmets for music from Wagner's *Die Walküre* and clown wigs for a program of circus music. We deployed a smoke machine on stage for a descriptive novelty piece called *Midnight Fire Alarm*, which went terribly awry one night when the machine was accidently set off before the piece had even started, much to the confusion of the audience. The band, shrouded in white smoke, was in hysterics unnoticeable to the audience through the thick haze.

POST-BOSTON

After becoming the CEO of The Cleveland Orchestra, my playing ca-reer went on hold for a while as I concentrated exclusively on manage-ment. The job was totally absorbing, and it became increasingly difficult to keep up my performing chops. In any case, my style of playing was deeply shaped by the BSO, a style totally opposite of Cleveland's. One of the fascinating things about percussion is orchestras have their own valid styles of playing that are not easily interchangeable. In Boston, the playing was sharply accented and with wide dynamic range. In Cleveland, it functioned more subtly as color in the orchestral palette, underplaying dynamics and supporting the sound, yet with awesome power when required. I loved listening to it, but it was not how I played.

After 13 years in Cleveland, the itch to perform reasserted itself. A fortuitous opportunity arose and I joined the Blossom Festival Band, a freelance Sousa-style ensemble assembled by The Cleveland Orchestra each summer to play concerts at Blossom Music Center, its summer home south of the city. The group had been performing there since the facility's opening in 1968. The conductor at the time was Loras Schissel, who works on the music staff of the Library of Congress and knows more about American music and concert bands than anyone I have ever met. We share a love of musical esoterica and the hysterical yet true stories that give color to the otherwise sober classical music world. Joining the ensemble brought me back full circle to my early love of band repertoire, and again *The Stars and Stripes Forever* loomed large. I still play with them, using the huge collection of cymbals I amassed over the years.

Firth and I stayed close friends long after I left Boston. We socialized when we could and I heard him perform as often as possible before he retired in 2002, after 50 astonishing years. I remember my last time seeing him play in the orchestra: it was a rehearsal of Mendelssohn's Symphony No. 3, the "Scottish." I was still awestruck by the precision of his rhythmic drive and the perfection of his sound, qualities that never abated from the very first time I saw him at Tanglewood years earlier. I was always fascinated by the evolution of his stick business, which in 2010 he merged with the Avedis Zildjian cymbal company. I last visited him two months before he died in 2015. Even with his health deteriorating, he was the same dapper, forthright individual I first met over half a century before.

Understanding Firth's influence now through the longer lens of time, I appreciate a profound lesson he taught me. He was the greatest artist on the timpani and being in such a famous orchestra gave him a huge bully pulpit. But for him it was not enough, and he simultaneously built a substantial commercial company. Even with this bifurcated life, he never lost his enthusiasm for the thrill of performing, partly, I

In action with the Blossom Festival Band in 2004

suspect, because he had the perspective from the outside as well as the inside. When asked if he ever got bored playing in the orchestra, he said, "No, it's still overwhelming to play great music with great musicians, but for slightly different reasons. When I first went in, it was like being on a fast roller coaster ride, and I was hanging on for dear life. Now the roller coaster ride is just as fast, but instead of hanging on, I might be pole-vaulting at the same time."[4]

Firth understood that continuing to play in the BSO was in fact the driver of his business success, giving visual presence and audible spirit to his company. He showed that it was possible to pursue linked interests simultaneously and to flourish in both. For me, it proved that passion for music and playing could be maintained while pursuing a professional path totally different from the one I had originally envisioned. And as I veered into management, I found a way to maintain just enough playing on the side to keep my hands directly on the music I loved. It was a perfect and fulfilling solution.

---

4 Mattingly, Rick, "Vic Firth: Beyond the Classical Stereotype," *Modern Drummer*, June 1982.

CHAPTER 2
THE DREAM JOB: ARTHUR FIEDLER

From an early age, I worshiped everything about the Boston Symphony, believing it the highest ideal of a successful and smoothly functioning orchestra. It was venerable, founded in 1881 by a wealthy Boston businessman, Henry Lee Higginson. He managed and personally paid for it until 1918, when, with his resources depleted, he incorporated it with a board of trustees. Since then it had achieved astonishing breadth, embracing not only the Boston Symphony but the Boston Pops, the Boston Symphony Chamber Players, the Tanglewood Festival and the summer music school, the Tanglewood Music Center. It owned two pieces of real estate, Tanglewood and Boston's acoustically renowned Symphony Hall. Every facet of the operation resonated deeply with me.

In May 1969, I began working for the BSO in the business office, feeling that I could absorb the exciting artistic atmosphere even though I was far from the nexus of what I loved, the music. At least I could enjoy many concerts and occasional rehearsals. My boss was the business manager, James J. Brosnahan, known affectionately as "Mr. B." Experienced and street-smart, he had a gentle demeanor that masked a determined strength of character and toughness, an earthy voice coarsened by years of heavy smoking and good whiskey, a disarming smile and an easy unhurried style. Brosnahan exuded wisdom and embodied the BSO's institutional memory — he had started as an office boy for the board treasurer and his career spanned more than 40 years. Even though he was not a musician, his common sense and practical experience in finance, business and people skills made him the no-nonsense glue holding the organization together. A framed sign in his office read, "If God wanted you to go to concerts, he would have given you tickets … JJBros."

Me and James J. Brosnahan in 1971

I was assigned to do the payroll, a tedious task. Though I had studied double-entry bookkeeping, journal entries and account structures at Wharton, I now faced these concepts daily, etching their logic and rules firmly into my brain. It was a crash course in financial practicality. Since everyone in the organization was touched by the payroll, it gave me a unique opportunity to meet them all quickly. And because every financial transaction went through our office, I had immediate knowledge of what was going on and how things worked. Whenever asked for advice about how to start in the music industry, I always advocate getting a working knowledge of accounting and finance by *doing*, instead of just *studying*, as the quickest way to understand an entire organization.

The BSO's quaint, charming offices were tucked away in spaces surrounding Symphony Hall's central auditorium. Brosnahan seated me next to him at a roll-top desk (one I was given when I left the BSO and went on to use throughout my career). Nearby sat the easygoing and immensely experienced Harry Shapiro, the long-time second horn player and the travel manager. The two taught me everything there was to know about the place — its history, culture, challenges, personalities, strengths and weaknesses. As a BSO groupie, I was an eager and willing student.

THE BOSTON SYMPHONY

With endless curiosity about all things BSO, I soon discovered an organization in an unexpected state of internal transition and uncertainty. The current music director, Erich Leinsdorf, was at the end of a seven-year tenure that had not been successful. Through my grandfather, I had met him years earlier when he was conductor of the Rochester Philharmonic. His Teutonic musical personality, while bringing needed discipline to the BSO after the relaxed years of Munch, was totally at odds with its tradition of French-Russian color. His brusque, abrasive manner rubbed against the genteel culture of the organization and of Boston, counteracting the impact of whatever musical success he had. Relations on stage were tense and brittle. Ticket sales were declining, a result not only of evolving audience habits and perfunctory marketing in the face of changing times but of Leinsdorf's waning popularity.

William Steinberg, music director of the Pittsburgh Symphony, had been selected as successor, to start a mere four months after I arrived. Given his other commitments and age, he insisted on no involvement in Tanglewood, previously overseen by the BSO music director. Ending the tradition of having a single artistic leader as the organization's internal and external face, a triumvirate was appointed to run the summer festival and school: frequent BSO guest conductor Seiji Ozawa, composer-educator Gunther Schuller and Tanglewood's most illustrious alumnus, Leonard Bernstein.

To destabilize the situation further, Steinberg fell ill during his third week on the job, shortly before a concert in Carnegie Hall. Never fully regaining his stamina, he was forced to cancel much of his Boston conducting during the three years of his contract. The usual replacement was Michael Tilson Thomas, the recently-arrived assistant conductor, who eventually led a majority of the concerts over those next three seasons. Extraordinarily talented and precociously gifted, Tilson Thomas at age 25 was not experienced enough to exert the effective institutional leadership needed in lieu of the absent Steinberg.

Recording had long been one of the pillars of the BSO — for prestige, visibility and money. In 1970, RCA terminated its long-standing recording contract for eight LPs annually with the Boston Symphony and 10 with the Boston Pops. The company thought that longtime Pops conductor Arthur Fiedler had already recorded his complete repertoire, knew Leinsdorf did not sell and had little in-terest in the prospect of Steinberg. Oddly, it had been RCA that, in 1962 after Munch's retirement, had urged the BSO to hire Leins-dorf, a conductor with whom it had previously made opera record-ings. Luckily, the German label Deutsche Grammophon, wanting to enter the American recording market, thought making records with the BSO was the right vehicle and had just signed a considerable contract. While seemingly good news in the face of RCA's aban-donment, the new recording situation was uncertain, given that DG had no real strategy for who would conduct the BSO recordings nor much interest in the Pops.

The chief executive was Thomas D. Perry Jr., who started working there in 1946 and became its head in 1954. Known as "Tod," he was articulate, elegant and very much the Boston gentleman, all of which had blended well with the genial Munch but not with the demanding and acerbic Leinsdorf. Since 1946, the BSO had been to-tally dominated by its board president, Henry B. Cabot Jr., a lawyer who was the crusty epitome of a stereotypical Yankee, with rumpled suits and a nasal Boston accent. Cabot decided everything and Perry deferred to him in all matters. Musicians with issues went directly to him, not to the management. The board was essentially just him. Lein-sdorf in his autobiography speaks bitterly about Cabot's domineering yet distant presence.[1] In 1968, he relinquished the board presidency, leaving Perry without a commanding board leader to depend on and defer to.

This was an organization — to the outside world a model of success, even though undergoing a major change in conductor — which was facing a plethora of underlying challenges without clear direction or leadership. To an ambitious young staff member, the situa-tion seemed surprising but filled with opportunities to make an impact.

---

1 Leinsdorf, Erich, *Cadenza: A Musical Career*, Houghton Mifflin, 1976.

INTERLUDE:
TOD PERRY'S UKASE ON SUITABLE DRESS

Perry had been an English teacher before running the BSO and was a clever and erudite writer. In June 1969, just before my first summer at Tanglewood and at a time when the informalities of Vietnam war protesters and the hippie generation were in full swing, Perry sent a broadside to all employees on the subject of suitable clothing to be worn at Tanglewood — a classic:

MEMORANDUM TO:
Tanglewood Staff Females, and Staff Males withal

In an ill-considered moment, I said I would shortly emit a ukase on suitable dress for working female staff members at Tanglewood. I have since had a number of conversations on this subject with females, notably my wife. We have discussed skirts, miniskirts, less-than-miniskirts, culottes, body stockings, plunging necklines, pants suits, no-pants suits and peekaboo as well as see-through garments. It's an interesting subject, surely, but complex, and the ukase that emerges is as follows:

1. That while on duty at Tanglewood, suitable and reasonable attire shall be worn, that the definition of "suitable and reasonable" shall be up to the department head wherein the female works, and that in general, extremes or extravagances of garb are to be avoided — that is, members of the staff are supposed to be helpful, friendly and not startling or unwantedly intrusive upon the attention of the people being dealt with.

2. The same general rules apply to staff males (with the inevitable differences, naturally, occasioned by differences of gender) — that "suitable and reasonable" attire shall be worn, one shall avoid clothing distracting as to its brilliance, informality or just plain sloppiness, and the department head is to be the arbiter of what's suitable for his department. The male species is complicated by the beard/hair problem, but the same general rules apply — you don't get to be sloppy, messy, grotesque or distracting in appearance.

3. At Tanglewood, but not on duty, reasonable decorum of dress is requested.

4. When you're not on duty and not at Tanglewood, you're on your own.

THE BOSTON POPS

And then there was the Boston Pops. Founded in 1885, a mere four years after the BSO, the 95-member ensemble comprised members of the Symphony minus its principal players, and the entire operation was, and still is, under the umbrella of the Boston Symphony Orchestra Inc. Higginson's stated artistic purpose was to broaden the audiences for his new orchestra by presenting lighter, informal concerts. These were originally called "Promenade Concerts," then "Popular Concerts," and finally just "Pops." It was a clever and practical innovation — to extend the employment of musicians when the regular classical season was over and to reach new audiences at affordable prices.

The BSO's stately home, Symphony Hall, built in 1900, was planned with remarkable foresight. It was the first concert hall designed according to acoustic principles, led by a young professor of physics at Harvard, Wallace Sabine, who more-or-less invented the science of acoustics. The result was a classic shoebox design based on the acoustically excellent old Leipzig Gewandhaus. In order to diffuse the sound properly and achieve optimal reverberation, Sabine directed that the interior's straight walls and ceiling be broken up and angled architecturally. To further reflect the sound, he designed niches over the upper balcony for 16 statues of mythological Greek and Roman deities and legendary figures, all plaster casts of old-world originals. Only one of the 16, of the Vatican's Apollo Belvedere, was in place when the hall was opened: the rest were cut from the design for cost reasons, but they were added one at a time a few years later, thanks to special funding from a generous group of supporters.[2]

For the Pops, Higginson insisted that the gradually raked floor be removable, leaving the entire downstairs area a vast flat space on which tables and chairs could be placed cabaret-style where light food, wine and champagne could be served during the concerts.

Each year, after the BSO finished its season on an early May Saturday night, a transformation began — the main floor seats and raked floor were removed, the tables and chairs installed, and the dark maroon walls around the floor repainted a bright, light green, and all to be completed before the first Pops concert three nights later. At the end of the season, the process was reversed, and the walls were repainted maroon. The resulting buildup of paint took its toll on the

2 Fascinating detail on the statues and the hall design can be found in "Symphony Hall: The First 100 Years," published by the Boston Symphony Orchestra, Inc., in 2000.

walls, which required complete replastering every 10 years due to excessive strain on the fragile plaster and wooden lath.

To brighten the mood further, fresh flowers nightly adorned the front of the stage and the conductor's podium. The programs were focused on the lighter classical repertoire, and almost from the beginning were structured with two intermissions so as to stimulate refreshment sales and enhance the atmosphere. Informality was the order of the day, with the goal of re-creating the ambiance of summer evenings in Viennese concert gardens.

By 1969, the Pops season lasted nine weeks through May and June, with concerts every night except Mondays. With a weekly schedule of six concerts and two rehearsals, plus at least 20 recording sessions over the season to make the necessary LPs for RCA, the schedule was brutal. A pickup ensemble was hired to perform the Sunday night concerts over the first eight weeks and the ninth week, giving the regular players much-needed relief. The summer Tanglewood season followed immediately thereafter.

One of the secrets of the Pops' success was building ticket sales on a wholesale, not retail, model — a radical, and clever, idea for an orchestra at the time. Group sales to community, civic and school organizations started in the 1930s and had matured to the point where 90 percent of the tickets to the entire season were sold through groups, in essence marshaling them into a vast retail sales force. Individual sales through the box office were minimal. With few tickets to be sold, programs were announced only two weeks ahead, printed inexpensively on long tear-off paper sheets called "snakes" which were hung weekly on a wall near the box office. Ingrained in the public's mind was the idea of "going to Pops," regardless of who was conducting or what the program was — a transaction with the institution itself rather than specific artists or repertoire. The concerts were always full. The group-sales model tied the orchestra closely to the civic, educational and social life of the city, and the Pops became a beloved and unique Boston tradition.

Attempts to replicate the model — melding light repertoire, an informal setting, a concentrated time of year and branded around a conductor — were few and short-lived: the New York Philharmonic's springtime Promenade Concerts conducted by André Kostelanetz from 1963 to 1978, the San Francisco Symphony summer season led by Fiedler from 1951 to 1978, and The Cleveland Orchestra summer pops series in the city's Public Auditorium directed by Louis Lane starting in the 1950s but discontinued in 1968 with the building of the Blossom Music Center.

ARTHUR FIEDLER

Arthur Fiedler was not the founder of the Pops, as is widely assumed, but its 17th conductor. Born in Boston, he joined the BSO as a violinist in 1915 at age 20. Industrious and ambitious, he demonstrated early musical versatility by also playing keyboard and percussion as well as conducting offstage musicians. Well-dressed and handsome, with dark hair and a stylish mustache, he quickly became a very eligible man about town, a role he played with relish. During his early years with the orchestra, as five conductors unsuccessfully cycled through leading the Pops, Fiedler watched with envy and dismay, frustrated at not being considered for the post. The turning point was his creation of free summer concerts at the Esplanade, Boston's outdoor concert venue on the Charles River. Their immediate success drew the attention of BSO leadership. In 1930, at 35, he finally got the job.

He threw himself into it with gusto, imposing a more regular structure on the traditional three-part program format conceived years earlier, with light classical repertoire to start, a standard concerto in the second portion and, in the third, American popular and show tunes, all of which had to be arranged for full orchestra from their original smaller forces. Years of making these arrangements built up a substantial library of pieces which became an integral and distinctive part of the brand. All were paid for by the organization, a considerable annual investment which ensured that the repertoire was up to date. They remained the exclusive property of the BSO, with no one other than the Pops or Fiedler allowed to perform them.

Fiedler possessed an innate sense of showmanship and a great ear for trends. His oft-stated philosophy was 'to play all kinds of music except the boring kind." In 1935, looking through a stack of scores in a music shop, he came across an unknown tango called *Jalousie*. Intrigued, he bought it, had it arranged for the orchestra and recorded. It became the first orchestral disc to sell a million copies. His early advocacy, in the 1940s, of Leroy Anderson, then a young composer at Harvard and its band director, paved the way for a remarkable body of cunningly titled pieces written for the orchestra, most to become wildly

Arthur Fiedler

successful hits on recordings and radio. All were amusingly scored and no more than three minutes long to fit on one side of a 78rpm record.

In the 1950s, with the rise of Broadway musical theater, Fiedler had medleys arranged of popular musicals — *Oklahoma!*, *Carousel*, *My Fair Lady*, *The Sound of Music* and *West Side Story*. In 1964, as the Beatles burst onto the scene, he commissioned an arrangement of "I Want to Hold Your Hand" that became a runaway hit, much to the consternation of some of the BSO's conservative Brahmin trustees. But Beatles tunes would continue to make regular appearances in programs and recordings well into the 1970s. Fiedler forged a distinctive programming brand for Pops concerts, and the embrace of this wide range of music, performed in an informal setting, resonated with the public. The inclusion of popular music alongside the light classical repertoire put the orchestra in sync with musical trends of the time, and the burgeoning record business gave it a national following.

Fiedler's conducting extended far beyond appearances in Boston. In the non-Pops season, he constantly guest-conducted orchestras all over the country. In 1951 he began leading an annual summer season with the San Francisco Symphony, which continued until just before his death. Starting in 1953, the Boston Pops Tour Orchestra, a pickup ensemble created for him, made months-long tours. And he had made a substantial number of records. Given his singular access to those arrangements of popular music, he was able to export his unique brand of programming to audiences year-round.

He determined early on that he did not want to compete for major music directorships by conducting the serious classical repertoire built around full-length symphonies by Beethoven, Brahms and Tchaikovsky. Instead, he carved out a distinctive niche in the light classical repertoire. He was well-schooled and experienced: he knew how to instill lilt in a Johann Strauss waltz, sparkle in a Rossini overture and froth in an Offenbach ballet. He had solid stick technique, a good ear and (a rare quality among conductors) an unshakable rhythmic sense — the ability to establish rock-solid musical pulse and maintain it over time.

I once attended a Pops recording session of Ravel's *Bolero*, a piece built on a steady, incessant snare drum rhythm. Two melodies alternate, starting quietly and gradually being embellished with greater instrumental density and color, all moving from double-*piano* to double-*forte* over 15 minutes. The solos are tricky to play, and the piece is hard to conduct with a totally steady pulse since the natural tendency is to slow down as it progresses and then speed up once it gets louder towards the end. The recording session started with a complete take of the piece. Inevitably, small errors occurred, made painfully obvious under the cold glare of microphones. Instead of recording the whole piece again, inserts are typically rerecorded where corrections are needed. For a piece like *Bolero*, it is critical that the tempos of the inserts exactly match the tempo of the whole take so that splices are not audible. Fiedler was astonishing in his ability to record corrections at precisely the same tempo as his steady first take of the whole piece so the producer could seamlessly insert them into the whole.

The amazing arc of his career was masterminded by him alone — he never had a manager or publicist. The scuttlebutt was that he didn't want to spend the money (he was a renowned skinflint), which was probably true but immaterial. Cleverly, Fiedler fashioned a public

persona as an approachable musical populist, through his programming and the informal Pops setting, while at the same time embracing
the aura of a remote maestro formally dressed in white tie and tails
who never spoke from the podium. He instinctively understood the
fine line between populism and serious classical artistry. A genius at
public relations and self-promotion, he never passed up an opportunity for a photo or interview. His long-standing passion for chasing
fire trucks — he accumulated an impressive array of honorary fire
chief hats from all over the country — only added to his mystique.
He was an authentic man of the people, seemingly known on sight by
everyone in Boston and addressed by all in idiosyncratic New England
twang as "Ah-thah." He had the distinct advantage of looking exactly
like a stereotypical conductor — elegant, handsome, slightly aloof but
with a twinkle in his eyes. And this was all wrapped in the mantle of
a distinctive national brand, the Boston Pops, of which he became an
integral part.

Fiedler was Boston's true musical celebrity, to the consternation of the BSO music director's elevated ego. Arriving once at Logan
Airport, Leinsdorf took a taxi to Symphony Hall, where he was to
lead a rehearsal. When the chatty driver asked him why he was going
to Symphony Hall, Leinsdorf grandiosely responded that it was "to
conduct the orchestra." The driver responded, "So, you must work for
Ah-thah Fiedler."

GETTING TO KNOW THE POPS

Upon my arrival in Boston, I immersed myself in the Pops, learning from Brosnahan and Shapiro the details of its history and how it
worked. I loved the whole idea: its elegance and perfection of execution, its broad repertoire and the sheer élan of the playing — a superb
concept, flawlessly executed.

How this huge machine was managed internally came as a surprise. With six revenue-generating concerts per week over two months
and substantial record royalties, the Pops seemed an almost self-per-
petuating cash machine for the BSO, somehow magically running itself and getting no attention from a management that rather grandly
focused more on the sober and proper business of running a world-
class symphony orchestra and a serious summer music festival. The
entire operation was handled in a bubble by Fiedler, assistant librarian

Bill Shisler, and Fiedler's secretary Harriet Littlefield, a colorful woman with a dark smoker's voice and a penchant for bourbon.

Littlefield handled Fiedler's other musical affairs as well, although Fiedler relished negotiating his own guest conducting fees (something he did alarmingly badly, consistently underselling himself). The substantial library was handled by Shisler, who also took care of the music for guest-conducting engagements. In addition, he booked and arranged for private concerts outside the Pops season with civic and convention groups, which was a highly lucrative business for both him and Fiedler, operated totally outside the control of the parent organization. I was shocked to learn of the BSO's apparent willingness to dilute control over its powerful Pops brand.

To my surprise, I discovered that Fiedler's conducting contract dated back to the mid-1940s and specified a total annual fee of $12,500 (over $200,000 today when adjusted for inflation), a laughably low sum for such a star and an amount that had never been increased despite his frequent entreaties to the board and management. But to supplement the low amount, he did get one-third of record royalties from RCA, which at one point amounted to six figures (over $2 million today), an office and secretary, and exclusive use of the Pops music library for concerts he conducted anywhere in the world. Despite his low annual fee, he proved a canny businessman who profited mightily from his position both financially and personally.

Fiedler's dominance over the enterprise was total. He conducted most of the concerts, leaving a few to be led by his assistant, Harry Ellis Dickson, a violinist in the orchestra and friend. Guest conductors were infrequent. Relationships with the ticket-buying groups were nurtured directly by Fiedler himself, who solicited repertoire suggestions from each, always having at least one work on the program to satisfy such requests. To further these relationships, he readily agreed to engage concerto soloists associated with them.

While it all appeared to function seamlessly, Fiedler, celebrating his 40th season as conductor when I arrived, was about to turn 75. I heard no mention internally of what might happen should the orchestra suddenly find itself without its famous maestro. And for the first time, he and the Pops were without a solid recording partnership when the RCA contract ended and the unfocused Deutsche Grammophon took over.

THE DREAM JOB: ARTHUR FIEDLER

I had first seen Fiedler conduct when the Tour Orchestra appeared in Rochester in 1953 and 1954 and first saw him direct a concert in Boston in the early 1960s. I had briefly met him when he visited Cincinnati as guest conductor in 1966. I was formally introduced to the great man a few weeks after arriving in Boston as he wandered into the business office to say hello to Brosnahan. He showed me his office, a laughably small cubicle tucked away between a bathroom and a staircase on Symphony Hall's second floor. It had barely enough space for a desk, a few chairs and some shelves for scores — hardly the grand command center I had pictured for such a major musical figure.

Through my first season, he and I became friendly, no doubt because I was genuinely enthusiastic about the Pops — something rare for a member of the BSO management, most of whom would attend concerts seldom and grudgingly. I was different, a star-struck fan who already had a working familiarity with the repertoire through recordings, radio broadcasts and live concerts. I loved the whole concept and went to as many performances as I could.

I gradually involved myself more and more in the operation — through my relationship with Fiedler, as well as performing occasionally as an extra percussionist. It gave me welcome ties to the music from my perch in the finance office.

EVENING AT POPS

In 1970, the fledgling PBS network proposed producing 12 hour-long television programs with the orchestra, to be called *Evening at Pops*. BSO management then was preoccupied with an unwell Steinberg and the need to find numerous conducting replacements, navigating the new recording relationship with Deutsche Grammophon and planning a European tour for April 1971.

Into the picture walked a producer from Boston's PBS station WGBH, Bill Cosel, who had directed many of the BSO's local television shows. I had met him in Cincinnati when he was a freelance director for a local television broadcast of the Cincinnati Symphony. We had bonded through our mutual affection for the BSO and Pops. Cosel asked me to become his partner in developing and planning the new series, and, given the management's other pressing priorities, Tod Perry thankfully agreed. Suddenly I was thrust officially into exactly the role I had yearned for: planning programs and concerts, and doing so with Fiedler, in addition to my regular business-office duties.

PBS thought the Pops' broad repertoire and informality would have wide appeal. Featuring an orchestra on television happened rarely, except for Toscanini's NBC Symphony and Bernstein's Young People's Concerts in the 1950s. The plan was for the programs to be taped at regular concerts in May and June and broadcast over the subsequent summer. A major soloist would join for roughly half of each program, the other half to consist of orchestral repertoire. Taping the series added considerably to both the complexity of an already intense season and the extreme discomfort of the players in the un-air-conditioned Symphony Hall, with scorching television lights added to the humid spring heat.

For *Evening at Pops*, Cosel and I would generate ideas and concepts, do research on possible soloists, and then present them to Fiedler. Once he signed off, Cosel would invite the artists, and we would all then make the musical programs. Since programs had traditionally not been constructed around star soloists, this became new territory for Fiedler, but he welcomed the collaboration. For the first time, and so soon after my Boston arrival, I found myself in real partnership with a major conductor.

Over successive seasons, innumerable solo artists appeared during the series. Cosel and I had enormous fun concocting what would become priceless moments: Julia Child of PBS's *The French Chef* narrating *Tubby the Tuba*; the Muppets from another PBS hit, *Sesame Street*, including Bert and Ernie singing "Rubber Duckie" in a fake bathtub in front of the orchestra, Cookie Monster taking a star turn saying "cookie" in Haydn's *Toy Symphony*[3] in place of the scored "cuckoo," and Big Bird making his conducting debut; Leroy Anderson talking about his famous pieces written for the Pops and conducting *The Typewriter* with Fiedler playing (not very well!) the carriage return; the Big Apple Circus, with the orchestra providing circus music under a real big top to accompany the tricks and acts; the Carpenters, with Richard Carpenter fulfilling his lifelong dream of performing Addinsell's *Warsaw Concerto* with Fiedler; and numerous singing legends — Ethel Merman, Marian Anderson, Ella Fitzgerald, Tony Bennett, Leontyne Price, Richard Tucker, Robert Merrill, Aretha Franklin, and more.

---

3 The piece has also been attributed to Michael Haydn, Leopold Mozart and Edmund Angerer.

INTERLUDE: RUBBER DUCKIE

When the cast of *Sesame Street* appeared on *Evening at Pops*, we had the hit song "Rubber Duckie" arranged for the full orchestra to accompany the Muppets Bert and Ernie. Throughout, all the musicians were supposed to squeeze real yellow rubber duckies, which had been donated by whoever makes rubber duckies. All was set, until one of the honchos from the American Federation of Musicians called to say that having members of the orchestra "play" rubber duckies on national television would constitute "doubling," a term meaning that musicians get extra pay for playing additional instruments not specified in their contracts. Because that would have cost thousands of dollars, I decided that just Fiedler and the percussion section, which is allowed to play all manner of sound effects without being paid for doubling, would squeeze them. But I vowed to give the union its comeuppance, and a labor negotiation a few summers later provided the opportunity.

The BSO labor contract had a long paragraph on doubling, specifying things like "flute includes piccolo but does not include alto or bass flute," which means that a flutist could perform on piccolo for no extra money but would get extra pay if asked to perform on alto or bass flute. After reaching final agreement on the contract without changes to the doubling provision, I impishly inserted into that paragraph, "Bassoon includes contrabassoon and rubber duckie." This made it through four drafts unnoticed and was included in the final signed agreement and in the printed version distributed to the players. Four months later on a tour bus, a member of the bassoon section suddenly screamed when noticing the clause. The whole orchestra was in hysterics and understood what had happened and who had done it.

The Pops season became increasingly complex as we walked the fine line between creating television shows and producing live concerts. Increasingly, Symphony Hall resembled a television set, with added lighting and stage decor. Air-conditioning became necessary for the comfort of both orchestra and audience under the hot TV lights, and a thrust stage was added to create a more dynamic visual setting for the soloists. With all this, a steady and subtle change started to occur, one that no one had foreseen, including me. The motivation for buying tickets "to Pops" regardless of conductor or program gradually eroded, as groups and the public gravitated toward televised concerts with star soloists, creating new sales challenges. When *Evening at Pops* first started, groups never knew if their concert might include a star or be taped for television — those were simply the luck of the draw. The change was perhaps inevitable.

Today, each Pops concert needs a theme or soloist, all publicized in advance — an unfortunate loss of one of the orchestra's distinctive assets, that the essence of the brand was the institution itself. Such a season is more expensive to produce and market, and it makes "going to Pops" similar to attending more generic concerts everywhere, an unfortunate and unintended consequence of the television series.

Cosel and I together planned the series until I left the BSO. It was a hit and ultimately lasted for 35 years, becoming one of the longest-running programs on PBS. And thanks to television, the already famous Fiedler became a rock star.

PROGRAMMING

Working with Fiedler on the television shows soon morphed into helping him plan the entire season. Making programs was a colorful and time-consuming process that involved Cosel, Shisler, Littlefield (and after she retired in 1970, her successor) and me crammed into his tiny office. Given the number of concerts and the concentrated schedule, the Pops had one large, revolving repertoire, constantly re-mixed in multiple ways for individual programs.

Fiedler designed binders separated into musical categories — "Marches," "Suites," "Waltzes," "Overtures," "Concertos," and "Medleys." Within each category, every piece performed was listed alphabetically by composer, followed by performance timings for each year — an orchestra member recorded the timings of each piece, and got extra pay for the task. These became an indispensable resource in our meetings.

Programs traditionally opened with a march, so we would consult the "Marches" section of the timing binder and make suggestions to Fiedler, who always asked, "How long?" Then came an overture, and the same process was repeated, and so on. Fiedler always made sure to include a specific piece requested by one of the large groups attending the concert. The sessions were hysterically funny — Cosel and I pushed for certain pieces, Fiedler pushed for others, and good-natured arguments and rampant jokes prevailed. Shisler, in a recurring gag, advocated Leroy Anderson's *The Waltzing Cat*, which Fiedler shouted down with a mix of good humor and theatrical drama.

A Pops performance started at exactly 8 p.m., opening with that loud march to get everyone's attention, followed by an overture as Fiedler got into the meat of the concert. Hearing these remarkable but seldom-performed gems — Suppé's *Poet and Peasant*, Offenbach's *Orpheus in the Underworld* or Hérold's *Zampa* — played by a great orchestra thrilled me. And the audiences. Following a quieter piece as a kind of *amuse-bouche*, the first third ended with something rousing. After the first intermission, the middle portion of the program offered a concerto or a more substantial orchestral piece like Ravel's *Bolero*, Tchaikovsky's *Capriccio Italien* or Respighi's *The Pines of Rome*. After the second intermission, the last part involved current songs, show tunes or film music, usually beginning with a medley from a musical comedy or an operetta. These specially-arranged short pieces were affectionately referred to by Fiedler and all of us in program meetings as "short crappy tunes."

Programs included a liberal number of unannounced pieces — "encores" — that Fiedler interspersed throughout, totally unlike the practice elsewhere of having them all at the end. Encores were triggered by a nod from him to his personal valet Joe Spotts, who stationed himself at the open center door at the back of the stage. At the signal, Spotts would raise a large sign announcing the title of the encore to the audience. This practice, gleaned from the Sousa Band, eliminated the need for Fiedler himself to announce encores, adding not only to the program's forward thrust but to his own detached mystique. In all my time in Boston, he spoke directly to the audience once, and that only after being prodded by singer Pearl Bailey on a television show to answer a question, after which she loudly proclaimed to the crowd's delight, "I got him to talk!"

With Fiedler's fixation on timings, all concerts ended punctually at 10 p.m. This nightly sequence — starting with a bang, providing musical substance, injecting a change of pace with a concerto and reserving the current tunes (never too many) to the very end — always left the public wanting more. Not performing encores after the final number only amplified the clamor for more, which audiences could get only by coming back to another concert.

He was a real showman in that final third of the program. The nightly grind of the Pops season led to planned and unplanned high jinks in concerts, some of which Fiedler gleefully joined or even initiated, including whistling during Alford's *Colonel Bogey March* à la *The Bridge on the River Kwai*, a dog barking in Piston's *The Incredible Flutist*,[4] funny sound effects added to some arrangements or conducting *The Stars and Stripes Forever* in three rather than four just because he felt like it. This was all done with a sly grin, and he loved seeing the effects of such pranks on the musicians' faces. This was another lesson I learned: a symphony orchestra requires hard work and classical music is serious business, but there is nothing wrong with a smile from time to time.

INTERLUDE: HIGH JINKS

Vic Firth and Fiedler had an avuncular relationship which created a safe zone for some fun. In Firth's bag of tricks was a carved wooden hand with the middle finger extended. At the end of a concert, Fiedler, heading offstage to a vociferous ovation, passed the timpani, which were positioned near the exit door. Firth would place the carved hand upright on one of the timpani as the maestro went by. Fiedler would wink and flick the carving over with his baton, only to see the hand reappear as he returned for a further bow, flicking it again as he passed. This went on night after night, to the guffaws of players and conductor alike. The audience had no idea

Through working with Fiedler, I learned his genius as a programmer. While there was a standard structure to a Pops concert, the magic was in how artfully he chose and ordered each piece. He knew how to build an emotional arc into a program, assessing both individual pieces and the relationships between them, conceiving the overall sequence as a single, cohesive experience for the audience. Building on the traditional three-part concert structure he inherited, he thought of programs as natural narratives with beginning, middle and end. I saw first-hand how hard he worked, taking nothing for granted, thinking everything through and agonizing over choices. He had an innate sense of what worked and what didn't, and he was usually right. Everything was geared toward creating events, performed at the highest of musical standards, that would produce palpable impact on the public. These programming and concert-producing lessons stayed with me my entire life.

An underlying premise of the Boston Pops was its foundation as a symphony orchestra that is not afraid to let its hair down by embracing popular culture, not as a commercial pop orchestra that plays regular classical pieces. In other words, the artistic *raison d'être* was validated

---

4 The composer was so taken with this effect, which occurred at the end of the "Circus March" at the first performance, that he subsequently wrote it into the published score.

by the first and second parts of a program, not the last, which is why Fiedler always referred to it as "dessert." Today, that basic premise is pretty much lost not only on the Boston Pops but on similar concerts across the country, with programs dominated by current tunes or the orchestra playing backup to soloists. That model does not effectively utilize or showcase the glories of a full symphony orchestra, negating the very reason for being of the institution. It has resulted in a plethora of pops-concert conductors more focused on being entertainers than serious musicians.

EXPANDED RESPONSIBILITIES

Through those early years, my BSO duties increased at a fast pace. While I was taking on *Evening at Pops* and having greater involvement in the Boston Pops, my role in the business office expanded into bud-

Fiedler at Tanglewood with one of the 1812 Overture *cannons —
the pose was his idea*

geting and financial strategy, property management and labor negotiations with the players and stagehands. When Brosnahan retired in 1972, I was promoted to business manager and my formal responsibilities grew even more. Three years later, I was surprised and gratified to be promoted to second-in-command under Perry. This took me out of the business office and thrust me not only into institutional planning and operations but creative matters for the Boston Symphony.

The institution's artistic leadership was changing as well. In 1973 following Steinberg's retirement, Ozawa was appointed music director, assuming full responsibility for Tanglewood as well and returning the organization to having a single artistic leader for all its Boston Symphony activities. A protégé of Munch and alumnus of the Tanglewood school, Ozawa had been a frequent guest conductor in Boston and Tanglewood for years. Having been involved peripherally with his appointment, I now started working with him regularly on planning and programming.

My new job also included working with Michael Tilson Thomas and Colin Davis, simultaneously appointed as principal guest conductors. It was Davis with whom I developed an especially close bond, finding his absolute devotion to music and deep humanity inspiring. I loved his conducting and admired his years of concentrated knowledge of and attention to Stravinsky, Mozart, Haydn, Berlioz, Tippett and more recently to Sibelius, whose seven symphonies became the cornerstone of his BSO recording projects during those early years. And it was Davis who took a personal interest in my early work and development. He became an important mentor — always encouraging me, always prodding me and always teaching me.

All of this was in addition to my work with the Pops. To my delight, Ozawa, given his reverence for senior mentors, paid attention to Fiedler and spent time with him, becoming the first Boston Symphony music director to do so. Fiedler now had visible support at the highest levels of the organization, something he had never enjoyed before. It was a far cry from the days of long-time BSO music director and founder of Tanglewood, Serge Koussevitzky, who, after finally inviting Fiedler to conduct a subscription concert in 1945, angrily withdrew the invitation on learning that he was going to conduct a concert elsewhere with a reigning pop idol. Koussevitzky wrote in a letter, "I strongly feel that since your name was associated with a Frank Sinatra show in Boston, it cannot remain on the list of guest conductors with the Boston Symphony Orchestra. That is my firm and unwavering conviction."[5] In 1955, after Koussevitzky was gone, Fiedler conducted the Boston Symphony for the first and only time at a subscription concert and then again at a special gala for his 75th birthday in 1969 — for him the ultimate present.

As the popularity of the Pops grew, it seemed natural to me to expand the enterprise. Seeing that Fiedler was spending most Decembers conducting the Boston Ballet's wildly successful production of *The Nutcracker*, I reasoned it would be better to have him conduct the Pops during the holiday period. In 1973, I created a series of Christmas programs (which included a surprise appearance on stage by Santa Claus) in the traditional tables-and-chairs set-up, and, a few years later, a New Year's Eve event, complete with dance floor in the center of the hall. Both became instant traditions, and the holiday concerts eventually expanded to multiple weeks.

The pickup orchestra became increasingly necessary as the Pops season itself was extended into July in the newly air-conditioned Symphony Hall while the regular BSO players were at Tanglewood, and for tours during the regular BSO season when the regular players were occupied. The pickup group was rebranded the Boston Pops Esplanade Orchestra. I moved the private concert business, previously run independently by Shisler, under the BSO corporate umbrella in order to control all elements of the Pops brand and to provide financial support for the parent company.

WORRY

The increasing concern was Fiedler's health. At 81, he still maintained a manic pace of guest-conducting, recording sessions and television programs as the expanded season itself became ever more taxing. Unsurprisingly, his energy began to wane. A turning point came in February 1976. The Boston Symphony embarked on its first European tour under Ozawa. Given his affection for Fiedler, Ozawa endorsed a concert with the Pops in London's Royal Albert Hall, the first time it would perform outside America. The preceding December, Fiedler

---

5 Moore, Robin, *Fiedler: The Colorful Mr. Pops*. Little, Brown and Company, 1968.

had become ill, exhausted by his incessant and grueling schedule. We all watched his health anxiously as the tour approached. While he had been relentlessly determined to go through with the prestigious occasion, a week before the trip he was forced to admit that it was beyond his stamina and reluctantly canceled. It was a serious blow to his pride.

Erich Kunzel, a young conductor I met while working in Cincinnati, had made a huge impact as an annual guest conductor since 1970, and his growing national reputation as a pops conductor had made him a potential candidate to succeed Fiedler whenever that time came. I engaged him to substitute in London, partly to help evaluate how plausible a candidate he might be.

The sold-out concert went fine — until an encore. Kunzel talked to audiences everywhere except in Boston: wanting the job, he happily complied with Fiedler's practice of never speaking to audiences. But unable to contain his enthusiasm in front of the cheering London crowd, he noticed a patron in the upper balcony getting up to leave and shouted out, "It's the second door to the right." I could hear the collective groan of the orchestra. While Kunzel continued to return as a guest conductor and went on to establish a stellar career with the Cincinnati Pops, the incident effectively ended his potential candidacy for Boston.

Fiedler subsequently recovered well enough to lead the Pops season two months later. Shortly thereafter, he reached the pinnacle of public acclaim with a nationally televised concert on the Esplanade celebrating the Bicentennial on July 4, 1976. While he had been conducting there for almost 50 years, he created a sensational production of Tchaikovsky's *1812 Overture* in 1974 by adding spectacular fireworks shot from a barge on the Charles River, military cannons and live bells from the surrounding churches to the score's already clamorous ending.[6] When the production was repeated in 1976, a crowd of 400,000 jammed the banks of the Charles River for miles. It was hailed by the Guinness Book of World Records as largest live attendance for a classical concert to date.

I rode with Fiedler amid a police escort from Symphony Hall to the concert site, both of us amazed at the turnout. The ecstatic crowd under the balmy night sky cheered him like the celebrity he had become. That night, since I was playing in the orchestra, I had a

---

6 A friend of Fiedler's, a Boston investor named David Mugar, volunteered to organize and finance the upgraded event, which he did for years and with military precision and anal-retentive attention to detail.

perfect view from the stage of the immense audience. During one of the encores, a swinging arrangement of the Andrews Sisters' "Boogie Woogie Bugle Boy," I witnessed this mass of humanity dancing to the music, waving flags and having the time of their lives. The image reminded me of sea grass energetically swaying in the wind.

The year ended triumphantly as Fiedler was awarded the Presidential Medal of Freedom by President Ford at the White House.

DECLINE

Though he conducted the 1977 and 1978 seasons, Fiedler's energy gradually and inexorably declined, resulting in increased guest-conducting cancellations and ending his longstanding series in San Francisco. I spent hours with him, reviewing his schedule, suggesting ways he could cut back and get blocks of time for planned rest. Alas, none of this succeeded as he stubbornly pointed to a small, framed sign on his office wall that read, "He who rests ... rots". I explained that by increasing his guest-conducting fees substantially to something more appropriate, he could earn more by working less, but to no avail. I cut back his Boston schedule as much as possible and, with his grudging agreement, began to add guest conductors. He continued to keep *Evening at Pops* to himself.

In the fall of 1978, I noticed an alarming deterioration in his physical strength and, even more striking, in his mental acuity. In meetings he seemed unable to focus and grew confused about simple scheduling questions. In December, he was finally hospitalized, with a buildup of fluid on his brain that seriously impaired his physical and cognitive functions. Doctors installed a shunt to drain the fluid, a risky procedure for an 84-year-old. After four days, he was out of intensive care and well enough to celebrate his birthday in the hospital, a riotous occasion joined by close friends with beer, whiskey and song. He remained fixated on the 1979 season, his 50th anniversary, and was determined to see it through.

Going home from the hospital to recover his strength, he focused on the May 1 season opening, which was to be taped for *Evening at Pops*. Heartbroken to have missed conducting a program as part of the Boston Symphony's historic tour to China in early March 1979, he rallied for a "welcome home" concert at Symphony Hall, conducting *The Stars and Stripes Forever*, a hopeful sign that he had recovered and was fit.

That spring, he was approached by a small pop label to record an album of disco arrangements to be called *Saturday Night Fiedler*, an obvious takeoff on *Saturday Night Fever*, then sweeping the nation. The Pops recording business had never really recovered after the glory days of RCA, and Fiedler readily agreed to the project over my cautions about its musical integrity and his health. The sessions were scheduled for late May. The label sent a photographer to his home to shoot pictures for the cover, with Fiedler in John Travolta's famous disco pose, complete with white suit. The photos showed a depressingly gaunt and emaciated figure, nothing like the dapper, sparkling image he had cultivated so assiduously.

He did rally for the televised opening night of the season, a huge personal triumph, and then once more four days later with flutist James Galway, also televised for *Evening at Pops*. Afterward, he collapsed in his dressing room. I was convinced the end had come, but after a frantic ride to the hospital, he revived, albeit seriously weakened, from what was only dehydration and exhaustion. He had made it to his 50th anniversary, but it was the last concert he was to conduct.

Even at that, he remained determined to go through with the *Saturday Night Fiedler* sessions two weeks later. I spoke with him every day and strongly advised against it. Finally, the day before the sessions, he told me I was right: he didn't feel strong enough and agreed to let his assistant Dickson substitute at the sessions. I was relieved, but knowing Fiedler well, I didn't trust the staying power of his decision. Just in case, I asked the orchestra's driver to alert me if he got a call from him in the morning, asking to be picked up for the sessions.

Sure enough, at 7:30 a.m. the driver called, saying he had just been summoned. I raced to Fiedler's house and found him morosely sitting in the kitchen, fully dressed for work. He appeared to have been expecting my arrival and wanting me to make the decision for him. I told him he could not do the sessions for the sake of his health, his reputation, his musicians and the project: he reluctantly agreed. I know it deflated his remaining strength and resolve to appear before the orchestra again, but it was necessary and right. Dickson did the sessions, and the project, as I had feared, was musically dreadful and a commercial bust. The recording was released several months later, with that horrible, sad picture of this great man on the cover.

I saw Fiedler twice more over the next month at his home. Sitting on his porch dressed in a bathrobe, he looked frail but still an elegant, if faded, presence.

On July 10 in the early morning, his daughter called with the not-unexpected news that he had died during the night. The saga had ended and a friendship was over. It was devastating but deeply meaningful for Cosel and me to work with the family in arranging the services.

His death was national front-page news and the press onslaught was overwhelming. It was in the middle of the extended Pops season, and I knew he would want the show that night to go on. Symphony Hall was abuzz with news media and an audience unsettled at witnessing the first post-Fiedler concert. Dickson mounted the podium at 8 p.m. sharp and asked the audience to stand as he made a few heartfelt remarks. He announced that the concert would begin with *The Stars and Stripes Forever* in Fiedler's memory, requesting the audience to remain standing and not to applaud at the end. Dickson gave the downbeat and then left the stage. The Pops performed Fiedler's signature patriotic march without conductor, playing it totally pianissimo until the final strain, which blared out at full volume, complete with traditional standing brass, blazing piccolos and the American flag dropping from the ceiling. The hushed silence at the end lasted for what seemed an eternity. The concert then continued — the simplest and classiest musical tribute I could imagine as the Fiedler era was laid to rest.

In 1984, a memorial was installed on Fiedler's beloved Esplanade, a six-foot sculpture of his head gazing paternally toward the Hatch Shell, where the concerts he started in 1929 were held. The sculpture is comprised of layers of aluminum plates: its image reads most coherently from afar and becomes more abstract as you draw near, providing a visual parallel to the elusive public persona of the man. Carved into the granite base is simply "Arthur Fiedler – Musician." Exactly.

While the history of the Boston Pops and the longevity of its heritage were remarkable, what impressed me above all else was the sheer audacity of the concept and how early in the BSO's history it was realized. While originally envisioned to achieve practical goals, at its core it had a strong musical vision: using a symphony orchestra to play concerts focused on light classical repertoire in an informal setting with refreshments. The Pops dared to alter the variables of traditional concertgoing in repertoire, setting, ambience, pricing, community positioning, marketing and messaging. Its schedule occupied a discrete and compact time of the year, a season within a season, and therefore existed as an entity, the complete opposite of designing individual concerts that occur in isolation. Such concentration means events feeding off themselves to reinforce context and identity.

In light of the virtually unchanged orchestra model since the turn of the last century, the Boston Pops was revolutionary in showing that thinking and executing differently was not only possible but successful. Key was doing it really well and having a leader in Fiedler who embraced the concept fully and assured its artistic quality.

The success of *Evening at Pops* made me realize the power of television in building brand recognition far beyond what was possible with just concerts and recordings. We were lucky to have in WGBH a local station which was experienced in televising orchestras and found sponsorship to finance the series, and in PBS a national network that wanted to broadcast it. And, of course, the Pops was a unique concept well-suited to the broad appeal that television provides.

Before getting to Boston, I could only admire the Pops from afar, but I soon learned that, by intensely sharing Fiedler's vision, it was possible to become an active partner in its realization, an involvement that enhanced my reverence for the institution and admiration for him. He was the first major artist with whom I developed a close professional and personal relationship, something unexpected and fulfilling. At its heart was not only a strong belief in the Pops concept but a mutual love of its repertoire and fascination with its programming. It taught me that the secret of working successfully with artists is not just the willingness to collaborate around shared goals but doing so in person, not muted through memos, phone calls or intermediaries. There is nothing like the back-and-forth that can occur sitting across a table, even in a cramped office like Fiedler's. This was a critical lesson I carried throughout my career.

Conductors are unique and, unlike instrumentalists or singers, can practice their craft only with an ensemble. This requires creative partnership with the management of institutions to organize those musical forces and realize the vision of artists. It is that dynamic, I was learning, which must always lie at the heart of running such an institution.

CHAPTER 3
ADVENTURES IN REPERTOIRE:
OLIVER KNUSSEN

Working for the BSO required spending summers at Tanglewood — not a hardship. It features concerts by the Boston Symphony joined by the world's most prominent conductors and soloists and is home to more than 150 young music students at the Tanglewood Music Center. The gorgeous grounds, dotted with studios, practice huts and concert facilities, was a beehive of sounds and activities, making it impossible not to be swept up in the swirling vitality of unceasing musical energy.

I thought I knew a lot of music when I started at the BSO, but I was soon disabused of that notion by the welter constantly engulfing me during my first summer at Tanglewood. Attending 24 concerts by the Boston Symphony, along with the wealth of chamber, vocal and contemporary music, added multiple dimensions to my range of exposure. I was introduced to opera, hearing *Otello* (my first Verdi stage work) and Berg's *Wozzeck*. It was the year that Tanglewood branched into rock music, under the stuffy banner of "Contemporary Trends." One artist presented was Janis Joplin, a performer who took my breath and heart away.[1]

My first regular exposure to new music had been at Princeton, where as a percussionist, I was regularly involved in working rehearsals of new works by graduate composition students. With a music faculty dominated by the likes of Milton Babbitt, Earl Kim and Roger Sessions, most of the new music I experienced was awash in astringent atonality. My years in Cincinnati added little to my knowledge, given that orchestra's conservative repertoire, so I had a pretty narrow view

---

1 Attending the concert was Erich Leinsdorf, apparently curious to take in such "contemporary trends." The BSO photographer captured his awkward backstage meeting with Joplin, two of the most unlikely artists ever to be photographed together.

*A collision of musical constellations: Erich Leinsdorf greeting
Janis Joplin at Tanglewood in July 1969*

of contemporary music. The BSO taught me quickly that there was a
much wider perspective, and I began to learn how much I didn't know.
I eagerly ate it all up.

OLLY

It was at Tanglewood in 1970 that I first met Oliver Knussen, or Olly
as he was known by everyone. He was an 18-year-old composition student of Gunther Schuller, one of the triumvirate running Tanglewood
at the time. A year later, I first experienced Knussen's music live, a performance of his Symphony No. 2. The piece was far from easy, but it
had immediate emotional appeal, already demonstrating the exquisite
craftsmanship and glistening sonorities that would come to character-
ize all of his works. I was moved and impressed.

During those two summers, I was dumbfounded by Knussen's
encyclopedic knowledge of and curiosity about music as well as his
complete command of the broadest range of contemporary repertoire. I found myself a total amateur next to him. How did someone

eight years younger than me know so much? He was an inspiring and infectious guide, expanding my own musical curiosity. Through those first summers, I tried to keep up with him, always motivated to learn whatever unknown pieces he enthused about. My record collection grew by leaps and bounds.

We discovered a shared, if twisted, fascination with the forgotten byways of the symphonic repertoire, such as the music of Leroy Anderson and Percy Grainger or the Tap Dance Concerto by Morton Gould (Knussen informed me it was one of two such concertos by Gould[2] — how could he know that?). And there was the Symphony No. 3 (*Ilya Muromets*) by Reinhold Glière. Not only did he know the piece, but he was familiar with its score and structure, and he knew Leopold Stokowski's sweeping cuts to prune its 78-minute length to a more manageable 37, as well as Eugene Ormandy's more judicious trimmings that reduced it to only 59 minutes.

Knussen was a big, cuddly bear of a man who, despite his somewhat shy demeanor, easily erupted into gales of laughter. He was fun to be around and never took himself too seriously, unlike the deadly earnest composers I encountered at Princeton. His joy in music, and in life, was captivating. He loved the ridiculous, relished gossip, enjoyed food and wine, and wrapped it all in a personality laced with a childlike sense of effusive wonder. While he could be private and guarded, he was always generous and warm, and totally undogmatic and clearheaded about his musical likes and dislikes.

He was brought up and schooled in London and showed precocious talent from the start. He composed his first symphony at age 14 and made his conducting debut with it in London a year later.

He came from a musical family. His father, longtime principal double bassist of the London Symphony and eventually its chairman, was domineering and somewhat distant but clearly proud of his son's early interest in composition. When Knussen decided to try conducting in his teens — believing he could do better justice to his own music than other conductors — his father gave him conducting lessons in the family living room, strongly insisting that musicians needed the conduc-

---

2 Gould's well-known Tap Dance Concerto was written in 1952 for the dancer Danny Daniels. In 1941 Gould had written an earlier one for dancer Paul Draper, but that piece was never performed and the score was lost. According to Loras Schissel of the Library of Congress, Gould actually wrote a third one in 1956, called "Concertette: 'Challenge' for Solo Tap Dancer and 3 Percussion." It was for a recording project that was never realized, and the score was never published.

tor's beat controlled and up high where it could be seen easily. Standing before his son with his hands outlining an imaginary three-foot-square box, his father would ask him to conduct along with a recording. Every time his son's hand strayed outside that imaginary box, he would slap it, not the most delicate way to teach conducting or establish loving rapport with one's child. But the young Knussen developed a fastidious technique, which no doubt contributed to the affection and respect orchestra musicians felt towards him throughout his life.

EARLY ADVENTURES

As we bonded over music industry gossip, our discussion usually turned to repertoire. With a sense of playful competition, we tried to out-nerd each other by bringing up obscure, terrible pieces. One was the Symphony No. 3 by Aram Khachaturian, which we agreed was perhaps the most amazingly ridiculous orchestral work ever. This forgotten gem had recently been given a new lease on life through a blazing 1968 recording by Stokowski and the Chicago Symphony. In one continuous movement, the work is immodestly scored for an immense orchestra, pipe organ and an extra 15 antiphonal trumpets. The last 20 of its 22 minutes seem to be one long, loud coda, roaring on and on with trumpets blaring, organ bellowing and percussion pounding. We agreed that it was truly terrible, not merely bad but "bad with an attitude" — what we came to call "great bad" music.

Knussen introduced me to the early four-movement version of Jean Sibelius's Symphony No. 5 and the absolutely mind-numbing *Ali Baba* Overture by Luigi Cherubini. In the Sibelius, all the sublime moments of the final, three-movement version are present, just not in the right places or proportions. I can imagine the conductor advising the composer after its premiere that, while the piece had good moments, it needed a "little work." It is truly awe-inspiring how Sibelius transformed the trainwreck of a symphony into the sublime masterpiece it became.

The Cherubini leaves you speechless. Even the brilliance of a committed and driven recording by Toscanini and the NBC Symphony fails to mask the comically incessant interjections by triangle, bass drum and cymbals, or to hide a theme in the coda reminiscent of *The Stars and Stripes Forever*. You can't listen to the piece without a guffaw. To me, it remains the gold standard for great bad music.

INTERLUDE: *ALI BABA* OVERTURE

In 1993, composer Peter Maxwell Davies guest conducted The Cleveland Orchestra. Much of his music is thorny and difficult, not necessarily what you might expect given his puckish sense of humor. During that same week, Peter Schickele conducted a benefit concert featuring the music of his alter ego, P.D.Q. Bach. For years, Schickele had presented concerts of "newly discovered" music by the mythical P.D.Q., all of which he had written himself. The music is full of gags, weird instrumentation and clever quotations, all presented with faux seriousness. Schickele was a genuinely funny man who delighted in skewering the stuffiness of classical music. He and Davies had never met until they spent a relaxed evening at our house and totally hit it off. One thing led to another, and, of course, we had to listen to the *Ali Baba* Overture, which neither of them knew. They were both convulsed. Schickele's priceless critique was, "I wish I had written that." Two years later, Davies outdid him, opening a program he conducted in England with it.

So began "The List", which we pledged would be the definitive catalog of "The 100 Best Bad Pieces of Orchestral Music." Over the years, we continually revised it, calling each other as we discovered worthy additions. It was shared with select friends for comments and reactions — early crowdsourcing — with the proviso that nothing could be deleted unless an alternative was proposed and approved by all. What was frightening was that we both came to know all these pieces. Eventually, we rechristened it the "Pedagogically United Research Effort on Symphonic History In Trash" — it took a mouthful to come up with just the right acronym.

Present at Tanglewood during those early summers was Michael Tilson Thomas, the recently-arrived BSO assistant conductor. He got to know Knussen and became an early champion of his music. In 1971, the BSO trustees wanted to reenergize Boston audiences frustrated by Steinberg's increasing absences, which had blunted the organization's artistic energy. They asked Tilson Thomas to devise an innovative series of concerts, experimenting with new and more informal kinds of presentation involving a degree of explanation and demonstration. Each program was built around a concept and full of unusual repertoire. The series was called Spectrum, and the energetic Tilson Thomas threw his considerable creative energies into it. His programs for Spectrum, along with his regular BSO subscription programs, were highly innovative in both repertoire and structure, providing me with a further crash course in contemporary composers and their work. It was through him that I first heard the music of Luciano Berio, Lou Harrison, Steve Reich, Carl Ruggles and David Del Tredici.

INTERLUDE: REICH'S *FOUR ORGANS*

The first Spectrum program, called "Music for Multiples," included *Four Organs* by the then-unknown American composer Steve Reich. Over its 20-plus minutes, maracas keep a steady pulse over which four amplified rock organs play a loud repeated chord that changes subtly and slowly. To the staid Boston audiences of those days, it was like music from outer space. During the live radio broadcast of the concert, the station was inundated with phone calls from irate listeners complaining that the "record" being played had a stuck needle. This caused the announcer, about 15 minutes in, to interrupt, reassuring the audience that there was no stuck record as this was how the piece really went. I still have a copy of the remarkable broadcast.

Two years later, when the BSO repeated the piece in Carnegie Hall, the audience erupted in a riot of catcalls, boos and cheers. One woman ran down the aisle and banged her fist on the stage, screaming, "Stop, stop, I confess."[3] With this concert, Steve Reich became a well-known composer.

Tilson Thomas thought Spectrum to be the perfect vehicle for introducing Knussen's music to Boston, and a few years into the series, he planned the premiere of his Symphony No. 3. The work was originally envisioned as a symphonic poem based on Shakespeare's Ophelia — her madness, her death and her funeral cortège. As the performance week arrived, it was unfinished, with only nine minutes of music completed, but Tilson Thomas decided to perform it as it was. Even incomplete, it was impressive work from a 22-year-old composer. Not until 1979 did Knussen, having rethought the whole project after the Boston premiere, complete its definitive 15-minute version, still with the shade of Ophelia hovering in its background. Unfortunately, his inability to complete works on time was to plague him, and his commissioners, throughout his career.

Through the 1970s and 1980s, I saw him infrequently in London, New York and Tanglewood, but we maintained vibrant telephone

---

3 Tilson Thomas, Michael, *Viva Voce: Conversations with Edward Seckerson*, Faber and Faber, 1994.

contact. The List continued to develop, with out-of-the-blue phone calls revealing newly uncovered candidates. During this time, for some reason I signed off to him as "Your Tomness," a name that stuck. Even his friends began referring to me that way, so I dubbed him "Your Ol-lyness." The nicknames held through the years.

My first visit to his home in London was eye-opening. The flat was packed, floor-to-ceiling, with books, scores, LPs, cassettes and tapes stacked everywhere except for a small pathway through the piles lead-ing to an enormous living-room sofa where he, his wife and daughter would watch television. Amid the chaos, he knew where everything

Maurice Sendak with Oliver Knusssen in 1984 at Glyndebourne

was, and, if asked about a specific piece, he would rummage through a particular pile and pull out the score and a recording. He listened constantly to live concert broadcasts on the BBC and was totally up to date on contemporary music everywhere.

Around this time, he composed two fantasy operas, *Where the Wild Things Are* and *Higglety Pigglety Pop!*, based on books by Maurice Sendak and with librettos by Sendak himself. The operas are remark-able not only for the sheer inventiveness and the magic of the music but as major exceptions to his practice of writing works less than 15 minutes long — one lasts 40 minutes and the other just over an hour. Produced all over the world, they are two of his most enduring com-positions. He himself always reminded me of a Wild Thing, with his large and imposing presence and robust sense of the ridiculous.

After writing these, Knussen found composing increasingly difficult. He took up more conducting, and his performing career blossomed. He became one of the artistic directors of the Aldeburgh Festival in 1983, director of Tanglewood's contemporary music activities in 1986, principal guest conductor of The Hague's Residentie Orkest in 1993 and music director of the London Sinfonietta in 1998.

PROGRAMMING

Though we were friends, our professional lives intersected for the first time only after I got to Cleveland. I had inherited a practice of annually inviting a prominent composer to conduct a week of each season's subscription concerts, so I invited him to make his conducting debut there in February 1993. As we started to discuss a program, he suggested including the première of an early Aaron Copland ballet, *Grohg*, the score and parts of which, assumed lost, had been recently discovered in the Library of Congress. After withdrawing the work, Copland had reused more than half in his *Dance Symphony*, but the original piece remained unperformed. Giving a major premiere of an unknown Copland work was a perfect way to introduce Knussen.

The composer for the next season was scheduled to be Witold Lutosławski, who died suddenly two months before his concerts. Aware that Knussen admired his music and had recently conducted his new Symphony No. 4, which was the centerpiece of our program, I called him to substitute. Thus began regular multi-week engagements that gave us a way to collaborate professionally in Cleveland on an ongoing basis.

Programming with him was a logical extension of the philosophy I had learned from Fiedler, always thinking of concerts as discrete journeys musically and emotionally. Knussen and I took advantage of the huge range of music he knew. He was partial to unusual and ever-changing structures — producing unexpected juxtapositions through an unconventional number and order of pieces. He firmly rejected "masterpiece" dependence and, of course, strongly advocated a major presence of new music. To provide variety and changes of pace, he loved inserting shorter pieces such as Ferruccio Busoni's hypnotic *Berceuse élégiaque*, Anatol Liadov's haunting *The Enchanted Lake*, Ruth Crawford Seeger's bracing Andante for Strings or Sibelius' mysterious *Valse Triste*. He also loved transcriptions, overtures, ballets and tone poems that had gradually fallen from favor, banished, for reasons that elude me, to pops programs.

Sharing our beliefs enthusiastically, we were in heaven creating programs that we could not just talk about but realize in performance. At one point, he wanted to conduct a second half of Edward Elgar's masterly symphonic poem *Falstaff*, a favorite of his. It is a great work, but at the end the music just stops, leaving the audience mystified and generating, at most, one clap — not a satisfying way to finish a concert. We needed a piece to provide closure that logically linked to *Falstaff*. Two days later, we both landed on the same idea: Elgar's over-the-top orchestration of Bach's Fantasia and Fugue in C minor for organ. *Falstaff* did indeed stun audience members into silence, but they went wild over the Bach-Elgar finale.

INTERLUDE: THE CONDUCTING SUIT

Knussen, a very large man, was not a fashion plate: he was usually dressed in baggy trousers and an old maroon sweatshirt. When he conducted, he was far from stylish on the podium, wearing a loose-fitting black shirt, voluminous black pants and seriously scuffed shoes. During his years as guest conductor in Cleveland, I heard increasing comments from patrons and musicians about his inattention to looking neat, one dowager going so far as to say that his appearance was an insult to the high standards of the orchestra. He frankly didn't care much, but even I thought he was looking pretty sloppy.

A year later for his next conducting appearance, I proposed, as part of his contract, sending him to a well-known tailor who would design and make, at our expense, a conducting suit. I was not insisting on tails or a tux or even a tie, but just something that would be comfortable and look good. He agreed.

The clothes arrived, and he looked terrific — new shoes, pants that fitted with a crease, a loose black shirt and a good-looking jacket. When he first appeared on stage, everyone took delighted notice of his improved appearance. Mission accomplished, or so I thought. He wore the suit everywhere he conducted, but after three years, on a return visit, I noticed that the shoes again looked terrible, the pants had reverted to the old baggy status, and the coat appeared different. I asked him what had happened to the conducting jacket and pants, and he said sheepishly that he had inadvertently left them backstage at the Royal Festival Hall in London and forgotten to retrieve them. Two steps forward, two steps backward.

Along with his frequent guest-conducting, Knussen signed a major recording contract with Deutsche Grammophon in the 1990s, thanks to my friend Roger Wright, the label's newly-appointed head of artists and repertoire, who had previously worked for me in Cleveland as artistic administrator. DG's interest in Knussen was predicated on his eclectic repertoire. We spoke regularly about what to record, ranging from major new works by Peter Lieberson and Colin Matthews to music by established 20th-century masters like Schoenberg, Stravinsky and Henze and to music by forgotten but important pioneers such as Seeger. Knussen's wide tastes mandated recording exotica like Stokowski's arrangements of music by Mussorgsky, including his kaleidoscopic orchestration of *Pictures at an Exhibition*. Cleveland was the beneficiary of this relationship, and together we made three discs over the next several years.

Increasingly interested in expanding the range of new music presented in Cleveland, I established a program for emerging composers, supported by a generous grant from philanthropist and friend Daniel R. Lewis. This enabled the appointment of a young composer-in-residence over a multi-year period, with the composer's works programmed and a new piece commissioned. To help in the selection process, I formally enlisted Knussen, whose knowledge in this area was vast. This gave us something else to collaborate on regularly.

In the late 1990s, he moved from London to a small, remote house in Snape, a village northeast of London that is home to the Alde-

Knussen at home demonstrating his toys, including the train clock I gave him

burgh Festival. While not large, the house had much more room than his cramped London flat. He promptly stuffed the added space with books, scores, CDs, cassettes, videotapes, an astounding collection of movies and television shows on DVD and an ever-increasing collection of toys and mementos collected on his travels. The house was a palace of wonder and of amazement, but it made for an abrupt change from his being in the center of London's busy musical life day-to-day.

At the same time, Knussen separated from his wife, Sue. They never divorced and maintained close contact, but without her at his side, he became more rudderless and his composing more erratic. A few years later, she died suddenly after a short illness. Devastated, Knussen was moved to compose the touching 12-minute *Requiem: Songs for Sue* for soprano and chamber ensemble, which has gone on to become one of his most frequently performed pieces.

INTERLUDE: TOYS

Knussen loved tchotchkes — as he said in a BBC documentary,[4] "Some people collect art, I collect crap." I shared his love of toys. On one of his visits to Cleveland, I showed him a tacky large clock with a small train that ran around its perimeter three times with whistles on the hour. He was transfixed, so I sent him one. When I visited his house in Aldeburgh, he proudly showed me his battery-operated penguin slide game, in which three miniature penguins climb a set of stairs and then slide down a curving chute — over and over and over. He loved it. I loved it too, so he sent me one. My wife found in a catalog a solar-powered figurine of Queen Elizabeth in a pink suit, clutching a handbag, her left hand poised to wave to her subjects. When hit by sunlight, the hand waved back and forth. We sent one to him as a birthday present.

This practice went on through the years. On one visit to Aldeburgh, we talked about children's musical records we had known. Two of my favorites were *The Little Fiddle,* narrated by Danny Kaye, and *Gossamer Wump*, the story of a little boy who played the triangle and got into hilarious adventures. I had long ago lost my 78rpm discs of these two gems. He, of course, knew both and promptly produced from the piles in his house not one but two CD releases from Japan containing both along with other children's favorites from that era. He gave me one, which I cherish and play for my grandchildren.

---

4 Gavin, Barrie, "Oliver Knussen: Sounds from the Big White House," BBC Television, 2001.

DUMB PROGRAMS

It was during this period we developed a second project, building on The List. Befuddled by and amazed at the plethora of terrible concert programs everywhere, we formalized a listing of the world's "best worst." One that was merely poor was insufficient for inclusion: it had to be spectacularly bad, with a strong dose of "dumbness." Our new tally, dubbed "Dumb Programs," memorialized examples that strained credibility by noted conductors. And they were, alas, not hard to find.

This list is extensive, having been added to over the years not only by us, but program geeks from all over the world. All are real, but my lips remain sealed as to the actual orchestras and conductors. We spared no one, and I admit to having included a few of my own — they looked good on paper at the time but sounded awful in reality!

The project started with what to me is the most insanely bad program ever, one which I am at a total loss to explain:

Gershwin: Piano Concerto in F

Bruckner: Symphony No. 6

The jazzy nature of the Gershwin completely fights the austere grandeur of the Bruckner. Each has real distinction on its own, but the combination is simply moronic.

But this one is not alone. Dumb Programs includes many stunners (remember, these are real):

Mussorgsky/Ravel: *Pictures at an Exhibition*

Stravinsky: *The Rite of Spring*

Ravel: *Bolero*

Beat the audience over the head. Then do it again. And then do it again. Just a bit of overkill?

Mahler: Symphony No. 9

Chopin: Piano Concerto No. 1

Inexplicable, but the theory must have been to put the contemporary piece first!

Mahler: *Das Lied von der Erde*

Mahler: Symphony No. 2, *"Resurrection"*

When deciding what to precede an 80-minute piece with, it is not a good idea to choose a 60-minute piece.

Inspired by the rampant dumbness, we did add a few invented programs at the end as examples of how far our twisted minds could go in outdoing the real ones. One of our craziest:

Elliott Carter: Variations for Orchestra
Carter: Piano Concerto
Carter: Symphony for Three Orchestras
Ravel: *Bolero*

Most orchestras, forced by their music directors to present contemporary music, resort to camouflaging the presumed discomfort by adding blatantly audience-friendly hits. We were certain this gem would be heavily advertised as *"Bolero!"*, annoying both the Carter lovers and those subjected to an hour of astringently difficult music prior to the 15-minute advertised feature.

My favorite mythical program:

Elliott Carter: *What Next?*
George Gershwin/Hershy Kay: *Who Cares?*

If only I had had the guts!

Our amusement notwithstanding, an essential reality emerged — the symphony world was overrun with programs which were dull and sometimes aggressively dumb, reflecting a complete lack of seriousness in thought and construction. A great program is necessary for sparking a committed performance from the artists and a transcendent experience for the audience. Creative and inspiring programs are great tools, all-too-often forgotten, for building audiences and community around institutions, but putting them together requires wide knowledge, an open mind, a sense of fantasy, and a willingness to work hard.

Program-making is a process that deserves an agonizing amount of attention — which pieces, in what order, with what forces, in what setting. Because assembling them is an inexact science, the best ones are usually the most unpredictable and riskiest — those that promise the biggest potential reaction also run the risk of failing the most spectacularly. Far too often, they are the product of casual and unthoughtful effort, becoming what has been derisively called "music from 8 to 10."[5]

---

5 This phrase has been attributed to Michael Steinberg by numerous people and I heard it directly from him, but I can find no definitive source in Michael's writings. It is vintage Steinberg.

CLEVELAND PICTURES

Given Cleveland's conducting relationship with Knussen, I decided in 1995 that we must commission a piece from him. But there was a problem: he was in a period of composing mostly short pieces with small instrumentation. As he explained: "The point is, I'm a big person, I'm just physically big, and I enjoy life. I don't know whether it's extremely significant or just something that's completely unresolved inside me, but I am profoundly drawn to miniature things, and fineness of detail and precision."[6]

I came up with what I thought was an ingenious solution, inviting him to choose a number of works at the Cleveland Museum of Art and write a series of miniatures, each based on an object from the collection — a kind of *Son-of-Pictures-at-an-Exhibition*. He embraced the idea. We spoke often about the project, giving it the working title *Cleveland Pictures*. Over the next several years he chose several that tickled his compositional fancy, including paintings, sculptures and a miniature animated Kremlin Clock Tower by Fabergé that entranced him. When he finally began composing in earnest, progress was slow. Additionally, his stamina began to decline as he gradually grew larger and larger due to his love of good food and wine and his lack of physical activity. When he experienced a few health scares, I was deeply concerned.

In the summer of 2002, I told him privately about my plan to leave The Cleveland Orchestra in two years, expressing hope that the work could be completed by then. He enthusiastically agreed and we scheduled the premiere for just before my departure. He worked feverishly, but with the premiere a month away, he had completed only 16 of the 25 minutes he envisioned. He was stymied by the ending, which was to be based on Turner's *The Burning of the Houses of Parliament*. He proposed that we present as scheduled what had been completed, promising to finish so we could perform it complete next season. I told him that I would rather delay until the whole work was done, thinking this would be an incentive to actually complete it. I was wrong. After the aborted premiere, two later performances were scheduled by my successor but then postponed, the work still incomplete.

---

6 Service, Tom, "I Had to Write It," *The Guardian*, Oct. 19, 2006.

LATE STRUGGLES

After leaving The Cleveland Orchestra but still living in Cleveland, I embarked on a slew of projects, the main anchor of which was artistic directorship of the Ojai Music Festival. My prime job was to choose a different artistic partner each year. It was there in 2005 that Knussen and I made plans to collaborate once more: I selected him as my first appointment. We worked enthusiastically on the programs, which were to include his recent Violin Concerto along with music by Mauricio Kagel and Percy Grainger, both passions of ours. His close friend and frequent collaborator Peter Serkin was invited to give a recital and perform Stravinsky's Movements and the planned American premiere of a Concerto for Piano and Chamber Orchestra that Knussen was writing for him.

Disaster struck a month before the festival, well after it had been announced. Knussen had been facing increasing health challenges which now required his hospitalization. By May, he had not sufficiently recovered to make the long trip to California and canceled. It was a deeply sad moment for both of us. I managed to find terrific replacement artists, but it wasn't the same. His planned Piano Concerto for Serkin was never completed.

We continued to see each other from time to time and spoke often. He guest-conducted in Cleveland several times, which allowed us evenings at home watching silly videos, listening to obscure music and laughing incessantly over much red wine. Throughout, we kept refining The List and Dumb Programs.

I never stopped trying to persuade him to finish *Cleveland Pictures*. He resisted, somehow having developed misgivings about what he had written. Hoping that hearing its glories played live would inspire completion, I helped arrange for him to conduct a private reading of the existing torso with the New World Symphony in Miami in 2009. The music was stunning, but he remained unhappy for some reason. My last attempt was to tie the premiere to the centennial of the Cleveland Museum of Art in 2016, but that also came to naught. The score remains unfinished.[7]

---

7 I helped arrange the first public performance of the existing torso in June 2022 as part of the Aldeburgh Festival's celebration of what would have been his 70th birthday. Even incomplete at 16 minutes, it was his longest orchestral work.

It was during a week spent at the Aldeburgh Festival in June 2018 that I last saw him. Thankfully, we were able to spend time together, but I was alarmed about his health. He had been diagnosed with a heart condition and was awaiting minor surgery. Having grown even larger, he moved cautiously and only with the aid of a cane. He expressed growing anxiety about reaching 66, the age at which his father had died suddenly of a heart attack. Frequent talks among our mutual friends always led to speculation of hearing one day that his weak heart, desperately trying to support his immense body, had simply given up.

Less than a month later I got that call — he died on July 8, two weeks away from turning 66.

His close friend, composer George Benjamin, summed him up eloquently at the celebration of his life in Aldeburgh:

> There's no question, our Large Friend was the most extraordinary musician of our time. First and foremost, as a composer, whose radiant, fantastical and poignant and supremely beautiful masterpieces will outlive us all. And of course, he was a sensational interpreter, conducting a vast array of repertoire — most, but by no means all of it, modern — with supreme intelligence, insight, sensitivity, precision and exuberance. But he was also a mentor and teacher of enormous influence, bringing to his younger colleagues a mixture of limitless enthusiasm, encyclopedic knowledge and phenomenal technical brilliance, all untouched by even a trace of dogmatism. These attributes alone, however, do not explain why he was so widely and deeply loved. He was completely idiosyncratic and individual, both in manner and look, and of course the funniest person in existence. And as a friend, he was the best – supportive, loyal, wise, tender and unlimitedly generous and devoted. How infinitely fortunate we have all been to have had this magnificent, glorious and utterly unique person in our lives for so many years.[8]

It is amazing to realize that Knussen was an influential force in my life for more than 45 years, touching my time in Boston, Cleveland

---

8 From handwritten notes by George Benjamin.

ADVENTURES IN REPERTOIRE: OLIVER KNUSSEN

Unexpected gift for my 70th birthday, to His Tomness from His Ollyness — an arrangement of "Happy Birthday" for percussion interlaced with musical gags occasioned by our mutual adventures.

and Ojai. I always felt his impact, even though, unlike with so many of my mentors, our working together was infrequent. The inquisitiveness he instilled in me during those early years in Tanglewood never stopped, and I always felt his gentle-yet-firm hand on my need to know more music more deeply, even when our contact was sporadic. And he was just fun to be around.

It was he who opened my curiosity to the wonders of contemporary music, a world that had been foreign to me. He pushed me into embracing a vast breadth of composers, whether Elliott Carter, Hans Werner Henze, Percy Grainger, Julian Anderson, Harrison Birtwistle, Toru Takemitsu, Morton Feldman or Arnold Schoenberg. He gave me insights into the process of composing itself, amplifying my growing habit of developing close relationships with creators, not just re-creators, of music.

Most memorable of all was his playfulness about life and music, and a willingness not to take himself and the music business too seriously, qualities I have always tried to emulate. This gentle giant, magnificent composer and dear friend, who served as a musical and intellectual anchor throughout my life, reminds me to this day that supreme artistry and serious intent are not inconsistent with having a smile and an open heart.

CHAPTER 4
SUCCESSION AND REALITY:
JOHN WILLIAMS

I was promoted to general manager of the Boston Symphony Orchestra Inc. at age 34, in September 1978, to replace the retiring Tod Perry.[1] It was the job I had long dreamed about, and I was thrilled that the BSO board put its trust in me at such a young age and with no experience as head of an institution. I now had full executive responsibility for the largest orchestral enterprise in the country, running the Boston Symphony, Boston Pops, Boston Symphony Chamber Players and a major summer music festival and music school at Tanglewood.

The not-for-profit BSO at the time was governed by a board of 25 community leaders. As in all American orchestras, reporting to the board was a chief executive (or "general manager" in the BSO's case) who had operational, financial and organizational responsibility for the entire institution, and a music director who had artistic responsibility. In addition to conducting, the music director's duties included setting overall artistic policy, supervising programming, overseeing the musicians and shaping the orchestra's basic style of playing, an inevitable consequence of being in front of the orchestra far more than any other conductor.

---

1 A note on the changing world of management titles: When I started in Boston, the chief management or executive officer was called manager, or in a few cases managing director. When I was promoted to the number-two position, Tod Perry, having been manager, was given the title of executive director and I the title of manager. When I took the top job in 1978 and Perry retired, my title became general manager. My successor, Ken Haas, was called managing director. When I went to Cleveland, I became executive director. Starting in the 2000s, the norm became president & CEO or chief executive. The board leader transitioned from president to chair. The major reason for this was the increasing corporatization of institutions and the perceived need to formally vest titular authority in the person who was leading fundraising efforts in the community. Throughout this book, I use the titles individuals were given at the time. The jobs are not much different over time, but the roles sometimes get confused because of the steady title inflation.

This organizational structure appears fraught with contradiction and conflict: two co-equal positions, the music director and the chief executive, each reporting to the board president — a structure I wryly refer to as the "Bermuda Triangle" because of its frequent internal turbulence. The design perplexes organizational experts, who typically advocate single lines of authority. But it can be totally workable with the right people in place, all united by a common vision. Real problems are more often caused by having the wrong leaders or a lack of mutual alignment than by the structure itself. The absolute prerequisite to success is the working partnership between the music director and the chief executive, as well as their relationships with the board president. Smooth functioning is entirely dependent on effectively managing the creative tension inherent in the structure.

As I moved into my new position, Seiji Ozawa was starting his fifth season as music director, an appointment that had promised excitement. His turtlenecks, beads and Beatles-like haircut gave the patrician BSO a hip and trendy image. He was a brilliant performer, a total master at marshaling the oversized forces of spectacular choral works — Schoenberg's *Gurre-lieder*, Berlioz's Requiem and Mahler's Symphony No. 8 — and in his element with the colorful Russian and French repertoire so ingrained in the BSO's DNA through years of Koussevitzky and Munch (the aberrant seven seasons of the Teutonic Leinsdorf notwithstanding).

INTERLUDE: MAHLER 8

In 1980 at Symphony Hall, Ozawa led a performance of Mahler's Symphony No. 8, a work for huge orchestra, antiphonal brass, organ, large chorus, children's chorus, and eight vocal soloists. It is not for the budgetarily faint of heart. Just before the final buildup to the concluding choral catharsis, a high soprano intones an ethereal call to heaven over a hushed sonority of flutes, harmonium, celeste and harps. To enhance the effect, we had the singer perform the part not from the usual place on stage with the other soloists but from an open doorway to the hall's second balcony, high above the side of the stage. The unexpected surprise was wondrous, even heavenly. Walking out after the tumultuous ovation, I overheard one elderly subscriber telling another, "This is indeed a magical place. Even the ushers sing."

SUCCESSION AND REALITY: JOHN WILLIAMS

My first year was intense and there was much to deal with. In December, just after President Carter opened diplomatic relations with Beijing, the BSO hastily organized a highly publicized tour to China three months hence. Ozawa, who was born there during the pre-World War II Japanese occupation, had earlier laid the groundwork for a possible visit by the orchestra when the time was right. With Carter's sudden announcement, that opportunity materialized. The flush of excitement drove the fast pace of the planning, leveraged by some immediate and well-connected funding from the Coca-Cola Company and Pan Am Airways, both anxious to expand their business interests in what was already the world's most populous country. While the trip turned out to be a staggering artistic and public relations success, putting it together on such short notice was stressful and completely consuming.

That was not the only foreign tour on the immediate horizon. The BSO's European presence had been sporadic, its only appearances being in 1957 with Munch, in 1971 with Steinberg and Tilson Thomas and in 1976 with Ozawa. To heighten our visibility, I planned the orchestra's first trip to high-profile European music festivals for the summer of 1979 with visits to those prestigious events in Salzburg, Berlin and Edinburgh. The highlight of the programs was Berlioz's *The Damnation of Faust*, an Ozawa specialty.

In addition, our recording strategies needed immediate rethinking since the considerable contract with Deutsche Grammophon was soon to expire. Though Ozawa had not been appointed when the agreement was initially made, the company dutifully made many recordings with him. Yet by 1978, enthusiasm had dimmed as his record sales failed to meet expectations. DG had never fully embraced Fiedler and the Pops, and those sales were likewise disappointing. A change was inevitable, so I negotiated a new agreement with Philips Records to record Ozawa and the BSO only. With Fiedler's faltering health, the Pops was without a recording relationship for the first time.

The success of *Evening at Pops* had persuaded PBS to start a second series called *Evening at Symphony*, this time with the Boston Symphony. It provided an ideal vehicle for building a national brand identity for Ozawa and the BSO. As with the Pops, programs were taped at live concerts in Symphony Hall.

What's more, the centennials of the BSO in 1981 and the Pops in 1985 were imminent, necessitating urgent planning on how to celebrate them.

POPS SEARCH

On top of all this, along with the normal stresses of running a large and complicated organization, Fiedler's physical decline was of growing concern. In spring 1979, I formed a Committee on the Future of the Boston Pops, consisting of five BSO trustees, two BSO overseers,[2] two members of the staff and three outside leaders from the Boston musical community. I framed a charge that included outlining a future vision for the Pops, defining the requirements for the next conductor, identifying and evaluating potential candidates, and determining a future role for Fiedler. These last two points were sensitive given his reluctance to relinquish any duties on the eve of his 50th anniversary. The committee set December 1979 as the goal for its recommendations to the trustees. My experience with the Pops made it crucial that I be central in the committee's work, and it came to dominate my second year of running the BSO.

An initial task was to coordinate evaluations of the upcoming season's guest conductors as possible candidates. One was John Williams, who was to direct two concerts in late May. He was known almost exclusively as a film composer through the runaway success of *Jaws* in 1975, the first *Star Wars* and *Close Encounters of the Third Kind* in 1977 and *Superman* in 1978. And these were just four of the 50 film scores he had composed to date. Few even knew what he looked like since most of his public conducting experience had been limited to occasional dates with the Los Angeles Philharmonic at the Hollywood Bowl. But he came warmly recommended by my friend Ernest Fleischmann, that orchestra's executive director. My only awareness of Williams, other than through his film work, stemmed from a decade-old recording of his Sinfonietta for Band, where he was identified on the jacket as "John T. Williams."[3]

The committee's work took on sudden immediacy with Fiedler's death in July 1979, but the effort was initially slowed by an organization consumed with the concurrent Tanglewood season and the European tour later that summer. One pressing matter was a Pops concert in January 1980 at Carnegie Hall, originally planned as part

2 The BSO Overseers were an advisory board of community leaders and supporters. They had no fiduciary responsibilities: they rather served the main Board of Trustees as an additional resource and way of expanding relationships into the community while not diluting the trustees' official governance role.
3 In his early Hollywood and recording days, he was also billed as "John Towner Williams" or "Johnny Williams."

of Fiedler's extended 50th anniversary celebration. Without him or a named successor yet for this high-profile date, we needed a substitute with star appeal, so I engaged Williams to conduct it.

The committee regrouped in September to address the urgent work of finding Fiedler's successor. The options at that time were surprisingly slim, as orchestras were just beginning to develop their own pops series. The Cincinnati Symphony became a bellwether, capitalizing on its long relationship with Erich Kunzel. He had arrived there in 1965 as assistant conductor (the same year I had started), soon rebranding his concerts as the Cincinnati Pops and establishing a substantial recording profile through a partnership with the fledgling Cleveland label Telarc. Fiedler and Kunzel dominated the American market for pops guest conductors. Both were classically trained and well versed in the symphony orchestra and its repertoire. Others starting to emerge, like Marvin Hamlisch, Skitch Henderson and Peter Nero, were more associated with the world of entertainment and popular music.

Recent guests seen as potential candidates included Mitch Miller of *Sing Along With Mitch* recording fame; the young American conductor John Covelli, who had achieved considerable success leading a few recent concerts; the longtime assistant conductor, Harry Ellis Dickson, who was 71; and Kunzel, who had conducted the Pops annually since 1970 but who effectively took himself out of the running with his behavior guest-conducting the Pops in London three years earlier. No one thought Williams was even a remote possibility, given his Hollywood career. As the committee deliberated and shared observations, no obvious successor emerged; each option had advantages, disadvantages and advocates. I arranged for Miller, Covelli and Dickson to replace Fiedler in a few previously organized private concerts and tour performances that fall so the committee could further assess them.

In October 1979, *The Boston Globe* ran a major story speculating on the search, focusing on the urgent need for a decision.[4] Not only was the next season just seven months away, but in mid-January, PBS would be considering whether to confirm the first non-Fiedler *Evening at Pops* season to be taped that May. It was time to get serious. First, I

---

4 Dyer, Richard, "Who'll Lead The Pops?" *The Boston Globe*, October 14, 1979.

had to get my own thoughts in order, so as to have a considered stance in working with the committee. I again consulted Fleischmann, who strongly recommended either Kunzel or Williams.

One long-shot idea that had occurred to me was André Previn, then chief conductor of the London Symphony, because of his strong grounding in serious classical, film and popular music. While I doubted that he would be interested given his burgeoning conducting career, I conferred with him at his home outside London. Politely and firmly demurring, he strongly recommended Williams, whom he had known well as a fellow musician in Hollywood since the early 1950s. Previn later paraphrased to the press what he had told me: "Anybody who thinks John Williams is just a Hollywood musician is completely wrong. He is such a good musician, so thorough, so completely schooled. . . . He is a very efficient conductor — there's no nonsense about him — he knows what he wants, and he knows how to get it. He knows the orchestra from the point of view of the man with the pencil, and that's quite rare among conductors. Did I say 'rare'? That's unique."[5]

INTERLUDE: COMPETITION

In November 1979 *The Boston Herald American* published a major story about the creation of the Philly Pops under Peter Nero,[6] although the real purpose of the piece was no doubt to tease out information on the search for Fiedler's successor (about which I remained stoically mum). I was asked whether this highly publicized venture might usurp the mantle from the leaderless Boston Pops. I succeeded, I thought, in appearing vague and unconcerned. Was I worried about competition from Nero and the Philly Pops? The paper characterized me as reacting "with Olympian amusement."

In late October, I dedicated a few quiet days to contemplate what to do, and employed a technique I often use to structure decision-making. The key question was determining the unassailably essential qualifications for a new conductor. I divided a sheet of paper

5 Dyer, Richard, "Mix Design and Mystery: You Get a Pops Maestro," *The Boston Globe*, January 17, 1980.
6 Pfeifer, Ellen. "Philly Pops 1980s Style: Can Peter Nero Give Boston a Run for its Money?". *The Boston Herald American*, November 12, 1979.

into two columns for positive and negative qualities, listing every item I could think of under each heading. There were obvious positives: "experienced conductor," "knows pops field," "popular with audiences," "good on television," "musical integrity," "ability as a public figure," "available" and "wants the job."[7] As negatives, I listed items like "sees Pops as a steppingstone to maestro career," "wants to maintain multiple pops positions," "primarily an entertainer," "unfamiliar with the Boston Pops" and "has never conducted the Boston Pops."

After considering the list for completeness, I crossed out every item that to me was not an absolute deal-breaker. The two left remaining were "musical integrity" in the positive column and "sees Pops as a steppingstone to maestro career" in the negative. This clarified the absolute need, above all else, to find someone with impeccable musicianship who saw the job as an end in itself. In my mind, this immediately and surprisingly narrowed the list of possibilities to one person: John Williams. Previn's advice had been sound.

Though Williams had not led many public concerts, he did have tons of conducting experience in the studio, where he was already a film-composer superstar. He was a Juilliard-trained musician steeped in the orchestral idiom, having almost single-handedly revived its dominance in film music from the glory days of Erich Wolfgang Korngold and Bernard Herrmann. I thought such experience was critical, since first and foremost the Boston Pops is a symphony orchestra. And Williams' two concerts the previous May had been successful with both the musicians and audiences.

Showmanship seemed to me an overrated qualification. Fiedler's public persona had been carefully shaped by the juxtaposition of his repertoire mix and genius for public relations with his cultivated mystique of a tail-coated maestro. In Williams' case, his Hollywood aura gave him a populist image without his having to act overtly like a showman, which by instinct he was not.

But there was a huge problem: would he even want the job? Because of his film career, neither the committee nor I thought so. Still, his proven musical integrity and the improbability of his appointment deeply appealed to me. My challenge was how to manage the committee's work while finding out whether he might,

---

7 I have included this item in every job description throughout my career. It may seem obvious, but it needs to be stated explicitly and assessed. Persuading someone to take a job if he or she is not emotionally all in is a recipe for disaster.

in fact, be interested. That October *Boston Globe* article speculating on possible names provided a helpful prod by including Williams as a dark horse possibility, and it triggered a surprising and timely letter from him: "The simple fact of consideration by the orchestra honors all the candidates, and I confess that my being included delights me."[8]

The next meeting of the committee was scheduled for mid-December, six weeks away. Because Williams' Carnegie Hall concert with the Pops was only a month after that, the timeline was extremely tight and demanded precise sequencing. Williams, who was working on the second *Star Wars* film, *The Empire Strikes Back*, was flying to London on December 15 to record the score. As the BSO was on tour in New York that week, he agreed to fly through New York a day earlier to secretly meet with members of the committee and Ozawa, another good sign.

He was instantly impressive. I found him a thoughtful musician, much more interested in discussing the symphonies of Ralph Vaughan Williams or Michael Tippett than the greatest hits of the day. He was elegant, soft-spoken, generous of spirit, understated and witty. He had a personality that completely contradicted my stereotype of the fast-moving commercial world of Hollywood. While it was abundantly evident that he was intrigued with the idea of leading the Pops, and therefore a more viable option than I had thought, sealing a deal was far from a certainty.

When the committee met three days later to review options, everyone was positive about Williams but measured, still thinking him unlikely to be interested. Our essential goals were to neither zero in yet on a single person nor preclude options. The committee delegated the final decision to the board chair, Ozawa and me. They asked me to ascertain Williams' clear position, giving me the needed maneuvering room.

My strategy was clear. I sent him a briefing paper on the needs, operations and schedule of the Pops. I would travel to London to talk seriously between his recording sessions for *The Empire Strikes Back*. I planned a full-court press; offer him the job, get him to accept, negotiate a deal with his agent, and then make the public announcement, all in time for his arrival in Boston on January 20 to rehearse for the Carnegie Hall concert two days later. If I could make this happen, that event would be his high-profile debut as conductor of the Pops, paving

8 Personal letter from John Williams, November 16, 1979.

the way for his first season in spring 1980. Total secrecy was essential in case he did not accept.

To be honest, I had no Plan B.

After arriving in London on New Year's Day, I accompanied him each morning to Pinewood Studios where the recording sessions were held, and we then spent evenings together discussing the job over a vodka and dinner.

He was a hard sell. The whole idea was foreign to someone far more comfortable conducting in the studio than in front of a live audience. And he did not want to leave Los Angeles or give up his film career. Yet it was clear he was intrigued. He liked the association with Boston and the revered nature of the position, and he thought he could achieve something musically exciting and rewarding with the orchestra. But getting a definitive yes out of him was proving elusive.

The situation changed abruptly on January 5, when *The Boston Herald American* published a front-page article reporting that Williams was the leading candidate and I was in London cementing the appointment,[9] a story apparently leaked by his agent. This opened floodgates of media speculation as well as the arrival of *The Boston Globe*'s music critic at my London hotel a day later. So much for secrecy. Yet the article provided the push I needed to close the deal with Williams since it was now public that he was the favored candidate. There could be no turning back.

The next day, Williams definitively said yes. When I returned home to inform the committee, the decision won unanimous approval and was endorsed enthusiastically by the BSO trustees. I negotiated an agreement with his old-line Hollywood agent, someone totally unfamiliar with the world of orchestras; the discussions were an adventure to say the least. A simultaneous press roll-out was planned in London, Boston, New York and Los Angeles on January 10. By happenstance, this would be six months to the day since Fiedler had died.

GETTING DOWN TO WORK

The announcement caught the musical world by surprise and was major news, with headlines like "A Musician's Musician,"[10] "A Thorough

---

9 Pfeifer, Ellen, "From Star Wars to Boston Pops," *The Boston Herald American*, January 5. 1980.
10 Dyer, Richard, "John Williams Is New Pops Maestro," *The Boston Globe*, January 11, 1980.

Musician,"[11] "A Wonderful Choice,"[12] and "Sounds of a New Era: Bravos All Around."[13] On January 21, after being introduced at a news conference, Williams held his first rehearsal as the Pops conductor. It was crawling with press, and he began by speaking directly to the players: "What I want to say most is that I am not here for career reasons. I never had time to be a symphony conductor. I am not here for the celebrity. I don't want that, and I don't need it. I'm not here for the money, though I have no reason to complain about that. I know it may sound patronizing, but the fact is that I am here solely and completely because of the music. The idea of conducting this great orchestra was an irresistible attraction to me. I need and welcome your help, and I am here for as long as you want me. That is how it is."[14]

Williams confirmed Previn's no-nonsense assessment by starting the rehearsal, of his own *Cowboys* Overture, by asking for a small deletion in the music, saying, "Let us begin, significantly enough, with a cut."[15] This was the first time most trustees and Ozawa had seen him at work. Halfway through the rehearsal, Ozawa, sitting with me in the balcony, suddenly clutched my arm and asked to speak privately in my office. Closing the door, he said somewhat breathlessly, "This man does not conduct very well." I reminded him how we had all acknowledged his lack of public conducting experience, but that his impeccable musicianship would more than win the day. Ozawa remained skeptical that first year but eventually became an enthusiastic supporter and friend. He saw the enormous rapport Williams developed with both audiences and the orchestra. And it didn't hurt that Ozawa's wife and two small children were thrilled to know the composer of *Star Wars*.

The Carnegie Hall concert was a triumph, and *The Boston Globe* proclaimed, "Williams Passes With Flying Colors,"[16] He was eloquent in the press. Responding in *The New York Times* to the inevitable question of whether he would now pursue a career as a "serious" conduc-

---

11 Dyer, Richard, "A Thorough Musician," *The Boston Globe*, January 11, 1980.
12 Dyer, Richard, "A Wonderful Choice," *The Boston Globe*, January 11, 1980.
13 Dyer, Richard, "Sound of a New Era – Bravos All Around," *The Boston Globe*, January 22, 1980.
14 Dyer, Richard, "Sound of a New Era – Bravos All Around," *The Boston Globe*, January 22, 1980.
15 Dyer, Richard, "Sound of a New Era – Bravos All Around," *The Boston Globe*, January 22, 1980.
16 Dyer, Richard., "Williams Passes with Flying Colors," *The Boston Globe*, January 23, 1980.

C3PO conducting the Boston Pops in 1980.

tor like his friend Previn, he said, "I know the orchestral repertoire pretty well, but my experience in conducting it is not that vast. ... The excitement of this appointment for me is a *musical* one. I've never aspired per se to the limelight. What's exciting for me is working with one of the world's great orchestras. ... It's not a big ego trip for me. But I don't know where it's going to lead down the line."[17]

Williams opened his first season on April 29 with a gala concert featuring guest appearances by the *Star Wars* droids R2D2 and C3PO. PBS, thrilled with the appointment, had renewed *Evening at Pops* and Philips now added the Pops to its new recording contract with the BSO.

Williams threw himself into the difficult grind of rehearsals, concerts, television tapings and recording sessions for the next two months. For him, the newness of it all was daunting. Arriving without much experience in conducting non-film music, he had an immense amount of repertoire to learn in order to direct the sheer number of concerts required during the season. I often forgot that when I arrived in Boston, Fiedler already had 40 years of accumulated experience and repertoire at his fingertips. Williams had little of either. There

---

17 Rockwell, John, "Traditionalist for the Pops," *The New York Times*, January 11, 1980.

were pieces to learn, programs to create, arrangements to commission, television shows and records to make — all on top of the stress of suddenly becoming a public figure.

As he planned to maintain his film career during the non-Pops season and continue living in California, he concentrated his Pops work on the Boston season and the holiday concerts and did not spend the rest of the year guest-conducting elsewhere. This was the opposite of Fiedler, who in essence occupied the role of Pops conductor year-round. Given his lack of experience, it was clear to me that Williams would require considerable support in basic planning, repertoire research and programming. Deeply invested in his appointment and its success, I actively provided it. I enjoyed working with him and we developed an easygoing partnership.

In August after his first season, Williams came to Tanglewood for the annual Pops concert. On arrival he learned that his longtime agent, Marc Newman, had suddenly died, and he was distraught. I accompanied him two days later to Los Angeles to attend services. Over a second Bloody Mary on the flight, he informed me that the work was really beyond what he had anticipated and he had decided not to continue beyond his two-year contract. To say I was surprised is an understatement, but I urged that we table discussion until after the funeral.

Two days later, we met at the 20th Century Fox lot, where Williams had worked for many years, with his longtime colleague Lionel Newman, the head of music for the studio and Marc Newman's brother. The Newman family was musical royalty in Hollywood: the famous composer-conductors Emil and Alfred Newman (brothers of Marc and Lionel) and a then-new generation of composers — Thomas, David and, of course, Randy of "I Love LA" fame. As we settled down to lunch at the studio commissary, I was introduced to numerous luminaries, including Mel Brooks, over whom I was more than a little star-struck. Newman noticed the president of production at the studio, Sherry Lansing, entering with three investor types. We watched as she worked the room. Arriving at our table and greeting Williams warmly, she introduced him to her guests as "John Williams, conductor of the Boston Pops," never mentioning *Star Wars* or *Jaws*. Hollywood, it seemed, was acknowledging that the appointment had bestowed exalted status, a perception that was not lost on him.

Seeing how Williams was viewed in Hollywood encouraged me to think he was not really ready to leave the Pops, but I didn't want to press the issue in the aftermath of his friend's funeral. We agreed that I would return to Los Angeles later in August to talk seriously about the future. Thankfully, it was becoming clear his resignation might not be a settled issue.

A month later, we talked through the challenges of his still being far from comfortable in this new role as well as what additional support could be made available to help him. It became clear that he would need even more of my direct attention to make his appointment a success, a commitment I knew would be difficult given my still-new responsibilities for the whole organization. And, of course, with one year already under his belt, he had already started to build repertoire and experience, so I knew everything going forward would be easier for him.

The meetings were successful; he not only agreed to stay, but we initiated discussions to extend his agreement for another two years to 1983, giving him a reasonable amount of time to grow in his new role.

INTERLUDE: DOPPELGANGERS

Arriving in Los Angeles in August 1980, intent on persuading Williams to remain as conductor, I surprised him by arriving at his door with a short beard, and wearing his trademark black turtleneck, an event captured in a series of pictures taken by his photographer wife. It was henceforth not lost on anyone that the real reason I hired him was that we looked eerily alike. When I started sporting a beard permanently in 1985, the likeness became widely acknowledged.

When he came to Cleveland in 1996 for the premiere of his Trumpet Concerto, we had a picture taken together in front of the full-length portrait of Severance Hall's benefactor, John Severance, whom we also both weirdly resembled.

In Vienna in 2020, I met Williams in the lobby of the Imperial Hotel just before heading to the concert hall for his debut with the august Vienna Philharmonic. Accompanied by security, given his superstardom, he headed out the front door with his party to waiting cars, saying he would see me at the Musikverein. I was surprised, as the hall was just out the back door of the hotel and across a narrow street. Was he becoming grand? I looked out that back door and was astonished to find the street jammed with hundreds of fans, waiting expectantly with cameras. I immediately understood why he had avoided this route. I stepped through the door, triggering a cheer and camera flashes as I was mistaken for him — the closest I ever came to true stardom.

Me and John Williams in Los Angeles in 1980

*In Cleveland in 1996 in front of portrait of Severance Hall benefactor
John Severance*

So began what were to be annual visits to Los Angeles each August to assess how things were going, leading, two years later, to another contract extension to 1986, a period that would embrace the 1985 Pops centennial. With each season, Williams' confidence as a conductor grew. He infused his artistic imprint on the institution, and his vast experience as an orchestrator led to a reinvigoration of musical arrangements with a whole new team of arrangers he knew in Hollywood.

Arranging popular tunes for live performance by a symphony orchestra without amplification is a specific talent. In addition to imagination, it requires deft balancing the individual instrumental parts so that harmonies and textures are clear in the live, unamplified environment — very different from arranging for the studio where these can be easily and instantly manipulated by sound engineers. The Pops repertoire broadened to include classic American Songbook tunes and, not surprisingly, more film music. Williams encouraged individual orchestra members to perform as soloists. His repertoire grew rapidly, as it had to with the sheer number of concerts he conducted.

On top of everything, he was proving extremely popular with audiences and PBS viewers. At the same time, escalation of his already-considerable fame was intensified by a particularly fruitful film period, yielding scores for such blockbusters as *The Empire Strikes Back*, *Return of the Jedi*, *Raiders of the Lost Ark*, *E.T.* and *Indiana Jones and the Temple of Doom*.

I once asked him his secret to writing film scores, how he approached a new project and what inspired him to capture the essence of a film so successfully in its music. Coming from the classical world, I was used to composers pointing to inspiration as the genesis of their work. To my surprise, Williams characterized film composing as much more about craft than muse. He would first view the film's rough cuts to grasp the feeling, tempo and emotional arc of the picture, jotting down a few key musical motifs. But he composed the score by then rigorously writing two-and-a-half minute increments of finished music each day, watching and carefully timing each to the corresponding portion of the film. The amount of time needed to finish a score thus depended on how much music the director wanted for the picture. He composed at the piano, notating in abridged score format the musical lines and harmonies along with indications of instrumentation. In this incremental way, he put a full movie score together.

TROUBLE

Everything appeared settled down until April 1984, when, out of the blue and formally in writing, Williams notified me that he wished to end his commitment at the end of the 1985 season because of the demands made on him by his film work as well as the stress of the job he was still struggling with.[18] As previously, I urged that we not discuss these life-changing decisions as the busy Pops season was about to begin, so we agreed to take up the matter in L.A. as usual in August.

But on June 12, in the middle of a rehearsal, he suddenly called an intermission, and stormed off the stage directly into my office. He announced with some heat that he would not continue in the position beyond the current season because of what he viewed as rude and insulting behavior by members of the orchestra. He had been rehearsing a new arrangement of music by Leonard Bernstein that received quiet hisses of disapproval from some players, an incident he said had occurred on several other occasions that week. He resigned, calling the decision irrevocable. I was stunned.

The orchestra committee met with him shortly thereafter, apologizing for the behavior of the offenders, but he was angry and told the committee of his firm intention to resign. He then informed the full orchestra, which visited him after the concert that evening. Not surprisingly, the news leaked to the press. Because he remained resolute, there was nothing to do but formalize an announcement and frame it in the best possible light. We worked out a mutual statement the next day, confirming his decision to leave at the end of the 1984 season. The news sent shock waves through the Boston public.

In a second meeting with the full orchestra a few days later, formal apologies were accepted by him, but there surfaced numerous issues of player malaise and discontent over the crushing schedule of six concerts per week for eight weeks plus rehearsals, recording sessions and television tapings. Such grumbling is not unusual for musicians when it comes to pops concerts since the motivating reason most join an orchestra is the serious classical repertoire. Williams was used to studio ensembles in Hollywood made up of musicians happy to have been engaged for the occasion, so I could understand how the players' kvetching annoyed him.

These cultural and scheduling issues resulted in formal discussions between members of the orchestra and board about the very

---

18 Letter from John Williams, April 14, 1984.

structure of the Pops season. Attending a special meeting of the trustees in June, Williams expressed willingness to work with the organization to address the underlying player unhappiness, a pragmatic position that gave me hope that he might reverse his decision. He agreed to defer the effective date of his resignation pending resolution of those conversations.

After numerous meetings over the summer, it was agreed that the season was indeed overly intense for the regular players. In addition, it was formally recognized that while some BSO musicians enjoyed playing Pops, others did not and would rather be excused. Such requests were handled on an ad hoc basis under a provision in the labor agreement for "optional leave," by which individuals can ask for time off without pay for any reason. Even so, the possibility of such requests being denied rankled the players.

A month later, it was agreed that the Pops season for the regular players would be reduced from eight weeks to six in 1985 and five in 1986. In addition, any musician would automatically be granted unpaid leave from the whole season unless committing to at least four of the weeks. In essence, the season was not only shortened but made optional. Finding replacement players was not difficult because of the freelance Esplanade Orchestra, whose members were steeped in the repertoire and Pops style. The solution calmed player unhappiness and pleased Williams. He formally rescinded his resignation and agreed to stay through his contract.

But this new structure had considerable financial impact. Because the eliminated Pops weeks were added to the subscription and Tanglewood seasons, the musicians' regular salaries were not reduced but redirected to those other activities. And the total length of the Pops season had to be maintained because of the considerable ticket revenues earned. The result was expanded use of the Esplanade Orchestra, in essence adding weeks of paying for two orchestras.

My own concerns lingered on whether this would erode the Pops as an artistic entity; however great the members of the Esplanade Orchestra were, the infusion of more substitute players might compromise the Pops' unique quality. One of the distinctive characteristics, which had assured its quality, was that the ensemble was made up of members of the Boston Symphony, who would now be less involved.

The schedule was indeed tough, but don't all major jobs have some elements that are less satisfying than others? To what degree was it the responsibility of all the BSO players, who were meticulously and competitively selected, to give their best to everything in the schedule whether or not they enjoyed it? How much of the unhappiness could be attributed to the normal grumbling of highly skilled, highly paid artists working under the unchanging schedule and rigid regulations inherent in the orchestra model? The underlying player discontent reminded me of the very reason I decided, back at Princeton, not to pursue a career as an orchestra musician.

POPS AT 100

Assured of Williams' continued commitment until 1986, we finished planning the centennial celebration. The Boston Symphony's 1981 centennial had featured a star-studded gala at Symphony Hall, a free performance of Beethoven's Ninth Symphony on the Boston Common on the mid-October birthday itself (for which the weather gods favored us), 12 commissions, plus a transcontinental tour and a trip around the world from Tokyo to the capitals of Europe.

As the quintessential American orchestra, the Pops demanded a different approach to its centennial. Large public events seemed in order, as did commissions that resonated more closely with its informality and spirit. Those commissions included an overture from William Bolcom, a special "research" commission to Prof. Peter Schickele to unearth the long-rumored and lost *1712 Overture* by P.D.Q. Bach, and Peter Maxwell Davies' *An Orkney Wedding, with Sunrise*, which has gone on to become his most frequently performed piece.

As the centerpiece of the celebrations, we organized a free summer concert on the steps of the Lincoln Memorial in Washington, televised live as part of *Evening at Pops*. In addition, there was a private performance on the South Lawn of the White House for the President and the diplomatic corps, followed by another free public concert in New York's Central Park.

The White House performance took place under the blazing sun of a hot, humid July afternoon. As it happened, President Reagan was hospitalized for minor surgery that day, so the atmosphere was tense. The audience included members of the Cabinet and the First Lady. Despite being continually refreshed with iced tea, she appeared visibly uncomfortable in the heat. About 30 minutes into the program, I was discreetly approached by an aide, saying she had asked that the concert end so she could graciously depart. I crept on stage at the end of a number, quietly telling Williams and asking that he cut directly to the final *Stars and Stripes Forever*. He and the orchestra did so without missing a beat. The news coverage and prestige of the event remained intact despite its premature ending.

DOUBTS AND TRANSITION

By 1985, Williams was firmly established and becoming comfortable in his position. It had been a tumultuous five years, and supporting the transition had taken far more of my energy and time than I had anticipated. With the large and complicated Boston Symphony Orchestra Inc. to run as well, I was finding the entire job difficult and frustrating.

In addition to the backbreaking workload, the partnerships between me, the music director and the board president were not functioning well. That should not have been surprising, considering that I had no experience running an organization when I was appointed. I was so anxious and thrilled to get the top job that I neither took the opportunity nor understood the need to establish at the outset a shared vision and ground rules for a working relationship with either the board president or the music director. While there are advantages to being promoted from within, there is the distinct disadvantage that thorough familiarity with strengths and weaknesses can blunt the immediate impact a new leader can provide. I naively treated the promotion as an expansion of my existing responsibilities. In fact, it was a totally different role that required galvanizing all parts of the institution — staff, musicians, board, volunteers and community — around a shared vision. It demanded far broader leadership skills in organizational, financial and fundraising planning than did the more transactional work of creating concerts and tours I was familiar with.

In addition, I felt a peculiar distance between the staff and the board, which I knew Perry had also experienced. The CEO and board need to be close thought partners, and that distance, a sense of "us" and "them," was difficult to bridge. I always suspected the issue was embedded in the inherent class culture of Puritan Boston, along with the very nature of how not-for-profits functioned in those times.[19]

Ozawa was a brilliant conductor. His physical conducting was incredibly elegant and balletic, and he was unbeatable in delivering visceral excitement that thrilled audiences. But he was much more of an instinctive than an intellectual musician, resulting in performances with more surface brilliance than deep musical insight. That had served him well in his early Tanglewood years, but not under the week-to-week scrutiny that a music directorship invites.

Then there was his repertoire. Under the domineering presence of his longtime manager, Ronald Wilford, head of the powerful agency Columbia Artists Management, he shifted away from the French and Russian repertoire in which he excelled to Germanic masterpieces — symphonies by Beethoven, Brahms, Mahler and Bruckner — in which he was far less comfortable. Despite his effervescent enthusiasm for the orchestra and complete mastery as a performer, I felt artistic drift and inconsistent quality in his performances, issues noticed by critics. There was regular hammering by *The Boston Globe*.[20]

While there were many moments of satisfaction and achievement, I was finding Ozawa neither very focused as an artistic leader nor the easiest collaborator. Because he was more impulsive than disciplined, thoughtful planning was difficult. Seasons seemed more like a series of brilliant-yet-unconnected events than cohesive statements. While on the surface informal, fun and a generous host (I had incredible eating experiences with him in astonishing restaurants), he was disorganized and mercurial, making it difficult to pin down decisions or even schedule meetings. All this was in direct contrast to the easy and efficient collaborations I had developed with Fiedler and Williams.

What's more, there were continuing issues with his physical presence in Boston. Ozawa always seemed to favor prestigious guest engagements and conducting opera in Europe over the BSO. He suffered frequent illnesses and perpetual jet lag, since working in Europe and the U.S. while living in Japan meant constant international travel.

19 In 1973 I remember hearing from the longtime manager of The Philadelphia Orchestra the news that he was finally allowed to sit at the board table during meetings instead of being relegated to a chair in the corner.
20 A good example is *The Boston Globe* chief music critic Richard Dyer's article, "It's Not Happening at the BSO," from May 6, 1979

It was an ongoing struggle to nail down time with him even to satisfy his contractual commitments.

Concerns over his leadership gnawed at me as we approached his 10th anniversary, and our relationship became troubled. Without the necessary alignment around common goals, a true partnership of mutual respect and equal acceptance of added value by each other was lacking. It was crystal clear to me which of us he thought worked for the other.

INTERLUDE: BLACKJACK

I once had to follow Ozawa on a ski vacation to Lake Tahoe to finish planning a season. It was indeed memorable talking about programs with him while riding up a chair lift, the only time he could offer to meet between ski runs, acupuncture sessions, Chinese feasts prepared by his live-in cook and late-night gambling in Tahoe City. One evening, we were playing blackjack in a less-than-glitzy casino, having an uproarious time and consuming a little too much scotch. Amidst the fun, Ozawa, not a novice gambler, was playing somewhat recklessly and losing. Distinctive-looking with his mop of long black hair and already a celebrity thanks to nationwide television exposure on *Evening at Symphony*, he had not yet been overtly recognized by anyone, something I could tell he noticed. The dealer, who had total control of the table with her affable banter, suddenly stopped after one spectacularly losing bet and, looking him squarely in the eye, said with perfect deadpan expression, "Hey bud, I hope you're a better conductor than blackjack player."

The BSO's board president, Nelson J. Darling Jr., a Boston lawyer and investment manager, was fixated singularly on the orchestra's finances. My concerns about what I perceived as inconsistent artistic leadership for the whole enterprise fell on deaf ears. Darling was steadfastly impressed with Ozawa's celebrity, energy, box-office draw and access to Japanese funding, and far more intent on keeping me focused on the never-ending quest to amortize the BSO's immense overhead than dealing with these other concerns. As a result, I found myself increasingly isolated from both the music director and the president. The board really wanted a general manager with unquestioned loyalty to and belief in Ozawa. That was not my understanding of the role: my primary allegiance was to the BSO.

With my enthusiasm, confidence and support eroding, I discovered that running the country's biggest and highest-profile orchestra was not the satisfying pinnacle I had envisaged. What I had naively thought to be a glamorous and creative position was turning out to be a slog. So, after a fast track of promotion from payroll clerk to the top job, in December 1985 at age 41, I resigned. It was a wrenching moment. While proud of what I had accomplished over seven years as the boss, I was worn out from the workload, emotionally exhausted from the stress and disenchanted with the orchestra business.

After a long search, the BSO chose as my successor Kenneth Haas, the longtime general manager of The Cleveland Orchestra. He and I were the same age, were close personal friends and had roughly similar career paths. When he called with the news that he was coming to Boston, I was surprised. I had thought him content in Cleveland, having recently appointed a new music director, Christoph von Dohnányi. Why leave? He said he did not want to risk becoming "boring," a statement recognizing the difference between taking personal responsibility for constant rejuvenation and not playing the victim by being "bored." It was a distinction that spoke powerfully to me throughout the rest of my career.

Haas started in Boston in March 1987 and paid me a visit a month later. He had just finished a long lunch with Williams, whose contract had been extended again just after I left. He arrived with an ashen face, shocked to have learned that Williams did not want to remain in the job after that season. I recounted that his ambivalence was not new, particularly as he got into the early grind of a Pops season, and advised Haas to put the matter aside and take it up in Los Angeles after the season was over. I have no idea what ultimately transpired between them, but Williams remained conductor of the Pops until 1993.

AN ICON

Williams has remained a close and important friend. After leaving Boston, I continued to visit him on the West Coast, and we spoke often. We worked together in Cleveland several times, including my presenting him and the Esplanade Orchestra at the Blossom Music Center in 1991, engaging him to guest-conduct The Cleveland Orchestra at Blossom in 1995, and commissioning his Trumpet Concerto in 1996.

SUCCESSION AND REALITY: JOHN WILLIAMS

Through the years, I witnessed the success his brave career shift to public performer had become. I knew how difficult it had been and how hard he had worked. Now in demand by every symphony orchestra, he regularly guest-conducts concerts of his music, and has recorded film scores with the Boston Pops, the Boston Symphony, the Los Angeles Philharmonic and the Chicago Symphony. He became America's composer of choice to write new works for patriotic and civic occasions, including a chamber work featuring Yo-Yo Ma, Itzhak Perlman, Gabriela Montero and Anthony McGill at the inauguration of Barack Obama. All this and his celebrated film scores have made him an American musical icon.

On January 18, 2020, Williams made his debut with the Vienna Philharmonic in a program of his music. It was also his conducting debut in continental Europe, hard to believe for a musical superstar about to turn 88. Hearing him so palpably excited about finally leading that most prestigious of orchestras was testament to his humility and unabated joy at making music, even at the lofty heights to which his career had taken him. It was an event I had to attend.

In Vienna, Williams' remarkable life came into absolute focus for me. Having known him so well for so long had perhaps blurred my appreciation of his fame and achievement — it is often hard to see clearly what is right in front of you. He was greeted by crowds of

John Williams conducting in Chicago in 2009

adoring fans outside his hotel, by a standing ovation as he took the stage, by cheers of delight at the beginning of each of his familiar scores, and, most importantly, by warm affection from the Vienna Philharmonic, an orchestra with a will of its own, as it embraced a new musical idiom and conductor with vitality and love. Here was the perfect example of a great musician from the world of popular culture being enveloped fully, and with the deepest of musical bonds, by the unquestioned symbol of the classical music establishment. The event was deeply personal for me, since it came almost 40 years to the day since his announcement as the new conductor of the Boston Pops.

At a dinner there, I reminded him of his telling *The New York Times,* on taking over the position in 1980, that he was not sure where this public conducting career would lead him. Now it was clear exactly where it had led. In those four decades, he never gave up film composing and scored an additional 60 movies. At the same time, he conducted the Boston Pops for 14 seasons and continues even now, as laureate conductor, to lead it annually. He has guest-conducted orchestras all over the U.S. and composed at least 40 orchestral and chamber works and concertos. In the process, he has become the quintessential American musician of our time. Through it all, he retained genuine enthusiasm, endless curiosity, thorough professionalism, self-effacing modesty and capacity for enduring friendships. He was always at my side, as an encouraging cheerleader and steady confidant for my own journey, and I am eternally grateful.

John Williams' appointment to the Pops was great for the organization and for him. He was more ready for the challenge than he realized, despite occasional bouts of ambivalence, and he embraced it with energy and commitment. His impact showed that institutions closely associated with longtime leaders, like Fiedler at the Pops, are more resilient than one might suppose. But a new leader's success depends on more than just an appointment. It requires actively having a tangible and positive impact, which in turn requires thoughtful and continual institutional support, a need I initially underestimated. One characteristic of successful institutions is that they are not, and must never be allowed to become, mere creatures of strong leaders. They are rather defined by a compelling vision given life by what the institution does, as the history of the Boston Pops proves.

SUCCESSION AND REALITY: JOHN WILLIAMS

I learned the awesome responsibility of leading a revered community institution with a national brand. It was an honor to have presided over this transition of the Pops' musical leadership, and I am immensely proud of the decision to hire Williams and to see him succeed. Likewise, I am proud of the work on the two centennial celebrations, escalating the BSO's international touring profile, and establishing major television presences for both the BSO and the Pops.

Thinking that running the BSO was the lodestar in my burgeoning career, I discovered that my fixation on the position and organization as a goal was false and misleading. Success is not just about getting a position. Ultimate job satisfaction and performance are built upon grasping challenges, building alliances, staying ahead of issues and executing well. How do you maintain artistic purpose in the face of organizational complexity? How do you forge true creative partnerships with artistic leaders? How do you instill a shared vision across the institution? How do you work effectively with a volunteer board and volunteer leadership? How do you simply survive an overwhelming workload? Being a truly effective institutional leader was a lesson I had yet to learn.

Leaving the BSO turned out to be the best thing that ever happened to me. It purged the false god I had set up, making me focus pragmatically on what was really important and how I could broaden my perspectives — great life realizations early in my career.

CHAPTER 5
BEING FEARLESS: PIERRE BOULEZ

My first experience seeing Pierre Boulez conduct was with the Boston Symphony at Tanglewood in 1969 just after I started working there. He had made his debut with the orchestra at Symphony Hall the preceding January, and the players were full of stories about his precise ear, fastidious technique and calm yet penetrating mind. The Tanglewood program ended with Debussy's *La Mer*, a Boulez specialty. With abundant patience and politeness, he tuned one chord sequence at a rehearsal meticulously, tirelessly and at some length. The BSO players were neither used to nor thrilled by such minute attention to detail, but the resulting performance was staggeringly beautiful in its subtlety and range of colors.

BEGINNINGS
Boulez was an unabashed modernist, well-known both as a composer and for strong and controversial opinions on music. It was not until the late 1960s and early 1970s that his conducting career took off, a result of his relationships with important and powerful mentors who shared his uncompromising commitment to the highest musical standards. These included BBC Controller of Music William Glock, New York Philharmonic managing director Carlos Moseley and The Cleveland Orchestra music director George Szell.

In 1968, Glock announced Boulez as principal conductor of the BBC Symphony, to start two years later. In February 1969, Szell named him Cleveland's principal guest conductor, making no secret of his dream that Boulez succeed him. But shortly after his debut with the New York Philharmonic that same month and to everyone's complete surprise, he was named that orchestra's music director, to succeed the charismatic Leonard Bernstein beginning in 1971. When Szell died in the summer of 1970, Boulez agreed to become Cleveland's musical advisor until a formal successor could be found, as his soon-to-be-starting duties in London and New York precluded him from being a realistic candidate. When Lorin Maazel was named the new Cleveland music director in 1972, Boulez relinquished his musical advisor post.

Here was a visionary leader, one who firmly advocated for what he believed in and then made it happen. His work in London and New York clearly reflected his beliefs in strong doses of contemporary music and unusual programs; he built relationships with composers and utilized different performance venues for new concert formats. In his four years with the BBC, he reshaped the repertoire and activities of the orchestra around music of the 20th century, distinguishing it from London's four other major orchestras.

In New York, he had less success, running up against an established audience used to the unrestrained glamor and populist energy of Bernstein and not kindly disposed toward Boulez's unfamiliar programming. His innovations to move the Philharmonic beyond the confines of the traditional concert hall setting — the Encounters series in downtown Manhattan and the Rug Concerts in a reconfigured Philharmonic Hall (the original name of the orchestra's home venue in Lincoln Center, later Avery Fisher Hall and now David Geffen Hall) — met with resistance and did not last beyond his tenure.

Everything changed when President Georges Pompidou invited Boulez back to Paris to set up and lead an institute specializing in musical research and technology at the new Centre Pompidou — what was to become IRCAM, the Institut de Recherche et Coordination Acoustique/Musique. It was an opportunity he could not refuse. Leaving his positions in London in 1975 and then New York in 1977, he withdrew from most conducting for the next ten years to devote his full energy and attention to IRCAM.

RÉPONS IN BOSTON

Our paths did not cross again during my early Boston years, except for my attending several of his concerts in New York. When he started at IRCAM, I lost touch with him for a few years.

While running the BSO, I was visited in 1983 by Nicholas Snowman, a co-founder (with Boulez and Michel Guy, then the French culture minister) of IRCAM's contemporary music group, the Ensemble intercontemporain. He wanted to discuss Boulez's new large-scale composition *Répons*, a showcase for the cutting-edge marriage of music and technology being developed at IRCAM. Until then, melding live performance with electronic sounds necessitated pre-recorded material or delayed processing. In *Répons*, microphones on the performers fed their sounds into computers for simultaneous processing and playback through an elaborate speaker system surrounding the spatial layout of the performers, creating a true aural circus.

Répons required an ensemble of 24 players and conductor in the center of the space, surrounded by six spatially separated soloists – two on pianos and one each on cimbalom, harp, vibraphone and xylophone/glockenspiel. The setup was extensive, with gigantic aluminum trusses surrounding the central performing space to support speakers and lighting. In those days, even with IRCAM's state-of-the-art technology, the electronics required for real-time signal processing were complicated and sprawling, a far cry from what is needed to perform *Répons* today.[1]

Snowman explained that the complex technology component and the necessary spatial setup of musicians and equipment required a flat, square space rather than a traditional concert hall, reassuring me that computer magic would counterbalance any acoustical challenges inherent in the space.

Boulez's idea was to bring *Répons* to New York, Los Angeles, Chicago and Boston, presented by each of their respective orchestras. Because this complicated work did not require a full symphonic ensemble and because of its highly complex musical language, Snowman's proposition was to perform the work with the Ensemble intercontemporain plus electronic equipment and technicians from IRCAM, all conducted by Boulez. His question was whether the BSO was interested in presenting the event in winter 1986.

The idea intrigued me. While the Boston Symphony had not been in the business of presenting non-BSO ensembles, I thought this a way for it to embrace cutting-edge thinking of IRCAM's frontier of technology and music. At the same time, we would build a relationship

---

1 In 2017, I attended a performance at the Park Avenue Armory in New York, and with the improvements in technology, the complete electronics package had been reduced to a laptop, though the realization still required the intricate setup of microphones, speakers and lighting.

with Boulez. I suggested that *Répons* be performed twice at Symphony Hall in the Pops configuration, with the musicians and electronics placed in the center of the flat floor and the audience seated around the periphery, in the two balconies and on the stage. The 1986 timing was fortuitous; the BSO would be on tour in Japan that February and the hall was free. To maximize the impact of the occasion and the presence of Boulez, I proposed he also lead the Ensemble in three subscription concerts (replacing the absent BSO), and then return later in the season to guest-conduct a week with the Boston Symphony. This would make him a significant presence in the season, showcased as conductor (of his Ensemble and of the BSO), as composer and as innovator through his work at IRCAM.

I surprised myself with how the *Répons* idea triggered such an expansive response. Perhaps it was the growing excitement of and knowledge about contemporary music that Knussen had instilled in me. Perhaps it was the idea of collaborating with Boulez, someone I deeply admired from afar. Perhaps it was the idea of injecting some contemporary energy into what I was feeling were predictable concert patterns in Boston. Perhaps it was increasing confidence in my own creative instincts. It was an exhilarating early instance of my taking a creative idea, expanding it, shaping it and contextualizing it, all in partnership with a great artist. I was intrigued with using the adaptable space of Symphony Hall for such a revolutionary piece. So I went for it.

Ozawa endorsed the plan, particularly having Boulez guest-conduct the BSO. The board was relieved about the costs, since performing three what-would-have-been-foregone subscription concerts would produce incremental ticket revenues to ameliorate the expense. The logistics would be relatively efficient since the empty hall allowed for the considerable set-up time with the BSO on tour.

Snowman was intrigued by the scope of my proposal. He initially expressed some acoustic concerns about performing *Répons*, with its massive electronics, in the reverberant acoustic of Symphony Hall, but said he would review the idea with Boulez. A few weeks later he reported that Boulez was extremely enthusiastic about presenting the high-tech work in the traditional setting of Symphony Hall, and he loved including his Ensemble and its distinctive contemporary programming on the more traditional BSO season. He was ready to proceed with the planning.

I had my first direct conversation with him several months later, when we met in Paris. I had always heard he had a ferocious intellect and was devastatingly opinionated. I expected him to be intimidating but found the exact opposite — a complete gentleman, easy to talk with, charming, smart, totally focused on musical ideals and far from the intellectual cold fish I had somehow expected. We bonded over the audacious juxtaposition of presenting *Répons* in the Boston Pops configuration of Symphony Hall.

During the considerable planning for the project, Boulez was always available and engaged, whether on the phone or in person when I was in Paris, and we were able to realize all aspects of the plan. I found working with him a delight, completely to the point and refreshingly free of intrigue and hidden agendas — a true creative collaboration, the kind that I had always envisioned working with great artists could be.

But then came my departure from the BSO, two months prior to the scheduled performances. After all the work up to that point, it was supremely disappointing that I would not be around for the final planning and execution of the project. Thankfully, fate intervened. The BSO asked me to manage and produce the event while key staff were on tour in Japan. It made sense and also pleased me. The event became the first artistic project in my post-orchestra life, one I enthusiastically threw myself into.

The two *Répons* performances were life-changing. Viewing this late-20th-century concert setup marrying instrumental and electronic sounds in this very 19th-century concert space was a moving statement on the possibilities of presenting music. The lighting, focused on the players and technology, left the surrounding space mostly dark, providing a visual cushion for the piece's stark modernity. The effect was magical as the subtly lit statues of Apollo and his fellow Olympian deities adorning Symphony Hall's upper walls appeared to gaze down on the future of music. Both performances were sold out and audiences were wildly enthusiastic. Here was a lesson about the power of creating compelling and uncompromising events.

The Ensemble's subsequent performances were astonishing in their virtuosity, even if the staid Boston audiences were somewhat taken aback by the choice of music. Boulez always eschewed traditional programming in his orchestral concerts. With the Ensemble,

Boulez's Répons *in Symphony Hall, February 1986*

he focused exclusively on contemporary scores, most of them brand new, and his Boston programs adhered to that model. After unknown and new works of Edgard Varèse, Elliott Carter, York Höller and Franco Donatoni, the program closed with what was for Boulez a standard potboiler, Arnold Schoenberg's Chamber Symphony, Op. 9. The work, written in 1906, is a mix of Schoenberg's emerging atonality with the Romanticism of the late 19th century. The concerts conclusively demonstrated that audience's predisposed aversion to Schoenberg dissipates when the music is heard in the context of more astringent works — the piece was suddenly appreciated as the logical extension of Mahler that it is.

To complete the whole project, Boulez returned a month later to conduct the BSO in a program of Stravinsky, Ravel and his own *Notations I-IV*. Away in Europe, I missed the performances but heard the musicians loved him. It is sad he was never persuaded to return to the orchestra after that. Knowing that he thrived working only with institutions with which he had intense creative relationships, it is clear my Boston successors were never able to establish one with him.

The *Répons* collaboration turned out to be precisely the spark I needed to rekindle my spirit from its post-BSO funk. At exactly the right moment, it whetted my appetite for what the music business could be like. Boulez stimulated my growing sense of artistic adventure, and I was transfixed by his total commitment to music and advocacy of 20th-century repertoire. Here was an artist committed to ideas and idealism, one with whom I could think about programming contextually and use concert spaces in new, reconfigured ways.

The central reason we worked well together was that the music was always primary and we were not afraid to dream boldly. What's more, Boulez was just fun to be with — attentive, open and with no unnecessary drama. Like Fiedler in a strange way, he was his own person — he had no press agent or manager. There was nothing complicated or extraneous about Pierre Boulez.

CLEVELAND

Répons started a long, enduring relationship between us. I visited Boulez in Paris several times, and at one point he asked for my help with his idea of including as part of the new Opéra Bastille a "*salle modulable*," a flexible black-box performing space for contemporary and experimental projects. But the idea dissipated when, to his considerable disappointment, the space was cut from the project.

We reconnected a few years later when I went to run The Cleveland Orchestra. He was emerging from his sole focus on IRCAM

With Boulez in Boston, February 1986.

and starting to conduct regularly again, including a return to Cleveland just before I started. In this and his earlier work in the 1960s and 1970s, he developed an affection for the orchestra's virtuosity and tonal refinement, and the musicians were deeply impressed by the clarity of his musical beliefs and fastidious conducting technique.

Reestablishing an ongoing connection between the orchestra and Boulez was an easy and immediate priority, and we began working together on a regular basis. For his annual two weeks, we had programs to make and, under his new contract with Deutsche Grammophon, recording repertoire to plan. He was always easy, relaxed and brimming with energy. I totally enjoyed the creative back-and-forth of making programs with him, and we were never at a loss for ideas. His performances in Cleveland sounded natural and fresh, and they were always highlights for me. While his musical chemistry with the orchestra members was extraordinary, he worked the musicians hard and never took preparation for granted. For every program, he requested — and used efficiently and completely — five rehearsals.

Boulez's conducting style was distinctive. His technique was neither showy nor dramatic, eliciting precision, expressivity and color from the orchestra. He never used a baton, preferring the flexibility of his arms, hands and fingers. He always conducted with a score, even in his own music, once explaining that it enhanced his concentration and obviated the need to worry about memorization. He never wore tails but was always dapper in a tuxedo, even with the orchestra in full dress. His stage demeanor was brusque and businesslike, but once conducting, he disappeared into the music, so what came through was the score rather than his interpretation of it.

Years earlier in New York, this spare conducting style, the jarring antithesis of his predecessor Bernstein's drama and flash, was caustically characterized in a *New York Times* article, "The Iceberg Conducteth."[2] While praising his leadership as music director, the article was less positive about his performances. Yet through all my years working with him in Cleveland, he met with only the warmest enthusiasm from audiences, musicians and soloists. Far from being arid and emotionless as suggested in the article, his conducting to me was highly expressive and fluid. This striking difference from his reputation in New York undoubtedly resulted from audiences' evolving acceptance of greater objectivity in orchestral performance style, much of which was the result of Boulez's

---

2 Rubin, Stephen E., "The Iceberg Conducteth," *The New York Times Magazine*, March 3, 1973.

advocacy over the years, as well as from his growth as a conductor. In New York, he was just entering his 50s, and his emergence as a master conductor came some 15 years later — there is much to be said for long experience and the wisdom that comes with age.

None of his programs were predictable, in repertoire or structure. Typical was a Cleveland one in 1993 that we also took to Carnegie Hall as his first major New York conducting appearance since he left the Philharmonic in 1977. It was full of nonstandard repertoire that was far different from what had become the standard masterwork-driven format, opening with Debussy's *Jeux*, the most elusive and diaphanous of his scores, and followed by Bartók's Piano Concerto No. l, a difficult piece for both the orchestra and the soloist. After intermission came Olivier Messiaen's *Chronochromie*, a wildly demanding work for huge orchestra with fiendishly virtuosic solo parts for xylophone, marimba and glockenspiel. The concert ended with Debussy's *La Mer*, the one familiar piece on the program and the same work I had first seen him conduct with the BSO almost 25 years earlier. I have never heard it performed more spectacularly than it was at Carnegie Hall that evening in that context.

My favorite program with Boulez was one we dubbed "The Great Shrinking Orchestra." It started with Stravinsky's *Song of the Nightingale*, a showpiece for a full 100-piece ensemble, followed by Messiaen's *Le Réveil des oiseaux*, for 60-piece orchestra and solo piano. The second half opened with Messiaen's *Sept haïkaï*, for 30 players plus solo piano, followed by Stravinsky's *L'Histoire du soldat* Suite for seven players. With the size of the instrumental forces on stage steadily decreasing with each piece, I asked the stage crew to remove the growing number of vacant chairs and stands from the stage as the concert progressed. The remaining players were increasingly concentrated in the middle of the empty stage on whom the lighting was ever more focused as the expanding empty space surrounding them stood in the dark. Here was a program against all conventions — totally unusual 20th-century repertoire, starting with the colorful explosion of a huge orchestra and ending with the focused intimacy of chamber music. The complementary production values magnified the sensation of the unusual program design. The result was mesmerizing. When the single percussionist finished the bravura solo at the end of the Devil's Dance that concludes *L'Histoire*, audience members rose as one in cheers.

In 1993, he also led the orchestra in Cleveland and Carnegie Hall in master classes before full audiences. Four young maestros rehearsed the musicians in two preselected pieces, with Boulez, guiding and coaching at their elbows, amplified so the audience could hear what was being said. While I expected the classes to be revelatory, I did not expect the reactions of wonder from members of the orchestra. Over their long history with him, they had developed a practice of shorthand communication — he never had to say much to elicit what he was after and why. Yet here, he had to explain to the young conductors precisely what he wanted and why. The players were not used to hearing him articulate the musical meaning of a phrase or a passage, why he beat it the way he did and how minute changes in technique could solve problems. He was direct, efficient, helpful and surprisingly entertaining.

A singular moment came when he tried to help one conductor negotiate a tricky passage in Debussy's *Jeux*. No matter what the young maestro did, nothing worked. Boulez would stop, explain and have him do it over. Finally, he decided to demonstrate how to manage the passage and, taking the podium, dispatched it effortlessly with his minimal yet precise beat. The young conductor was bewildered, obviously daunted to be standing in front of The Cleveland Orchestra. Wanting to convey the necessity of projecting total confidence and authority, Boulez said, "They will do exactly what you show them. They are very impressive, but you must not be impressed."

In 1999, I got a letter from a guest conductor who had been a potential candidate to succeed Christoph von Dohnányi. Angry at having been passed over, he withdrew from all future engagements, including two weeks booked for the next season. Boulez was already engaged for his regular two weeks, and I quietly ascertained that he was free for the suddenly open time slots. I explained the problem to him and proposed that he come for those weeks as well. As further enticement, I suggested that for the second week, he conduct a concert performance of Debussy's opera *Pelléas et Mélisande*, a project we had discussed but never realized. Doing an "easy" program the first week would allow the additional rehearsal time needed for *Pelléas,* given its length and the fact that the orchestra had never played it.

He cheerfully agreed and proposed as his "easy" program:
    Stravinsky: *Fireworks*
    Anton Webern: Six Orchestral Pieces, Op. 6
    György Ligeti: Piano Concerto (Cleveland premiere)
      intermission
    Stravinsky: *The Rite of Spring*

This music is as hard as it gets. The orchestra had often performed *The Rite* with him, so its intense challenges were well worked-out. But the Ligeti, which they had never performed, and the Webern, which they had done only rarely, were fiendishly complicated. We laughed about this "easy" program throughout his life, and I dubbed it "the Pierre Boulez pops program" to his high amusement.

Boulez was a fanatical advocate for music from the first half of the 20th century, as well as for contemporary works. But through time, his repertoire expanded judiciously into the Mahler symphonies and, true to his French roots, back into Berlioz. He had recorded the *Symphonie fantastique* and its companion piece, *Lélio*, early in his career but then, with rare exceptions, left the composer untouched. I persuaded him to return to Berlioz with the *Symphonie fantastique*, the complete *Roméo et Juliette*, a work he had conducted only once before, and the Requiem, a piece totally new to him.

Through the 1990s, he expanded his conducting activities, concentrating on ensembles he admired and had relationships with — The Cleveland Orchestra, Berlin Philharmonic, Chicago Symphony, Ensemble intercontemporain, London Symphony, Los Angeles Philharmonic and Vienna Philharmonic. Under his expansive new agreement with DG, he rerecorded his core repertoire (most of which he had initially done for Columbia Records in the 1960s and 1970s) — Bartók, Stravinsky, Webern, Berg, Schoenberg, Ravel, Debussy and Varèse — plus works new to him, including the complete symphonies and orchestral song cycles of Mahler, some Berlioz, Richard Strauss and Szymanowski. He also ventured into opera: Debussy's *Pelléas et Mélisande* and Schoenberg's *Moses und Aron*. In 1996 the Vienna Philharmonic invited him to conduct and record Bruckner's Symphony No. 8 at the Abbey Church in St. Florian, Austria, where Bruckner had been organist; Boulez had reached the pinnacle of acceptance by even the Austrian musical establishment.

INTERLUDE: THE CAPTAIN

In the 1990s, Ara Guzelimian, then artistic advisor of Carnegie Hall and another long-time Boulez friend, and I adopted a private, affectionate nickname for him: "The Captain," symbolic of his immense influence on us as teacher, guide and mentor. In 2000, he recorded Schoenberg's Piano Concerto with Mitsuko Uchida in Cleveland, a project dear to both of them. When Philips released the CD, its cover featured an arty black-and-white picture of the two, with the heading in block letters "SCHOENBERG, PIANO CONCERTO, MITSUKO UCHIDA, PIERRE BOULEZ." On receiving the CDs, I had a friend in the marketing department doctor the cover to read, "SCHOENBERG, PIANO CONCERTO, CAPTAIN & TENNILLE," after a well-known 1970s pop duo. I sent a CD with the doctored cover to Guzelimian without a note (see next page). He later told me he received it at his office in Carnegie Hall and dutifully put it on his desk. Only a few hours later did the heading register, and we had a great laugh. On a late visit with Boulez, we tried to explain the joke to him; alas, it did not translate.

OJAI

It was through Boulez that I first visited California's Ojai Music Festival. Ever since we met, he had talked about it, clearly smitten with the place. He would get misty-eyed recalling his first time there in 1967, coming over the surrounding mountain ridge in a convertible before dropping down into the citrus-tree wonderland of the Ojai Valley and meeting a wall of pungent orange-blossom scent. He loved the festival's free spirit of adventure and always considered it one of his important musical homes, returning as its music director in 1970, 1984, 1989, 1992, 1996 and 2003.

At his urging, I made my first visit in 1996, when he was there conducting the Los Angeles Philharmonic. I was immediately transfixed by the music, setting and audience. The concerts take place at the Libbey Bowl, in a picturesque park in the middle of the town, with the audience seated on uncomfortable wooden benches beneath spreading sycamore trees. When I returned in 2003, the festival ended on a very hot Sunday afternoon with Boulez conducting Mahler Symphony No. 9. During the piece's sublime finale, two squirrels chased one another on tree limbs above the audience, chattering loudly and jumping from branch to branch. Such is the magical marriage of nature and music at Ojai.

My favorite photo of Boulez – taken at his last Ojai appearance in 2003

Boulez was thrilled when I became artistic director there in 2004, and the festival was always a prominent topic of our conversations. By then, almost 80, he felt he could no longer undertake the grueling trip from Europe, so sadly we never worked together in Ojai. I often consulted him on my plans and ideas, and he followed everything with an intense and supportive eye, always urging me to be more daring.

BADEN-BADEN

Through all our working together I regularly visited him in Baden-Baden, a small and wealthy town in Germany just over the French border from Strasbourg. He also had a large apartment in Paris, as well as a small house on the outskirts of the city and another near Aix-en-Provence, but he always considered Baden-Baden to be home. While it might seem curious that the most famous living French musician resided in Germany, he told me he was making an intentional statement, as he felt that earlier in his career the French had not accepted him.

His house was a four-story stone structure on a hillside overlooking the city. It had a somewhat menacing Gothic look that I told him reminded me of Norman Bates' house in *Psycho*. Furnished in a spare modernist style, it was full of books and scores, with original paintings by Mondrian, Picasso, Klee and others adorning the walls. His assistant Hans Messmer lived on the ground floor, and Boulez occupied the upper three.

Visiting was always a pleasure; he was a generous and welcoming host. We talked about politics, art, music and a favorite of his, music business gossip. He relished being kept up to date on what was happening, the latest scandals and stories, and offered news of his own. He was very droll and loved to laugh. An avid walker, he started mornings with the steep hike down to the town center where he would buy a daily collection of newspapers. Along the way he was warmly greeted by friends and shopkeepers, and he always reciprocated.

In the late 2000s, his eyesight began to fail, causing difficulty reading scores. Retiring from conducting, he settled full-time in Baden-Baden. During those final years, I visited him every four to six months, joined on many trips by our mutual friend Ara Guzelimian, a predecessor in Ojai and at that time Provost and Dean of The Juilliard School.

INTERLUDE: VEGETARIAN

In 2014, when Guzelimian and I visited Boulez in Baden-Baden, he was, as usual, the consummate host, though by then his vitality and stamina were seriously compromised, and he was finding it harder to communicate. Over lunch, we carried on with news about the music business, which he was always keen to hear. At one point, Guzelimian asked me to tell Boulez the big music news from New York. He stopped eating and looked up, asking me what the news was. I told him that two days earlier, conductor Lorin Maazel had announced he was turning vegetarian. Boulez's mouth turned up in a wry smile and he said quietly but pointedly, "Without bones."

With each visit, I found Boulez increasingly frail. It was heartbreaking to see his strength and vigor erode so steadily and completely. 2015 saw 90th birthday celebrations for him around the world, including at Ojai, where I arranged for performances of several of his major works and a multimedia program on his life. Sadly he was not well enough to attend any of them. He died peacefully at home on January 5, 2016.

Guzelimian and I traveled to Baden-Baden for the private funeral in a Roman Catholic church, attended by close friends and colleagues (a more public memorial service would take place in Paris a few days later). The funeral itself was surprising to me. Over the course of our friendship, I had not known him to be particularly religious, but I learned that during his last months he was visited regularly by a Catholic priest. While the music performed at the public service in Paris was by Messiaen, Debussy and Boulez himself, nothing played in Baden-Baden was French, just Bach, Berg and Webern, a nod perhaps to his deepest musical heroes as well as a final comment on his relationship with France. He was buried under a simple gravestone on a hillside overlooking the town.

Boulez entered my life at exactly the moment I needed to be reminded of the exhilaration in planning musical events together with great artists, focusing totally on creativity. I realized how much I had been craving the unfettered stimulation of a conductor consumed with a strong vision of what music must be and unafraid of being adventurous. The Boston *Répons* experience represented everything I had yearned for in the music business and laid the foundation for my increasing fearlessness about programming and concert presentation through the rest of my career. In curious symmetry, it was later, in Ojai, that the creative seeds Boulez planted in me were to reach their fullest realization.

For me, accepting Boulez as one of the seminal thinkers and musical intellects of our time goes without saying. His legacy as a composer is unquestioned, and the standards he set as a conductor and programmer are unparalleled. Through his tireless advocacy, he brought 20th-century orchestral music into the regular repertoire, so that today the music of Stravinsky, Bartók, Schoenberg, Webern and Berg appear frequently on programs. His conducting evolved from seeming cool and detached to being highly flexible and expressive. He was a selfless performer, never inserting himself between the music and the listener.

By the end of his life, this outspoken critic of the status quo and advocate of the new was fully embraced by the very centers of the musical establishment he had railed against — Vienna and Berlin — and celebrated for his uncompromising views of repertoire, programming and concert presentation. His perspectives on musicians and institutions were huge influences on me, and a crucial lesson I learned was to have unshakable belief that clear artistic principles are the basis for decision-making. He demanded of everyone a point of view, something he possessed in abundance.

Pierre Boulez was relentless in forging close and sustained relationships with those with whom he felt a common bond through commitment to similar artistic values — people such as William Glock, Carlos Moseley, George Szell, Ernest Fleischmann and Ara Guzelimian. That was what really mattered to him. Those relationships went deep and were long-lasting. For over 30 years, I was honored to be included in that company as colleague, collaborator and friend.

To Tom – One of the Boulez mafia , smiling and happy as I am . with affection – May 16th 2000

The "Boulez Mafia" at Carnegie Hall in 2000 – Carlos Moseley, me, Ernest Fleischmann, Boulez, Franz Xaver Ohnesorg (of Carnegie Hall) and Ara Guzelimian

CHAPTER 6
CLARITY FROM THE TOP: WARD SMITH

Boston left me certain I was done running orchestras. But I had no idea what I was going to do next, even though there was no doubt it would somehow relate to music. After managing the BSO, the largest and most complex orchestra organization in the world, where else was there to go?

Thanks to an introduction by Dutch conductor Bernard Haitink, I found myself, in summer 1986, advising Amsterdam's Royal Concertgebouw Orchestra about fundraising strategies. The engagement partnered me with Thomas Harris, an American living in Holland who had consulted with them before.

At that time, the funding situation in Europe stood at a critical juncture as open-ended government subsidies were coming to an end. This created urgent challenges for performing institutions such as the Concertgebouw, where money from the state and city amounted to close to 90 percent of its budget. Needing additional revenues, the orchestra thought private sponsorships were the answer but was unfamiliar with how to enter that market. Unlike government subsidies, by then taken for granted, private support is a transaction between donor and institution that must be sought out and justified. Americans with expertise in this area, such as Harris and myself, were suddenly in demand.

This job led to further consulting projects with Harris in Europe over the next 18 months. Assignments usually began with advice on how to raise private money but would typically evolve into helping clients rethink the prerequisites necessary to support this new source of revenue. The work expanded into issues of broader organizational and board development, strategic planning and financial strategies, engagements in which our clients were always boards of directors. Looking at organizations entirely from the outside gave me new understanding of and appreciation for how they did and did not function. Without the distractions of day-to-day operational responsibilities, the work provided perspectives I had never gained in Boston. Up to this point I had not stepped back to appreciate the importance of the board in setting and owning policy or the role of the CEO in ensuring that the underlying premises of well-functioning institutions be established and maintained.

The consulting work surprised me with how easy it was to see clients' critical challenges — organizations are far more transparent than they think they are. I came to understand how addressing issues head-on and getting them right are essential; there is no hiding real problems. Alignment within the organization, starting at the board level, is essential to provide context for decision-making, and it must be centered on mutual understanding of what the institution stands for, why it exists and where it is going.

THE CALL

In October 1986, with my consulting business flourishing, I received a call from Ward Smith, board president of The Cleveland Orchestra. We had met several times over the years and hit it off. A lawyer and business executive, Smith had joined the board in 1972, becoming its president in 1983.[1]

An elegant man with a full head of white hair, he was engaging, smart, had an infectious sense of humor and used colorful language that somehow did not offend because of his open and friendly manner. In his casual and breezy way, he greeted everyone with playful nicknames. Mine, for some reason, was "Petunia," and it stuck for as long as I knew him.

The purpose of his call was to inquire if I would consider running The Cleveland Orchestra, replacing Ken Haas whose acceptance of the BSO job had just been announced. I explained that I had no interest to be head of another orchestra and put the idea out of my mind.

Over the next six months, I immersed myself in consulting. It was stimulating, but subconsciously and then consciously, I began to

---

1 A note on the changing world of board leadership titles: In the 1980s, the lay leader of the board held the title of board president. By the 2000s, as the title of the chief management officer escalated to president & CEO, the volunteer board leader became the board chair, and what was formerly the board chair became the honorary chair or chair emeritus.

CLARITY FROM THE TOP: WARD SMITH

Ward Smith

question if it sparked my true interests. Its allure faded as three gnawing feelings emerged.

First, consulting — delivering diagnosis, analysis and recommendations to the client — was removed from implementation. I missed making things happen and became frustrated at being so far from planning concerts. Being around these amazing European organizations and musicians whetted my appetite for getting back into the trenches.

Second, I missed the process of building teams to address opportunities and solve problems, something I really enjoyed. Consulting did not provide the opportunity of working operationally with others and I missed the messy vitality of the back-and-forth.

Third, I was fatigued from monthly international travel and in a constant state of jet lag. Moving to Europe, given my growing misgivings about consulting, was not an option.

In April 1987, I answered a second call from Smith. He asked again if there were any circumstances under which I might consider the Cleveland job. I had not expected the question but totally surprised myself by not immediately saying there were none. Instead, I explained that I had come to believe that for a performing institution to be truly great, clear artistic principles must drive decision-making, thereby building a compelling case for attracting the necessary funds. In other words, settle on a vision and do what is necessary to fulfill it rather than scaling aspirations to what is thought to be affordable. Even so, I reminded him that my background in finance guaranteed that I understood the necessity of fiscal prudence. If Cleveland subscribed to that basic premise, I told Smith, we could have another conversation. A few days later, after conferring with his board colleagues, he confirmed complete agreement with my premise and invited me to meet in Cleveland. I suddenly found myself a serious candidate for a job back in the orchestra world.

I later learned that the real reason for this second call had been a reference check on someone being strongly considered. Smith had not expected my opening the door to being a candidate, so the reference was never checked and that other person was put on hold pending my visit.

I knew The Cleveland Orchestra through both recordings and live performances. A late entrant into America's so-called Big Five (Boston, Chicago, Cleveland, New York and Philadelphia)[2], it was widely considered a "musicians' orchestra," and known for its impeccable chamber-music quality and stunning virtuosity. It had a distinctive style and sound, combining flawless balance, crystalline clarity, smooth homogeneity and characterful musicianship by its stellar principal players. Performances were notable for their extreme dynamic range, starting with the most gossamer of pianissimos.

Most people attribute these qualities to the exacting leadership of Szell, but they were carefully nurtured by his successors — Pierre

---

2 The origin of the term "Big Five" American orchestras is difficult to pinpoint, but no doubt it was established by music journalists in the 1950s. At first, there had been the Big Three (Boston, New York and Philadelphia), justified by those orchestras' ongoing presence in New York and recordings. The artistic emergence in the 1950s of the Chicago Symphony under Fritz Reiner and The Cleveland Orchestra under George Szell gave rise to the Big Five. Managers of the group started meeting to discuss joint concerns in the 1960s and commissioned aggregate studies, further formalizing the group.

By the 1970s, as the overall quality of American orchestras increased, and critical recognition of others escalated, the boundaries for membership blurred; the Los Angeles Philharmonic and the San Francisco Symphony in particular pushed for a Big Six or Big Seven. The term Big Five today, while faded from public consciousness, is still understood to have represented the Boston, Chicago, Cleveland, New York and Philadelphia orchestras years ago.

Boulez (briefly as interim), Lorin Maazel, and at that point Christoph von Dohnányi. One of the secrets of The Cleveland Orchestra's ongoing distinctiveness was always having music directors who were superb trainers, relentlessly demanding about internal balance, phrasing and intonation. This is not unlike how a coach drills sports teams on basic conditioning. Given the orchestra's extraordinary work ethic and virtuosity, the challenge for any conductor in Cleveland was never getting the musicians to play the right notes and rhythms, which were well in hand by the first rehearsal, but making musical sense of the piece and producing a cohesive interpretation.

The acoustical quality of the orchestra's home, Severance Hall, was an additional factor in its inherent style. The auditorium seating capacity, only 2,000, was well below that of its peers (Boston's Symphony Hall, for example, holds 2,625). This smaller cubic volume did not require the players to exaggerate dynamics, and the fine onstage acoustics allowed them to hear one another with exceptional clarity.

Szell's 24-year tenure steeped the orchestra in the Classical style of Mozart, Beethoven and Schubert, as his splendid recordings attest. Maazel maintained those high standards and added tonal brilliance. The result was an ensemble with an old-world European hue coupled with American precision, always conveying an overall impression of elegant restraint. It was stylistically the complete opposite of the swashbuckling color and in-your-face ebullience of the Boston Symphony. The difference intrigued me.

I wondered whether I was genuinely interested in the job or merely running away from exhausting travel and unfulfilling consulting work. I sought perspective from Colin Davis, with whom I had forged a close relationship in Boston. I had always found his advice thought-provoking and laced with wisdom. He knew Smith well, having guest-conducted in Cleveland and been approached by him to be its music director several years earlier. He adored the orchestra but had declined, about to assume the music directorship of the Bavarian Radio Symphony in Munich as he was winding down his tenure at London's Royal Opera. He seemed a perfect sounding board.

At a long dinner in Munich, I asked him point blank whether I was crazy to consider the job after my Boston disillusionment. He answered by recounting his recent experience conducting Dresden's Staatskapelle Orchestra in Vaughan Williams' Symphony No. 6, paired with Bruckner's Symphony No. 7. He pondered what had possessed him, a British conductor, to lead a quintessentially Germanic orchestra in a very English symphony in Dresden, a city still in ruins from the Allied bombing of World War II. The work, which starts violently, ends with a graphic musical portrait of the nothingness of post-nuclear devastation — music that is timeless, eerie and still, yet with an ominous undercurrent, a startling reflection of the city's surrounding desolation. Davis said he personally heard the Vaughan Williams followed by the Bruckner, although appearing contradictory, as a spiritual and meaningful totality. It reminded him that all music exists in a context that can amplify concentration and impact.

And that, he explained, was why I needed to take the job. Cleveland did not have the cosmopolitan allure of Boston and was not large — by 1984 it was only the 12th largest metro area in the United States[3] and its population had been shrinking for years — but it had one of the world's greatest orchestras, which it had supported and nurtured over the years. Davis saw how deeply Cleveland needed its orchestra as the center of its self-esteem, which he likened to the mystique of a diamond forged in a bed of coal. He was certain that because of this context of intense community pride, I would be able to achieve things there that were never possible in Boston.

Two weeks later I headed to Cleveland, almost screwing up everything at the outset. A veteran traveler, I was in the habit of arriving at airports at the last minute and proud of never having missed a flight. This time, I cut it too close, arriving at the gate five minutes after the plane departed. Rebooking thankfully delayed my arrival for only two hours, but it did require an embarrassing call to Smith. It was not the best way to begin a job interview, but it cured my bad habit.

From the airport, Smith took me to a stuffy men's club steeped in burnished wood paneling, hushed silence, high ceilings and uncomfortable furniture. We met in a private room with two other board members: Alfred Rankin Sr., Smith's predecessor as president and now its chair, and Richard Tullis, head of the personnel committee. I had met Rankin before but never Tullis. Over a predictably bland lunch of creamed chicken and peas, we chatted cheerfully but aimlessly for an hour.

Deciding to get to the point, I asked if I were offered the job, what would they want me to *do*? I remember Smith's answer clearly: "The Cleveland Orchestra is one of the greatest in the world, possibly

---

3 Estimated CMSA population data for 1984 according to the United States Bureau of the Census.

the best — we know that, and you know that. But frankly, it is not good enough, so I expect you to make it even better, and I fully understand my responsibility as board president to support that effort."

I was deeply impressed by his elegant clarity, which Rankin and Tullis echoed. It seemed that this was an organization that understood what was important and what would provide a common foundation on which to build— it was all about the music. They never produced a job description, which didn't bother me since such comprehensive lists are ultimately neutered by sheer length and attempts to cover all the bases. Being able to answer succinctly what they wanted me to do in a way that cut to the essence of the job was more than sufficient.

After lunch, Smith took me to meet Dohnányi, who was just finishing his third season as music director. I had met him briefly in Europe and knew his recordings. He came from a remarkable family. His paternal grandfather was the Hungarian composer Ernst von Dohnányi. An uncle, the renowned German theologian Dietrich Bonhoeffer, was executed by the Nazis in 1945, along with two other uncles and his father, for highly developed plots to kill Hitler. Before Cleveland, his orchestral career was somewhat limited, as most of his work had been in the opera house, both as a conductor and in running the companies in Frankfurt and Hamburg. Despite his being a widely admired musician, the Cleveland appointment caught the music world by surprise, resulting in an oft-repeated quip, "Christoph von Who?"

As a conductor, he had a reputation as a fierce taskmaster, always well-prepared and fixated on the basics of phrasing, balance and tuning during exacting rehearsals, very much in the tradition of his predecessors. While a strong advocate of composers like Hans Werner Henze, Arnold Schoenberg and Alban Berg, Dohnányi was well schooled in the central European repertoire so deeply in the blood of the orchestra. He appeared to be in many ways the perfect stylistic successor to Szell.

This was our first extended conversation, and I found him deeply committed to music and impressively intelligent, with an easy manner. He had done his homework on me, so we spoke primarily about his artistic goals, a discussion unlike any I had experienced with Ozawa.

At the end of the meeting, he pronounced us in sync about basic musical beliefs and tastes. Almost as if I had already accepted the job, he declared to be looking forward to our working together and outlined his ground rules: we would work together on his programs but as music director he would have final say and first call on reper-toire; because of my knowledge of conductors and repertoire, I would control the selection of guest conductors and their programming. This was refreshing; most music directors jealously guard those authorities. Dohnányi was certain that since we agreed on basic musical values, his programs and those of guests would convey a unified and cohesive ar-tistic profile for the institution. I found his concept of a true collabora-tion invigorating — a classic alignment around mutually agreed-upon values and goals.

Smith then drove me around Cleveland's gorgeous suburbs, which I had never seen, all previous visits having been limited to down-town and around Severance Hall. Here was the ultimate, and effective, soft sell that this was a lovely place to live. Dropping me back at the airport, he promised to be in touch quickly. I returned home excited that both Smith and Dohnányi appeared to be the kind of institutional partners I had yearned for.

Still slightly unsure that I really wanted to run another orches-tra and as a reality check, I went to Carnegie Hall a week later to hear Cleveland perform. I bought a ticket at the door and melded into the crowd, not wanting to alert anyone I was there. The choice of mu-sic was typical Dohnányi — intelligent and serious, with the complex Symphony No. 4 of Charles Ives followed by the mighty Fourth Sym-phony of Brahms. I was overwhelmed by the program and the perfor-mance, leaving the hall convinced that I truly loved this astonishing orchestra and what it stood for.

Smith formally offered me the job, and I immediately accepted. The appointment was announced in June, catching many orchestra colleagues, thinking I was done with orchestras, by surprise.

Over time, the perception became that Haas and I had simply switched positions after spending 17 years with our respective orchestras. The reality was far different. Haas's BSO appointment was announced ten months after I had left there and well before the idea of Cleveland was on my radar. My serious conversations with Smith did not start until another six months after that. By the time I started there in September 1987, Haas had been in Boston for more than seven months.

DISCOVERING THE ORGANIZATION

The Musical Arts Association (MAA), the corporate entity of The

Cleveland Orchestra, had a smaller budget than the BSO, even though both owned their concert halls and summer venues. Big differences were Cleveland's lack of either a separate pops brand or a summer music school. This narrower scope of operation resulted in a greater focus on the genuine musical values embodied by the orchestra itself.

I spent my first months getting to know the organization and the city. Surprising was how different the culture was compared to Boston. Cleveland was not as large and nowhere near as cosmopolitan, and it felt much more relaxed and friendly than the more uptight and frenetic culture of the East Coast. As an outsider coming into the community to run one of the city's crown jewels, I was welcomed with open arms, quite unlike the polite standoffishness I always felt in Boston. Part of this could have been because it was the first time I had ever moved to a city to take an executive position, an experience that was never to repeat itself in my career.

It did not take long to discover a palpable culture of cohesion and spirit within the organization. The musicians seemed genuinely happy, without overt bitterness or competing cliques. There was easy and open friendship between staff and board. All in all, a very positive vibe.

That openness and collegiality was embodied by Smith, who not only knew most musicians and staff by name but socialized and played golf with many of them. He was friendly and cheerful but also laser-sharp and focused when needed. Clearly devoted to the orchestra, he took the position seriously (as he did his numerous other volunteer roles, including as an active board member of Case Western Reserve University). He was invested in the institution and community and was widely respected and well-liked. As Colin Davis had said, the orchestra was central to the psyche of the city, no doubt because it was, along with the Cleveland Museum of Art and Cleveland Clinic, one of the biggest not-for-profits in town. In Boston, educational institutions dominated the landscape, none more powerfully than Harvard.

Right from the start, Smith and I forged an open and direct working relationship. He was always available despite his considerable corporate responsibilities as CEO of NACCO Industries, a former coal mining company which he diversified into materials handling and consumer kitchen products. He never interfered with my work, instinctively understanding the fine line between governance and management. At the same time, we were able to establish an enduring personal bond. I spent more time with him over my first several months than I had in seven years with his counterpart at the BSO.

> **INTERLUDE: FILLING THE TANK**
> Shortly after arriving in Cleveland, I visited a gas station in our Cleveland Heights neighborhood. As those were the days before self-service gas pumps, an attendant filled the tank. He started chatting, noticing Massachusetts plates still on the car and asked if we were visiting. I said we had just moved from Boston. Out of the blue, he expressed delight for us, adding: "You will really love it here. Not only is it a wonderful place to live, but we have the world's best symphony orchestra."

A first priority for me, as I had learned years earlier in Boston, was mastering the organization's finances. They were slightly out of balance, despite strong ticket sales. The endowment was miserably low for such an orchestra and annual fundraising was tepid — I was surprised to find that the largest annual gift was only $25,000 (adjusted for inflation, about $65,000 today).

A key to the finances had been support from summer pop music concerts at the MAA-owned-and-operated Blossom Music Center. Built in 1968, Blossom is a glorious outdoor amphitheater 40 miles south of Cleveland, with under-cover seating for 5,000 and capacity on the surrounding lawns for another 10,000, not unlike Tanglewood. The orchestra performed about 25 concerts there each summer, with the remaining nights used to book rock and pop bands, concerts produced and managed by the orchestra staff. By 1987, the net financial return to MAA from this business had seriously deteriorated. Competition in the market had dramatically increased with the addition of new promoters and venues; the number of tickets for sale for summer music events had doubled over five years. This divided the audience and drove up artist costs through competitive bidding, both factors cutting MAA's bottom line in half. Further declines were projected, and the result was a growing financial imbalance that needed immediate attention.

Smith and I decided drastic action was required to shore up this diminishing business. He and a fellow board member, an expert in corporate mergers, led the negotiation to license off the pop music business to MCA Concerts (which has since morphed into Live Nation), in exchange for which it paid MAA a percentage of gross income from the rock concerts and assumed the full costs of operating the property. Dates were carved out for MAA to present its own orchestra concerts at its own risk. The reduction in costs and increased risk-free income stream from the pop business helped stabilize MAA's finances, and, by eliminating the need to manage Blossom, allowed us to concentrate fully on the orchestra.

A major surprise for me was how different the staff culture was from Boston. Haas and I were friends and respected each other's accomplishments, but our leadership styles were completely different. Mine was informal, open and often lighthearted, while setting lofty goals and delegating authority to a self-starting team of lieutenants. Haas was the opposite, more centralized and formal, with most decisions coming to him. He signed all checks personally. I found myself being addressed as "Mr. Morris," the opposite of the total informality I was used to. Haas had been, and still was, "Mr. Haas" to everyone, even my assistant, whom I had inherited from him — whenever I asked her to call Haas in Boston, I overheard her saying "Mr. Haas, Tom wants to speak with you." I came to understand that there is no single right way to do a job; different styles work effectively for different leaders in different situations.

As a result, everything in Cleveland initially came to my desk, as it had with Haas. While it was easy to change "Mr. Morris" to "Tom," it took time to move decision-making and initiative down into the organization. I inherited his senior staff members, who were outstanding but imbued with his style. I needed a team that reflected my philosophy, and Smith totally supported these changes. Beyond having great people who took initiative, my goal was a culture that valued music first and engendered a nurturing environment for artists and composers. I wanted to create an atmosphere of joyful enthusiasm — classical music is a serious art, but that does not negate the idea of having fun while working hard. I strove to foster this by exuding it myself and attracting people who shared it.

My first hire was a director of marketing — occasioned, luckily, by the sudden resignation of the incumbent, who surmised quickly, and correctly, that we would not see eye-to-eye. The new one was Gary Hanson, who was to remain with the orchestra for almost 30 years, the last 12 as my successor at the top.

I found the artistic planning predictable and somewhat muted. The small size of the city dictated a subscription season shorter than others, leaving weeks to be filled each year with other activities. The result was a surprising amount of touring, both domestically and abroad, activities that seemed put together more out of the need to fill unused weeks of employment for the musicians than building strategically focused projects. While the healthy partnership with Dohnányi I had hoped for was happily materializing, I felt the need to beef up the institution's artistic support resources given Smith's mandate. My second move was adding someone in charge of artistic administration — a new idea for Cleveland, as that work had previously been handled by the operations staff. The arrival of the BBC's Roger Wright in this post, along with Hanson, fundamentally changed the internal culture and depth of planning.

INTERLUDE: HOW NOT TO IMPRESS YOUR NEW BOSS

Eager to take stock of everything the orchestra was doing, I attended an education concert soon after I arrived. This particular one featured projected images over the orchestra of the composers whose works were being performed. Fine — until the conductor announced the next work to be Paul White's *Mosquito Dance*, a short and extremely vivid musical picture of the insect's annoying buzz, capped at the end by an enormous swat played by the slapstick. It always brought down the house. The composer was totally unknown and this was his only piece anyone had ever heard of. It had been popularized by Fiedler and the Boston Pops, so I knew it well. Cleveland's education director didn't, or couldn't, find any information about White in order to project his picture over the orchestra so he faked it by projecting a picture of some anonymous person, pretending it was White. Alas, I, his new boss, was watching and I actually knew the composer through a strange coincidence — he had been the conductor in Rochester when I was growing up. After the concert, I confronted the hapless fellow, saying that the projected image was not Paul White. He turned beet-red and stammered something about not being able to find his picture. I explained not only that I knew White but, driving home my command of the situation, suggested he could easily have procured a picture from Cleveland's timpanist Paul Yancich, who was also from Rochester and who I knew was White's grandson.

It took me another several years to replace the director of development and director of finance, moves that, with hindsight, I should have made earlier. Development was especially critical because the orchestra's fundraising was not robust. Despite this, Cleveland had a history of generous philanthropy, which was why such a small city possessed the jewels of a great orchestra and art museum. Knowing this, I was encouraged by the potential for substantially greater fundraising. By 1993, we doubled annual giving from the board and mounted the orchestra's first major fund drive in years to coincide with the orchestra's 75th anniversary, adding $25 million to the meager endowment. With these boosts and the MCA Concerts deal, the finances were back in balance.

GOVERNANCE

One area in which Smith proved particularly insightful was board governance, for which he was responsible. In Boston, I had not viewed the board as a partner and never forged a real relationship with it or its leaders — to me it had seemed more of a necessary evil. I was wrong. As I learned in consulting, the key to success is the effectiveness of the board and its leadership. It has to own what the institution is about. It has to advocate in the community for the orchestra's importance. It has to be engaged. It has to add value. And it has to be supported.

Smith taught me how governance works, not by being dogmatic but simply by attending to it on a daily basis. The role of boards had changed significantly in the 1970s as organizations got more complicated, seasons longer, the need for raising money greater and the role of ensuring fiduciary prudence more essential. It used to be that a strong and dominant chair was more than sufficient, with the rest of the board more or less rubberstamping decisions rather than having much to do. This had been the case in Cleveland prior to Smith, as the board had been dominated for 30 years by two strong leaders in Alfred Rankin Sr. and Frank Joseph.

But now, board leadership needed to be shared to take care of the growing responsibilities. Well-functioning committees — finance, fundraising, audit, investment and governance — were necessary to handle these myriad functions. All this required changes in the board's culture and a willingness by its leader to share responsibility — easier said than done. One of Smith's greatest achievements was presiding over this transformation. Knowing he could not do everything himself, he delegated the real work to committees, choosing strong committee chairs and giving each clear charges. He opened the board to wider segments of the community in terms of age, race, gender and religion. He expanded the board's size — which, at 60 members, was already much larger than Boston's 25. Most important was giving it something to do, such as the fundraising drive and the leasing of Blossom's pop concert business. And he did it all with a gentle but firm touch, never forgetting that great boards, like great orchestras, need ongoing nurturing and inspiration.

I spent a lot of time "managing up" and made certain that board and committee meetings were always excruciatingly well-prepared. I became a true believer in rehearsing presentations and meetings, since they are, after all, quasi-performances. I paid steady attention to working closely with Smith, who was a persistent yet patient teacher. It not only made the organization function smoothly but ingrained in my mind the firm precept to always "know your boss."

The triangle of Smith, Dohnányi and me functioned smoothly because we were aligned, making any structural ambiguity irrelevant. Inevitable conflicts never became issues of control or power. We each understood our respective responsibilities and accountabilities, accepting that the process of solving problems required persistent collaboration.

I found Smith's initial assurance that decision-making would always be predicated around artistic principles was deeply engrained in the board's culture. He was adamant that its job was to support what was being done artistically, and he was insistent that artistic decisions and the management of the institution were responsibilities respectively of the music director and executive director, subject, of course, to normal budgetary and governance oversight.

In any orchestra, debate about art versus money is inevitable, though I believe it to be a false dichotomy. The board annually approves a budget, one proposed by management in the context of overall goals and scheduling realities. Artistic planning is always a matter of making choices within some limiting parameters, whether schedule, resources or vision, and the discipline of doing so stimulates creative thinking. But it is the sole responsibility of the artistic and administrative leaders to advocate for and allocate those budgets accordingly.

As Dohnányi and I sharpened the orchestra's profile by adding more adventurous repertoire and new program structures, the public, not surprisingly, noticed. When patrons shared their opinions eagerly and vociferously, Smith and the board were unstinting in their support and steadfastly refrained from interference, fully understanding

The Bermuda Triangle in a light moment.

the fine line between governance and management and never blurring the distinction.

SURVIVING THE WORKLOAD

Running a big orchestra is stressful and intense by definition, as I knew from experience. Concerts are produced year-round — there is no let-up — and I attended two or three times weekly. And following performances there were frequently dinners with visiting artists. This was all after working in the office all day, sometimes six or and occasionally seven days a week. In addition, there was travel — tours, meeting artists, planning tours and recordings or making myself visible at important musical occasions in order to give the orchestra a constant presence worldwide. It was exhilarating but exhausting. My international travel was so extensive that Smith once wryly commented that I occasionally came to Cleveland from Europe.

I drove myself hard, arriving in the office early and often staying through the evening's post-concert meal, but I had learned the importance of being rested for maximum effectiveness and efficiency. The relentless schedule made it impossible to manage my time reasonably on a weekly or even a monthly basis, but I could do so on a quarterly basis, taking blocks of time off every three months. Making sure I had adequate rest was one of the key points I insisted upon when hired.

A key element in Cleveland, I realized, was the need to have fun doing the work, a perspective Smith shared. We traveled together, went on tours together, ate together, drank together and joked together. He was a total mensch. At artist dinners when he was not attending, staff members present would say in unison, "Thank you, Ward," as I signed the bill. He once returned an expense account, on which were frequent meals at a favorite Asian eatery, with the notation, "Petunia, did we buy a Japanese restaurant?"

INTERLUDE: BEN AND JERRY'S

In June 1994, Ben & Jerry's Ice Cream announced that Ben Cohen, its CEO, was planning to retire. In keeping with its flair for over-the-top marketing, the company took out full-page ads in major newspapers headlined, "Yo, We Want You to Be Our CEO." It asked those interested to submit no-more-than-100-word essays explaining why they should be named CEO, enclosing the top of a Ben & Jerry's ice cream container. The winner was promised the job, but second prize, free ice cream for life, was the real incentive. All other applicants would receive a coupon for a free pint of ice cream plus a rejection letter personally signed by Ben and Jerry that was "suitable for framing." To the company's utter amazement, it received 50,000 applications. The possibility of second prize was too irresistible to pass up, even at the risk of getting the job, so I applied (see opposite page). Alas, I was one of the 49,999 receiving the rejection letter, which, suitably framed, has prominently hung on my office wall since (also see opposite page).

SUCCESSION PLANNING

In Cleveland, the expectation was for board presidents to serve from eight to twelve years, even though by statute they were elected annually to renewable one-year terms. This was unlike most orchestras, which elect presidents for three-year terms, after which a successor takes the post. The assumed longer terms demand care in the nomination process and a greater commitment to the institution from the individual; this provides continuity and accountability by keeping leaders in office long enough to deal with the consequences of their decisions.

THE CLEVELAND ORCHESTRA
CHRISTOPH VON DOHNÁNYI • MUSIC DIRECTOR

SEVERANCE HALL
CLEVELAND, OHIO 44106
(216) 231-7300
FAX: (216) 231-0202

Thomas W. Morris
Executive Director

June 27, 1994

Ben and Jerry's Homemade, Inc.
P. O. Box 240
Waterbury, Vermont 05676

Dear Sirs:

I am a fifty-year old CEO, who has spent the last twenty-five years running two of the world's greatest symphony orchestras.

I am creative, smart, committed, successful and interested in new challenges. While I would not normally consider entering the for-profit world, the manner of your search appeals to me as representing a corporate culture to which I could relate, and to which I could contribute. In short, yours is a world I could sink my teeth into.

Besides, I love great ice cream, and I promise not to rename the company "Tom and Jerry's".

Yours sincerely,

Thomas W. Morris

TWM:hs

The Musical Arts Association operating
THE CLEVELAND ORCHESTRA, BLOSSOM MUSIC CENTER and SEVERANCE HALL

Cleveland's long average tenures, coupled with a tradition of choosing outstanding individuals, were major factors underlying its history of success.

After 12 years, Smith felt it time for his own transition of board leadership. He taught me that successful succession planning is better addressed when the organization is enjoying the best, not the worst, of times. Having recruited and prepared a number of potential successors, he managed this transition seamlessly and effortlessly. On leaving the position, he became board chair, a largely ceremonial position, for another seven years, still very much involved but completely supportive of his successor.

In 2003, he relinquished that position, unfortunately in declining health battling cancer. A year later, he was able to speak at my Cleveland retirement party, which he did in his usual avuncular style, uproariously recalling many of our mutual travel, dining and work escapades. For his memorial service six months later and in keeping with his good cheer and zest for life, he requested a performance of not a funeral adagio but "Seventy-Six Trombones."

Davis's advice that I go to Cleveland was absolutely spot-on. I often remarked that if Boston lost the Boston Symphony, the city would be sad but consoled, knowing it still had Harvard. In Cleveland, loss of the orchestra would be a death blow. That need, plus the shared vision Smith, Dohnányi and I forged, made it the ideal situation in which I could flourish. My ambivalence about returning to orchestras had not been about the business per se but rather about the lack of clarity and values at the BSO and my own unpreparedness for that job. There I had coveted the position, but in Cleveland I really wanted the job.

One of the secrets of Cleveland's success is the very institutional philosophy that Smith conveyed to me during my job interview — that all decision-making would be measured against artistic vision and principles and his charge to make the orchestra ever better. Throughout my tenure, that compact was never breached by Smith, any of his successors or the board. We had disagreements, we had challenges, but that foundation was validated over and over. For that, I say loudly, "Thank you, Ward."

CHAPTER 7
NOT NUMBER TWO:
CHRISTOPH VON DOHNÁNYI

As soon as my appointment was announced but before actually starting the job, I immersed myself in the critical issues facing The Cleveland Orchestra. Ward Smith's clarion charge, to make it better, motivated me to quickly establish a positive rapport with Christoph von Dohnányi and zero in on pressing artistic matters.

EARLY DECISIONS

Two months before my official start, I visited him in London, where he was guest- conducting the Royal Opera. I felt an urgent need for clear focus on three topics: upcoming tours, recording agreements and relationships with key guest conductors. I considered these issues critical to building a distinctive international brand —particularly for Cleveland, given the greater name recognition of its peer orchestras' cities — Boston, Chicago, New York and Philadelphia.

INTERLUDE: WHERE FROM?

For a mid-1990s tour performance in London, a prominent board member and community leader invited a London business associate to join him at the concert. The friend, a true music lover, was thrilled to hear the orchestra in person for the first time, having collected its recordings and been a fan for years. The board member was puffed up with pride by his friend's enthusiasm. Entering the Royal Albert Hall, the business associate, in all seriousness, suddenly asked a question that showed the power of the orchestra's brand relative to that of the city, "Where is The Cleveland Orchestra from?"

Tours bring an international orchestra into competitive arenas, providing exposure and enhancing reputation. They must be consid-

Christoph von Dohnányi's gala welcoming concert in 1983.

ered strategic opportunities for achieving key goals rather than ways to fill time in the schedule, and then planned with purpose as to frequency, location and programming. Everyone likes the prospect of good reviews, but they are unpredictable and never enough to justify the enormous effort and expense of touring. More important is using them to build a global network of advocates, and my robust contacts and musical friends provided a fresh platform on which to build.

From what I was hearing, the Cleveland-Dohnányi image, now three years in, was cloudy at best. A year earlier, the orchestra had undertaken a four-week European tour at a time when the musical partnership with the conductor had not fully jelled. Programming was predictable and did not showcase Dohnányi's reputation for the new and unusual. Ticket sales were not great and the critical reaction was mixed. A fully committed tour to Asia was set for October 1987, shortly after I was to arrive, with an inefficient itinerary of a week in Japan followed by a week in Taiwan, and then back to Japan for a week around Tokyo. A second four-week tour to Europe had been booked for May 1989, but programming was not yet finalized. Addressing that was urgent.

In New York, America's most competitive and glutted market for classical music, the orchestra was vastly overexposed, generally performing five programs annually at Carnegie Hall and another at Avery Fisher (now David Geffen) Hall. So many appearances made it impossible to ensure that each added incremental value to the orchestra's impact. For 1987-88, the New York concerts were already under contract, and there were evolving plans for another visit in January 1989. The only firm commitment for that one was to superstar soprano Kathleen Battle as soloist at Carnegie Hall. I could hardly imagine an artist less compatible with Dohnányi musically or temperamentally, given her growing reputation for capricious behavior. But she was under contract and guaranteed a full house. The programming would be absolutely crucial.

Having a major association with an international record company is prestigious and creates the aura of external validation. In addition, it provides a promotional partner for tours and financial support, particularly in those days when recording costs were borne totally by the label, which then paid the orchestra royalties. Exclusive recording contracts had long been a major part of the American orchestra scene. Digital technology and the advent of the compact disc in the early 1980s motivated record companies to sign ensembles, conductors and soloists to re-record repertoire in the new technology — an expansionary time for the recording business.

The Cleveland Orchestra had no exclusive relationship during the Maazel years, but it did make a lot of recordings on a project basis, mostly with Decca but also with Columbia and Telarc, a young audiophile label in Cleveland. Such was the case over the first three Dohnányi years — Telarc had recorded four Beethoven symphonies plus symphonies by Schubert and Tchaikovsky, and Decca the last three Dvořák symphonies. In addition, one good outcome of that first European tour had been inspiring Hamburg's Teldec label to record Brahms' Symphony No. 1.

With positive critical reaction to these early discs as they started to reach the market in spring 1987, Decca suddenly proposed a major five-year exclusive contract with Dohnányi and the orchestra. What motivates record companies to offer such contracts always mystified me, and one of the weirdest reasons seemed to be preventing artists from making recordings with others. Dohnányi was understandably thrilled by the offer, and I decided that it needed to be dealt with promptly, seeing it as a way to achieve an early and substantial win before my actual start date.

With Decca, I insisted on carve-outs for Teldec to complete a Brahms symphony cycle to follow its first recording, and for Telarc to complete a Beethoven symphony cycle to round out its earlier recordings. To be honest, I did not know at the time if either label was committed to completing the two cycles. To my utter surprise, Decca agreed; my insistence on the carve-outs seemed to make them more eager to make the deal. Luckily, the other two labels then both happily agreed to complete their respective cycles, motivated in part by Decca's expanded interest. Such were the strange motivations of record companies. I signed an "exclusive" recording contract with Decca plus "non-exclusive" ones with the other two labels for the Brahms and Beethoven symphonies plus any other works with Decca's approval. So much for "exclusive," but I was able to arrive in Cleveland with substantial new recording commitments.

Over the previous several years, the orchestra had developed a relationship with the eminent Russian conductor and pianist Vladimir Ashkenazy. He had positive musical rapport with the players, and together they had already made a few recordings for Decca, with which he had his own exclusive contract. Prior to my being hired, serious discussions had been initiated about his being named principal guest conductor and leading the orchestra for four weeks annually, doing some touring and making additional recordings. I learned Dohnányi suddenly got cold feet for some reason and the deal was falling apart, upsetting Ashkenazy. I was well familiar with the perceived threat to a music director by another titled conductor, having watched Colin Davis' long-time Boston position as principal guest conductor be gradually undermined by Ozawa. Since the position had already been offered and accepted, I told Dohnányi it was too late to renege and formalized the appointment. Privately, I welcomed it since I thought Ashkenazy's passionate conducting style a perfect complement to Dohnányi's more cerebral approach.

In addition, Boulez had returned the previous November to conduct in Cleveland for the first time since 1972. His appearances were warmly welcomed by the orchestra and community. I told Dohnányi that we needed to rekindle regular engagements with Boulez for multiple weeks annually, something I knew he would welcome and the musicians would embrace. As with Ashkenazy, I found Boulez's conducting style and repertoire affinities made him a complementary presence to Dohnányi. I consummated the deal, which, given Boulez's busy commitments, would start a few years later.

THE FIRST SIX MONTHS – A STAKE IN THE GROUND

Upon my arrival, the announcements of the new recording agreements and Ashkenazy's appointment established an immediate burst of forward momentum. Now Dohnányi's and my priority was to start building on this positive energy and make immediate and visible differences in what the orchestra had been doing.

First I needed to understand the essence of the musical chemistry between him and the musicians. I attended early rehearsals to see how they interacted and saw that his working style was intense, insisting not only on interpretive matters but on the basics of balance, phrasing, and intonation. He left nothing to chance and used every last minute of each rehearsal. The musicians seemed to appreciate his exacting expectations. Their own work ethic was extraordinary, and they came to first rehearsals fully prepared, already able to play pieces better than most orchestras do after all rehearsals.

The first concerts after my arrival featured Bartók's Concerto for Orchestra, a work commissioned and performed often by the Boston Symphony, so I knew it well. After the first performance, Dohnányi pulled me into his dressing room to ask what I thought. Two things struck me: I could hear the inner voicings of harmonies clearly, not just the bass and treble, such was his internal balancing of the orchestra; and I found the piece not as relentlessly loud as I was accustomed to in Boston. Its sheer volume was overwhelming in only two places — at the huge climax two-thirds through the first movement and at the very end. Opening the score, an amused Dohnányi pointed out that these were the only two places in the piece notated triple-forte, with all other climaxes marked double-forte or below. While most orchestras play either loudly or softly, Cleveland had an infinite palette of gradations, starting with the quietest pianissimo. Dohnányi insisted on such distinctions, as were clearly marked in the scores. Furthermore, the orchestra's innate concept of fortissimo had more to do with focusing and projecting the sound than with sheer amplitude — loud passages penetrated through you rather than knocking you over.

Over those early weeks, the orchestra gave me a sensation of wondrous awe; they consistently played with exquisite refinement, immense musicality and taut discipline, far beyond anything I had ever heard and a tribute to both its heritage and Dohnányi's exacting rehearsals. My only reservation was that the playing was so refined that it sometimes lacked outright emotion and passion. Before starting the job, a major New York presenter had said to me, "The Cleveland Orchestra always impresses you, but it does not always move you." As I considered future planning, it became clear that establishing a compelling and competitive musical profile would require a mix of brain and brawn — truly distinctive programming that embraced unusual music and interesting juxtapositions of pieces, coupled with the exquisite discipline of the playing. Both elements showcased Dohnányi's strengths and would speak positively to the critical community. And working towards these goals aligned perfectly with my beliefs and skills.

From my time at the BSO and my own personal experience in attending concerts, I had come to believe in the critical importance of programming and that great programs must always contain an element of risk and unpredictability. It was a principle Dohnányi and I shared. We both favored unusual structures, different numbers of pieces, plenty of contemporary music, unfamiliar works and high contrast, all in order to ensure variety, vitality and an ever-present element of the unexpected. I had implicit faith in audiences, firmly believing that this energy is what attracts them to the thrill of live performance. My credo was for all concerts to possess some element of the unexpected, whether in repertoire, program structure and format, production values, or artists' interpretations — all of it constructed into a compelling arc of musical narrative. Each concert must pack an emotional wallop, not merely look good on paper. Doing this effectively is not a dry intellectual exercise that appeals only to sophisticates; the results speak powerfully to any listener, who will always know when the outcome is exactly right. All that is needed is imagination, curiosity and flare to transform what is ordinary and predictable into something special and impactful. Routine is to be avoided at all costs.

Take this example, constructed according to the template that dominates most orchestra concerts today — a short opening piece, followed by a concerto, and after intermission a big Romantic symphony — the "19th-century masterpiece model" that theoretically ensures audiences buy tickets:[1]

---

1 Orchestral programming before 1960 was very different in repertoire and program structure. For example, look at Toscanini's tour programs with the NBC Symphony in 1940 and 1950, as detailed in Mortimer Frank's *Arturo Toscanini: The NBC Years*, Amadeus Press, 2002.

Suppé: *Poet and Peasant* Overture
Prokofiev: Piano Concerto No. 3
   intermission
Beethoven: Symphony No. 6, "Pastorale"

There is nothing specifically wrong here, but there is also nothing really right, just three good pieces placed together in a predictable way. In striving to make every concert special, I see infinite possibilities of repertoire and structure, opportunities much more enticing than this conventional thinking. How much better to replace the Prokofiev, which is terrific, well-known and a stylistic contrast to the Suppé and Beethoven, with something more unusual, more of today and more surprising, such as H. K. Gruber's *Frankenstein!* This is a fantastical and whimsical piece for speaker and orchestra with a text based on children's rhymes and crazy orchestration that includes numerous toy instruments. It adds unexpected fizz but is still a piece in the Austro-Germanic tradition of the other two. Then flip the order so the concert opens with the Beethoven, better placement since its unassertive ending makes a limp concert closer. The Suppé is a rousing potboiler, usually relegated to pops concerts, guaranteed to bring down the house at the end, which is precisely where the cumulative energy should lead.

The result:

Beethoven: Symphony No. 6 "Pastorale"
   intermission
H. K. Gruber: *Frankenstein!* for speaker and orchestra
Suppé: *Poet and Peasant* Overture

While this program's structure is upside-down from the traditional format, it makes total sense for the poetry of the Beethoven and the peasant humor of the Gruber to be summed up by the "poet and peasant" of Suppé. And the temperature increases as the concert progresses.[2]

Dohnányi and I developed a lively working relationship based on trust and mutual confidence, with a healthy give-and-take. I found him completely engaged, full of ideas and easy to work with, always putting in the necessary time to make the programming as perfect as

---

2 This is a real program I constructed with Franz Welser-Möst in Cleveland in 2002.

possible, strikingly unlike my experience in Boston. His instincts were outstanding, and he was always willing to take risks. No matter what the creative process, we never forgot the ground rules we had agreed upon — he was the one on the podium, so his judgment was final for his performances, and I made certain that the selection of guest conductors and their programs were not only artistically complementary to Dohnányi's but conveyed a unified philosophy to the season as a whole.

With the 1987-88 concert year already underway, the impact of our work would not become fully visible until the following season. Our goal was to make that one a clear manifestation of our beliefs and tastes, obviously different from those that had come before and making a strong statement about the future. The timetable was tight, with the marketing announcement less than five months away.

The resulting 1988-89 season did look different, which was widely noticed. This fully cemented our partnership, setting the stage for the years that were to follow. A good example of our reconceived programming and how we worked together was the opening concert, announced as Wagner's Prelude to Act I of *Lohengrin*, Ligeti's *Atmosphères* and, after intermission, Bruckner's Symphony No. 9. The first half was unusual structurally and provided a heady prelude to the Bruckner — not your typical season opener. Shortly before the rehearsals started, Dohnányi suggested reversing the two opening works and performing them *attacca* (with no break in between). The Ligeti, a gauzy work all about textures, is extremely quiet. It dies to nothing at the end, where, written in the score, are three bars of silence that the conductor continues to beat, making stillness an integral part of the ending. Going from this, without pause, into the hushed high violin harmonics of the Wagner created a magical impression of the two works as one continuous experience. The sustained reverence of the Wagner, with its gradual crescendo to overpowering climax and then return to the quiet of the opening, seemed to grow organically out of Ligeti's mists. The *attacca* effect changed the way audiences listened — one patron asked why we had not performed the Wagner, thinking it part of the Ligeti. The original order was already interesting, but the revision made it memorable. Our willingness to make the alteration, only days before rehearsals started, established what was to be a recurring practice of never being afraid to make programs better, even at the last minute.

NOT NUMBER TWO: CHRISTOPH VON DOHNÁNYI

The season was full of many unusual programs, such as Beethoven's *Leonore* Overture No. 1 and Symphony No. 1, followed by the violin concerto *Offertorium* by the Russian composer Sofia Gubaidulina. The concerto is a difficult yet moving work based on Bach, and its importance mandates that it be the only work on the second half, not sandwiched, as such new works so often are, between two marketable war horses, a misguided practice that I call "trying to disguise the contemporary piece." It never fools audiences and always cheapens programs.

Ashkenazy offered an all-Shostakovich program: the little-known Five Fragments for Orchestra, Piano Concerto No. 2 and Symphony No. 14. The symphony, written for two vocal soloists with a chamber orchestra of just strings and percussion, is one of his bleakest works, far from the bombast of his other symphonies. Here was a concert that showed a totally different side of the composer, consisting of works hardly ever heard, in a provocative program.

The season sold well and audiences noticed the change; by midyear, The Cleveland Orchestra's programming was a hot topic around town. Because we had deliberately lightened up on contemporary works in the second half of the year, audiences forgot some of their heated reactions to the first half — just as subscription renewal forms went out for the next season. It was all part of how we employed precise strategies in constructing seasons. The new direction was firmly established, and Dohnányi and I never let up.

BUILDING THE BRAND

The real challenge was creating plans over the next five to ten years that escalated the orchestra's visibility and reputation. This fit with one of the realities of the classical music business, the need to plan multiple years in advance given the span of artists' future commitments.

Music directors in the U. S. usually conduct nine to eleven subscription weeks, so as to thread the fine line between maximizing the impact of their presence and not risking over-exposure. Having a strong roster of guest conductors is critical to filling out the schedule and providing complementary artistic viewpoints. Enticing opportunities lie in the choice of particular guest conductors and how they relate artistically to the music director, rather than simply filling weeks with those available.

Ashkenazy assumed his principal guest conductor role immediately, and Boulez started returning regularly in 1991. By then, the two were with the orchestra for a total of six weeks annually plus an occasional tour. We also benefited from the steady presence of the orchestra's young resident conductor, Jahja Ling. Between Dohnányi, Ashkenazy, Boulez, and Ling, the orchestra enjoyed stability and continuity in its conducting roster for three-quarters of its 24-week subscription season, minimizing the churn of guests.

As important as building conductor relationships was ending some of them. Erich Leinsdorf, briefly Szell's predecessor, had been guest-conducting for multiple weeks annually since the early 1980s. Just before my arrival, he had been engaged for an additional week to lead concerts in the newly renovated Playhouse Square, a rehabilitated complex of old movie houses in downtown Cleveland. His hosts told him that, for that extra week, they needed the luxurious guest house, where he usually stayed for a family wedding. True to form, Leinsdorf took high umbrage and imperiously cancelled the week, so upsetting the interim management between Haas and me that he was not re-engaged for two seasons hence. He then wrongly conflated his not being invited for that season with my appointment, which was announced shortly thereafter. When he returned in February 1988 for two weeks that had already been contracted, he treated everyone — musicians, patrons and me — rudely and disdainfully. His unpleasantness led to concerts that were not very good, making everyone even unhappier. When the players complained about his behavior, I told them that while I was not responsible for his being disinvited in 1988-89, I took full responsibility for his not coming back after that.

INTERLUDE: ADVICE

Leinsdorf was never at a loss for barbed comments. In the summer of 1971, during the orchestra's search for George Szell's successor, the musicians conducted an informal preference poll of the leading candidates. The results showed 76 for István Kertész and only two for Lorin Maazel. Worrying that the decision was heading toward Maazel, the orchestra committee leaked the poll results to the Cleveland *Plain Dealer*. Two months later, an uproar erupted when the Maazel appointment was announced. Leinsdorf reportedly said, "I suggest that Maazel's first act be to fire the two musicians who voted for him, thereby uniting the orchestra."

NOT NUMBER TWO: CHRISTOPH VON DOHNÁNYI

One essential responsibility of a music director is making personnel decisions — hiring, seating, casting, disciplining and, if necessary, firing. Such procedures are enshrined in the orchestra's collective bargaining agreement. In Cleveland, unusually among American orchestras, the music director has final hiring authority, with a players' committee providing only advice. I attended auditions and learned firsthand that because of the orchestra's unique sound and style, everyone knew precisely what was wanted in a new member beyond being able to play the instrument well: have no ingrained bad habits, possess a sound able to blend, bring added value artistically and, for principal players, have profound musical personality. Dohnányi had superb judgment in choosing new members, never opting for mere expediency and always willing to search further if no outstanding candidate emerged in an audition. This practice taught me the indelible lesson that when hiring, never settle for just good enough and if there are any doubts, do not say yes.

I saw this in action at an early audition for principal trumpet. The players' committee, Dohnányi and I listened as each candidate appeared in turns at the center of the empty stage for 10 minutes to play a concerto excerpt and a pre-announced selection of orchestral excerpts. It is a brutal process. Among the candidates was a star member of another major orchestra, certain he had the job. Sauntering onto the stage, he showed off his technical brilliance and confident presence but played way too loudly. Dohnányi, unimpressed, quickly dismissed him, to his obvious consternation. Next came a player with an understated manner who had beautiful sound, musicality and selfless sensitivity. He was hired, even though his experience had been limited to two years as fourth trumpet in the Houston Symphony. That was Michael Sachs, who remains in the position to this day. Everyone was focused on finding someone not with flash and fame but with the right musical character to fit the orchestra's innate style as well as with the promise of growth.

As for tours, I was committed to making each one really matter in enhancing the orchestra's reputation. Given the effort and expense involved, the return had to be measurably broader than just financial. Key were programs that would signal the new profile and establish a national and international foundation on which to build. My personal relationships with important presenters were essential not only to secure the desired dates but to control the programming and not be forced to play only greatest hits in order to supposedly sell tickets.

Given our overexposure in New York, starting in January 1989, I created scarcity by reducing the number of Carnegie Hall concerts from six to four per season, three with Dohnányi and one with Ashkenazy. I made sure the dates were mostly concentrated in blocks, avoiding the dilution created by separated single dates, and I ensured that this more compact pattern would persist over future seasons. For programming, needing unusual works that would attract attention in that glutted market, we landed on Ferruccio Busoni's Piano Concerto, a rarely performed 60-minute behemoth from 1904 with a fiendishly difficult solo part and a men's chorus in the finale. I always had a soft spot for it, as did Dohnányi, so we immediately made it the centerpiece of one of the concerts.

Then there was Kathleen Battle. Fretting about her German pronunciation, Dohnányi insisted on no Richard Strauss or Mozart. I suggested Heitor Villa-Lobos' *Bachianas Brasileiras* No. 5 for soprano and eight solo cellos, a wordless text that seemed perfectly suited for her high light voice. To go with it, we decided on a Bach cantata. At the rehearsals, Dohnányi fussed about Battle's diction in the Bach and worried about negative critical reaction to his complicity in scheduling it with her. At one point, he gave me a recording of Dutch soprano Elly Ameling singing the same piece and asked it to be given to Battle so she would "understand how it goes." I overlooked the request and reminded him that she would guarantee a full house at Carnegie, with reviews concentrated on him and the creativity of his programming, not the superstar soloist. We devised a spectacular and unusual program: Bartok's energetic *Miraculous Mandarin* Suite followed by the Villa-Lobos, and after intermission, Bach's wedding cantata BWV 202 and Edgard Varèse's *Amériques*. The latter is an overwhelming onslaught, requiring an oversize orchestra of 130 players. Here was a program that defied all conventions in the pieces selected, in their order and in the extraordinary contrast of styles and sonic magnitude.

The resulting three Carnegie programs — the Busoni, the Battle program and a third that included Beethoven's "Eroica" Symphony plus music by Delius and Tippett — totally changed the Cleveland-Dohnányi image. With their varied structures and unusual repertoire, with only one so-called "greatest hit" and no pot-boiler concerti, they played to our strengths and attracted audiences. The reviews were as I predicted.

For the already-committed European tour in May 1989, the only flexible element for the over-long four-week schedule was programming. Three concerts were devised featuring works tied to simultaneous recording releases — Mahler's Symphony No. 5 on Decca, Schubert's Symphony No. 9 on Telarc and Brahms' Symphony No. 1 on Teldec. Beyond these were unusual works by Bartók, Delius, Webern, Schoenberg and Tippett, plus pianist Krystian Zimerman playing a Beethoven concerto. The programs' creativity and variety created the desired result.

INTERLUDE: MAHLER 5 IN BERLIN

Percussionist Joe Adato, the orchestra's master of the cymbals, was a unique character. He was never afraid to tell anyone bluntly what was on his mind. When asked once by a young percussionist how to play cymbal crashes softly, Adato answered, "Don't hit them together too hard, kid." In May 1989, the orchestra under Dohnányi performed Mahler's Symphony No. 5 at the Berlin Philharmonie. The piece opens with a trumpet fanfare followed by a loud outburst from the orchestra, complete with crashing drums and cymbals. Everything then settles into a solemn, ominous funeral march. In the Philharmonie, the percussion section was on the top riser in the back, in full view of the audience. After the opening outburst of the Mahler, Adato set his cymbals down on backward facing chairs in front of him, cushioned by pieces of carpeting, and sat down during the somber funeral march. Suddenly at a very quiet moment, the cymbals slipped to the floor off their precarious position on the chair with a deafening crash. I remember Adato looking quickly around, as if to say, "Who did that?" The sound was a shock, causing a few titters in the orchestra and audience. But the performance continued to the end. Dohnányi was apoplectic about what had happened and furious at Adato, expecting at least an apology after the concert. Nothing. The next night, at the Schauspielhaus in Berlin, Dohnányi, still fuming, heard no apology. Finally, at the end of that concert and unable to stand it any longer, he summoned the orchestra's assistant conductor, Michael Stern, and asked that he bring Adato to his room. Stern, who had a vicious sense of humor, knew exactly what was up and proceeded into the backstage area, shouting, "Joe Adato, drop everything. Dohnányi wants to see you." I don't remember what happened next because we were all laughing so hard.

Turning my attention to future touring, I resolved first and foremost to limit each trip to no more than three weeks, two if possible. Anything longer tires out an orchestra and diffuses impact. Ideal are multiple appearances in important venues in major cities. For the promoter, the desired outcome of a successful concert is securing a return engagement, given the general paucity of tour dates from in-demand artists and ensembles. The best way to do this is viewing dates not as one-time events built around marketable repertoire and soloists but as part of a longer-term relationship showcasing and selling what the orchestra and conductor stand for.

I felt an urgent need to return to Japan with better routing and stronger programs, resetting the orchestra's image after that ill-conceived October 1987 tour. I planned a three-week trip in May 1990 built around mini-festivals of four concerts each in Hong Kong and Tokyo. Taking a page from my Boston experience, I also planned a three-week trip that summer to major European music festivals. The centerpiece was a return to Salzburg, the orchestra's first since 1967, with other appearances at the equally prestigious Lucerne Festival and London Proms. The programming for both was distinctive and unique.

I wangled an invitation from Haas to perform the closing weekend of concerts at Tanglewood in 1991 while the BSO was to be in Europe. I was determined professionally and personally to outdo ourselves with the programs. The final one was a given: Beethoven's Symphony No. 9, the traditional close of the Tanglewood season. For the first concert on Friday, Mitsuko Uchida, who had made her Cleveland debut the previous winter performing the Schoenberg Piano Concerto, played a concerto by Mozart. That program opened with Webern's early Romantic score *Im Sommerwind* before the Mozart and closed with Schubert's "Unfinished" Symphony and Strauss' *Till Eulenspiegel's Merry Pranks* — distinctive music in an unusual structure. Saturday became the challenge. We knew Varèse's monster *Amériques* was the closer, and Dohnányi wanted a first half of Schumann's "Rhenish" Symphony. But how to open the second half before the Varèse? With the print deadline looming, we agonized until, entering a New York restaurant for lunch, we heard over the sound system Mozart's *Eine Kleine Nachtmusik*. "Eureka," we both said. Placing that slender Classical work with only 30 string players as prelude to the Varèse juggernaut would make the later sound even more overwhelming.

What resulted were two unconventional programs preceding Beethoven's Ninth with a wide mix of standard and nonstandard repertoire. The visit created a sensation. I will never forget the breathtakingly quiet opening of the Webern, emerging eerily out of the din as the welcoming ovation subsided, triggering rapt attention from the enormous crowd. *The New York Times* called the juxtaposition of the delicate Mozart with the massive Varèse "an elaborate practical joke … with an impish humor that Mozart himself might have relished." Of the performances, the paper went on to say, the Varèse "was quite simply the most stunning display of mass virtuosity and sonic splendor this listener has ever heard. . . . The impact reminded this listener of a physics professor's observation, dimly recalled after many years, that if the members of an orchestra were somehow able to align their sound waves perfectly in phase with one another, the sound would have a focus and force comparable to that of a laser beam. On this occasion, The Cleveland Orchestra seemed to approach that impossible ideal, and the experience was awesome."[3]

Back home, as a result of the deals I had put in place, the orchestra began recording at a furious pace, producing a staggering 35 CDs with Dohnányi over the first five years. The repertoire included all the symphonies of Beethoven, Brahms and Schumann, plus symphonies by Mahler, Bruckner, Dvořák and Mozart, as well as works by Berlioz, Bartók, Ives, Varèse and Richard Strauss. It all reached such a fever that in 1990, when Dohnányi conducted his first ever performances of Shostakovich's Symphony No. 10, I excitedly urged Decca to add sessions two weeks later to capture it. The label readily agreed, despite having recorded the same piece months earlier with Solti in Chicago and Ashkenazy in London. Such were the seeds of the market oversaturation soon to come.

Over this same period, an additional 13 CDs were recorded with Ashkenazy for Decca and Boulez for Deutsche Grammophon. Ashkenazy led the five Beethoven Piano Concertos from the keyboard and began a survey of the major orchestral works of Richard Strauss and the complete Brahms symphonies. Boulez concentrated on his core repertoire, beginning with Stravinsky's *Rite of Spring*, a piece he had recorded with the orchestra 22 years earlier for Columbia in

---

3 Oestreich, James, "At Tanglewood, Beethoven's Ninth and a Sonic Blast," *The New York Times*, August 27, 1991.

pre-digital sound, plus major orchestral works of Debussy and Messiaen. We were in the recording studio constantly and the whirlwind of releases gave rise to a frequently touted tag line, "America's Most Recorded Orchestra."

A final programming initiative in those first years was opera, a natural choice given Dohnányi's background. The orchestra had presented staged operas in the 1930s in the then-new Severance Hall. Regular multi-week appearances in Cleveland by the touring Metropolitan Opera ceased in 1986, so there was an unfilled market. In 1991, we revived opera with concert performances of Henze's *The Bassarids*, of which Dohnányi had conducted the world premiere in Salzburg in 1966. This was followed in 1992 with Beethoven's *Fidelio*.

Dohnányi and I had clearly established a fantastically creative partnership, which allowed us to think through together not only *what* we wanted to do, but *why*, *when* and *how*. Scheduling had evolved well beyond the challenge of how to fill the calendar. The results of our careful work over these initial years in framing how the orchestra played, what it played and where it played visibly sharpened its image and reputation.

Dohnányi's musical preparation was always first-class. He was well-read and informed about the compositional and historical context of what he conducted. He was meticulous in rehearsals and

---

INTERLUDE: NICKNAMES

In homage to Ward Smith's penchant for nicknames, I bestowed several memorable ones. In the office, all of us referred to each other by our initials. In Dohnányi's case, since I abhorred and refused to use the ubiquitous "maestro," he became "CvD." With the recording frenzy, this morphed into "Compact von Disc."

For years, the orchestra had broadcast its concerts on the local classical radio station, WCLV. The longtime head of the station, Robert Conrad, was a regular presence on the radio and the announcer for the orchestra broadcasts. He had a stentorian voice and spoke with measured assurance, the dramatic pauses between his words sometimes extending to interminable lengths. Broadcasts ended with his trademark closer, "And that......was... another broadcast concert......by.......the Cleveland........... Orchestra." Except that in his delivery, the final "d" of "Cleveland" was elided and attached to the concluding "Orchestra". As a result, I officially dubbed the orchestra "The Dorkestra," a name that persists in some circles to this day.

---

understood the need to keep the basics of intonation and balance in shape. The orchestra's playing, thanks to his scrupulous preparation and coupled with imaginative programming, resulted in concerts that were noticed. Our strategy was working. The orchestra was suddenly in demand, concerts were full and critics were abuzz, so much so that we started to hear the phrase "Cleveland-type programs" in the music industry.

Feeding the external national and international reactions to touring back to Cleveland helped to shape the case for the necessary and needed expansion of fundraising — everyone responds well to external validation. We developed a tag line that was to become ubiquitous: "Hear What the World is Talking About."

REFINING THE BRAND

Two unique opportunities unexpectedly presented themselves as centerpieces of our objective to refine the brand going forward, the Salzburg Festival and Wagner's *Ring*. The orchestra's appearance in Salzburg in 1990 turned out to be fortuitous. The festival's longtime artistic director Herbert von Karajan had died the summer before; Gérard Mortier, general director of La Monnaie (the national opera house of Belgium), was named his successor, to assume the post in 1991. Dohnányi and Mortier knew each other well, having worked together years earlier at the Frankfurt Opera. He was a brilliant and fearless impresario, determined to blow the dust off Salzburg's crusty conservative traditions. He lost no time shaking up the dominant presence of the venerable Vienna Philharmonic by proposing three residencies for The Cleveland Orchestra, to take place in the summers of 1992, 1994 and 1996. This idea was exactly the step we needed in our foreign tour strategy, putting Cleveland head-to-head with Vienna on its home territory.

The first visit consisted of three concerts, to which I added three dates at the London Proms, one to be televised by the BBC. Ever the strong advocate of contemporary music, Mortier wanted 1994 centered around a big, genre-busting new piece. At one of our planning meetings, I suggested Harrison Birtwistle's *Earth Dances*, a work premiered in London in 1987 (a performance I had attended) and staggering in its difficulty and complexity. The piece is 45 minutes long, scored for huge orchestra and, as with all of Birtwistle's music, hard on performers and audiences alike. Mortier found the idea exactly what he was looking for, and Dohnányi immediately embraced the suggestion, trusting Mortier's and my enthusiasm but not knowing the piece or much of the composer's music. His willingness to take on such complex challenges was one of the reasons I loved working with him.

The work went over like a lead balloon with the Severance audiences, who were taken aback by its length, complexity and gnarly textures. It is a tough piece to listen to; the trick is surrendering to its shifting masses of sound and complex waves of overlapping rhythms. In Salzburg, the audience erupted into opposing camps of raucous cheers and vociferous boos, exactly the kind of controversy Mortier loved. *Earth Dances* received a friendlier reception at the Proms in London, Birtwistle's home turf. Dohnányi subsequently became an advocate of Birtwistle's music, conducting further works in later years.

In 1996, in addition to the third and final Salzburg summer residency, the orchestra toured Europe in April, visiting London, Berlin, Budapest and Amsterdam, performing at the Lucerne Easter Festival and presenting a concert and a conducting master class in Paris with Boulez. But it was with the three Salzburg residencies that Cleveland-Dohnányi was officially adopted by Europe.

Wanting to further sharpen the orchestra's profile in Asia, we returned to Tokyo in October 1993 to perform all the Beethoven symphonies plus two Beethoven piano concertos with Uchida in Suntory Hall. The goal of this third visit to Tokyo with Dohnányi was to cement the orchestra's classical bona fides in music-hungry Japan, and to do so in the city's preeminent concert venue.

As for New York, I thought the orchestra still overexposed and ended the annual visits to Carnegie Hall, deciding to skip the city entirely in 1993-94 to create additional scarcity. A year later, we started a biennial pattern of concentrated mini-festivals. The first featured four concerts focusing on Brahms and the Second Viennese School and included the Birtwistle (which Decca had just recorded). The series closed with a concert performance of Berg's *Wozzeck*.

With so much recording over the first five years, a key question was how to maintain momentum, particularly with so much of the central repertoire already on disc. The answer was opera, and a surprising idea took shape. Dohnányi was invited to conduct Wagner's *Ring* in 1992 at the Vienna State Opera. This cycle of four

INTERLUDE: DANGEROUS

In November 1991, I received a phone call from Dohnányi in Hamburg, asking if I had heard the new Michael Jackson CD, *Dangerous*. I told him I had not and, perplexed by the question, asked if he had. He said his teenage daughter had just played it for him, claiming that The Cleveland Orchestra was on it! One track, he said, opened with an excerpt, lasting over a minute, from the finale of our Telarc recording of Beethoven's Symphony No. 9. Not knowing anything about it, I asked how he knew it was our recording. He said the intonation was at A = 440, the pitch level the orchestra played at. Others tune higher to A = 442 or 444. He also claimed to recognize his phrasing in a particular passage. I thanked him and said I would look into it.

I called Bob Woods, president of Telarc Records, to ask if he knew anything about it. He didn't. I bought a copy of the Jackson CD and listened to it. Sure enough, there was a 67-second verbatim excerpt from the last movement that certainly sounded like Cleveland. As a CD junkie, I had all three of its recordings of the Ninth Symphony — Szell's from 1961, Maazel's from 1979 and Dohnányi's from 1986. I carefully compared the passage on *Dangerous* with all three. It was without question the recording under Szell. I checked back with Woods who had done his own analysis, concluding independently that it was definitely Szell. I called Dohnányi to tell him that it was in fact our orchestra, but it was the Szell recording, not his. He was totally unconvinced. Use of such an excerpt from a commercial recording requires not only the permission of the artist but also a licensing fee. What was done here was neither right nor legal. I wrote to Sony, which owned the Szell recording through its Epic label, on which was also *Dangerous* — asking for an explanation. My letter drew no response, so I wrote a stiffer one a week later. With still no response, I engaged a tough, well-known New York media attorney, who wrote a third letter demanding resolution and threatening suit. This got Sony's attention, and they said they would look into it. Nothing further happened, so I instructed the lawyers to sue Sony and Michael Jackson for damages. News of our $7 million suit reached all the major media, making Sony and Jackson look silly. We reached a financial settlement two months later.

My goal had been to make the point that this was an unauthorized use. My real hope, since *Dangerous* was released at the height of Jackson's fame, was a credit sticker for the orchestra on the *Dangerous* CDs and, ideally, a benefit appearance with Jackson and the orchestra. We had nothing to lose. We got the credit sticker and some money but no benefit performance. After the settlement, Dohnányi pointedly and good-naturedly asked for his cut of the settlement, since he was the one who found this. A lengthy tongue-in-cheek back-and-forth followed, and I promised him a fancy thank-you dinner.

operas lasts over 15 hours[4] and is a mammoth undertaking requiring a huge orchestra and with dozens of difficult singing roles. Given its length and complexity, performances are necessarily spread across multiple days. Conductors see it as a pinnacle of validation, so it was no wonder that Dohnányi was thrilled by the Vienna invitation.

Even more intriguing was Decca's idea of recording it, but Dohnányi cleverly proposed doing so in Cleveland. The label agreed, surprisingly given the immense cost, but thought the plan fit into its longer-term strategy of expanding his recording profile into opera. I eagerly embraced it, not only as a way to enhance orchestra's own Decca presence but as a long-term project around which to focus Dohnányi's future Cleveland seasons, building upon previous years' concert opera presentations. The original idea was to perform each *Ring* opera in successive years as part of the Severance season, and to make the recordings immediately thereafter. Each opera would necessitate three weeks for rehearsals, performances and recording sessions, a plan that was efficient operationally and financially.

Die Walküre, the best-known *Ring* opera, was presented first, in November 1992, and then *Das Rheingold* in December 1993. As with all vocal projects, the casting was critical, and since Decca was financing the recording, it appropriately held the right to approve singers. The most difficult role to cast is Siegfried, a brutally taxing tenor part that appears only in the last two operas, *Siegfried* and *Götterdämmerung*. Both were tentatively scheduled to be performed and recorded in 1994 and 1995, giving time for finding the right singer. But this proved more elusive than expected, and in 1993 Decca decided to delay recording the last two operas until 1996 and 1997 to provide yet more time. This seemed reasonable and practical. To maintain the presence of opera in the Severance Hall season, we scheduled Berg's *Wozzeck* for January 1995.

But the decision to delay proved fateful. It was at just that moment that the classical recording business began to implode through oversaturation of CDs, both new recordings and reissues, and just as the retail market started to give way to online sales, a phenomenon Decca and other labels did not see coming. By 1994, to cut losses, record companies worldwide were slashing their plans; projects were dropped and contracts reduced or terminated. The expansionary days were over.

---

4 *Das Rheingold* lasts about two-and-a-half hours (without intermission), *Die Walküre* and *Siegfried* four hours each and *Götterdämmerung* four-and-a-half hours.

NOT NUMBER TWO: CHRISTOPH VON DOHNÁNYI

Decca installed new management to deal with the new reality, and Dohnányi and Cleveland became prime targets for cost-cutting. While the company was initially reassuring about its intention to complete the *Ring*, orchestral projects ceased. The numbers tell the story — between 1993 and 1997, the number of CDs recorded with Dohnányi dropped from 35 over the previous five years to 16, six of which were the first two *Ring* operas. Of the remaining 10, only two were recorded in 1996 and 1997, in addition to a few final projects with Ashkenazy and Boulez. By 1997, Decca dropped all pretense of finishing the *Ring* despite my attempts to find a compromise for financing it.

Notwithstanding the inglorious end of the Decca relationship, these five years saw a maturing in the public positioning of the Cleveland-Dohnányi partnership. Central to our strategy was seeding our public relations work by repeating over and over that "the three great orchestras of the world are Vienna, Berlin and Cleveland," at once cementing the orchestra to its European sensibility and distinguishing it from its American rivals. To further burnish our reputation locally, we adopted another tag line, "Renowned around the world, committed to its community."

My policy was never to use our own superlatives promotionally but to freely use those of others. Conveniently, *Time* magazine in 1994 declared that "Cleveland has become the best band in the land"[5] in its survey of the American orchestral scene. Superb press often led to Dohnányi being asked whether the orchestra was really the "best," to which he slyly replied, "I cannot answer since I would be accused of bias and self-interest. But I can tell you definitively that Cleveland is not number two."

REASONS TO STAY
In accepting the Cleveland job, I had told Ward Smith that I expected to stay no longer than 10 years, which seemed a natural tenure for running an orchestra — long enough to remain effective while avoiding the risk of becoming "boring," as Haas so aptly put it. Approaching my ninth anniversary, the comment began to haunt me. Should I leave? Was I ready to leave? Were there compelling reasons to stay?

After serious reflection, I determined there were three specific challenges that would wholeheartedly convince me to stay: proactively oversee an inevitable transition of musical leadership, given that

---

5 Walsh, Michael, "The Finest Orchestra? (Surprise!) Cleveland," *Time*, January 10, 1994.

Dohnányi would have served for 16 years by the end of his contract in 2000; manage a renovation of Severance Hall, a project Dohnányi had long advocated and I felt was essential; and, at a time of extraordinary economic growth, mount a major fund drive with the goals of funding the hall renovation, adding substantially to the endowment and expanding annual fund support. I presented these challenges to Smith and Richard Bogomolny, a local businessman who had succeeded Smith as board president. They were unequivocally enthusiastic about addressing all three, providing clarity on what they wanted me to do. I was not yet ready to leave.

Bogomolny and I wanted to handle the inevitable music director transition smoothly and positively, yet in a way that genuinely celebrated Dohnányi's remarkable achievements. Our goal was to ensure a seamless hand-over of leadership. A music director search needs a minimum of five years — two years for the actual search and, given the lead time that conductors are booked in advance, another three after the announcement before any selected candidate would be free to take up the post.

We commenced discussions with Dohnányi about the future. He had already been thinking about transition and expressed the desire to begin reducing his time commitment, something to which we could not agree. We soon reached the mutual decision of extending his agreement by two years to end in 2002, which would make his the second-longest tenure in the orchestra's history. The decision was announced in June 1997, providing us the time needed to find, reveal and install a successor.

Severance Hall was designed in 1930 as a theater with an orchestra pit and fly space above the stage for hanging scenery. For concerts, the stage was enclosed by a flimsy canvas backdrop and the auditorium itself was covered with heavy carpeting and drapery, both of which made for dead acoustics. Szell pushed hard for a renovation in 1957, which resulted in the installation of a permanent stage shell and removal of the carpeting and drapes. The shell walled off the fly space, effectively ending theatrical presentations, but also sealed off an Aeolian-Skinner pipe organ, installed in space above the stage when the hall was built.

The resulting acoustics were vastly improved and considered "very good" if still somewhat hard and dry, no doubt due to the rigid stage wall surfaces. While this was the sound Szell preferred, Dohnányi wanted something warmer and more reverberant that still maintained the hall's storied clarity. He strongly advocated moving the organ from its purgatory to its rightful position at the back of the stage, allowing performances of works with prominent organ parts. Beyond the acoustics and organ placement, further goals included restoring the hall interior to its original Art Deco brilliance, which had faded over the years, and improving and enlarging the public spaces.

With the help of a board committee to oversee the project, architect David Schwarz and acoustician Christopher Jaffe were hired. Plans and designs were made, budgets established and funds raised. In March 1999, the orchestra moved from Severance to the Allen Theater at Playhouse Square in downtown Cleveland for the 10-month duration of the renovation, a period carefully calculated to span two half-seasons in order to avoid negatively affecting ticket sales by being out of Severance Hall for a single complete season.

The $36 million project, managed masterfully by Gary Hanson, was on budget and on time. All of the objectives were achieved. Severance Hall went from "very good" to "outstanding." The new design of the stage, with the organ beaming proudly at the back, took its cues from the Art Deco detail of the hall's interior, making it one of the most strikingly beautiful anywhere. And the expanded public spaces hugely enhanced the audience experience. The hall reopened on schedule in January 2000 with a private concert for the project's construction workers to thank them for their hard work, letting them be the first to hear the results of their labors. The next day was a gala concert, that included a commissioned fanfare from Birtwistle. The project proved a lasting tribute to the Dohnányi era.

As for fundraising, it seemed to me a stretch goal was in order, something far in excess of the 75th anniversary endowment push for $25 million. I liked the sound of raising $100 million by 2000, a third of which would respectively fund the renovation, add to the endowment and provide annual support over four years. The number got everyone's attention, and it was heartening that by the end, $116 million was raised, far exceeding the goal.

CELEBRATING DOHNÁNYI

After announcing in 1997 Dohnányi's departure, we had five seasons to celebrate his extraordinary tenure. We continued to intensify the pace of foreign tours with trips to Japan, Hong Kong and China in 1997-98; to Europe and the Canary Islands in 1998-99; to Vienna and Cologne in 1999-2000; and to open the Edinburgh Festival in summer 2000.

In New York, we generally maintained our alternate-year Carnegie Hall strategy, returning in 1997 for three programs built around Schubert, in 1999 for two concerts each conducted by Dohnányi and Boulez, and in 2000 several times for multiple concerts and Carnegie's season-opening gala.

Two memorable events occurred in this period. In October 1996, Ken Haas experienced cardiac arrest in the middle of the night, suffering considerable brain damage. No longer able to run the BSO, he required 24-hour custodial care, which was expensive and not covered by health insurance. Worried about the financial consequences for his family, a few of his orchestra management friends organized a benefit concert to fund this need. Haas was beloved, so it all came together quickly and effortlessly. We assembled an all-star ensemble with volunteer musicians from orchestras he had worked for — New York, Cincinnati, Boston and Cleveland. Boulez, Dohnányi, Kurt Masur and Seiji Ozawa agreed to conduct, with Itzhak Perlman

Severance Hall after 2000 renovation

as soloist. The concert took place in April 1998 in Boston's Symphony Hall. The program — just music and no speeches — opened with Paul Dukas' Fanfare from *La Péri* and "Nuages" and "Fêtes" from Debussy's *Nocturnes* conducted by Boulez. Dohnányi followed with Strauss' *Till Eulenspiegel*. After intermission Masur led Tchaikovsky's *Romeo and Juliet*, and Ozawa closed with Perlman playing John Williams' music from *Schindler's List* and, to close, Ravel's *La Valse*. The $1 million raised was put in a trust for the sole benefit of funding Haas' care. That support, critical to the family, would have been sufficient for years, but sadly he died in January 2001. The concert was one of the most meaningful I was ever involved with.

The other event was the first and only appearance with the orchestra of long-time Chicago Symphony music director Georg Solti. Dohnányi had long tried to lure him to guest-conduct, as they knew each other from their time together at the Frankfurt Opera years earlier. We finally succeeded and Solti made his debut in April 1997 in a program of two favorites, Bartók's Concerto for Orchestra and Beethoven's Symphony No. 5. Curious how this fiery and passionate maestro would work with the cooler Cleveland style, I eagerly attended his first rehearsal. He began with the Bartók and conducted the first seven minutes before stopping. In his thickly-accented English, he said that he found the playing elegant — in fact, too elegant. For this folk-like music, he wanted a heavier and earthier sound. I forget his exact phrase, but it was something to the effect that "this is not Mickey Mouse music." Starting again from the beginning, Solti totally transformed the sound as the players followed his instructions exactly, making the orchestra suddenly sound like the bold, brash Chicago Symphony while retaining that Cleveland elegance. The musicians fell in love with him, and the feeling was mutual. He was so taken that, when I spent an evening at his house in London two weeks later, he expressed not only his wish to return immediately but to take the orchestra on tour and re-record Wagner's *Tristan und Isolde* for Decca with Cleveland and not the Vienna Philharmonic. His enthusiasm was heartening, although the *Tristan* idea was risky given his age and unwise given Decca's abrupt dropping of Dohnányi. Solti told me over his favorite malt whiskey about upcoming plans to conduct Bach's *St. John Passion* and Berg's *Wozzeck*, both for the first time. For a superstar of 85 to exude such energy and curiosity was inspiring. Sadly, that was the last time I saw him; he suddenly died four months later.

TRANSITION

The big focus over this period was the search for Dohnányi's successor. Immediately after the announcement of his departure, we appointed a search committee of three members each of the board, staff and orchestra, plus the concertmaster. Inclusion of orchestra members in such searches is both good practice and a condition in the labor agreement. This was my first search for a music director; the closest I had ever come was finding Fiedler's successor almost 20 years earlier.

Over time, I had come to the firm conclusion that hiring for any critical position involves much more than finding someone with the competency to do the job. Essential is understanding what the candidate brings to the organization, what they stand for, and how they will fit. These require the organization be laser-focused on what it wants the music director to do (as with my experience of being hired by Smith). Searches are much more about the *what* than the *who*.

Given Cleveland's distinctive and clear musical personality plus the continuity of its music directors' artistic profiles, the committee focused on the need for someone steeped in the Classical repertoire and style to build on the orchestra's artistic heritage. Needed was a conductor skilled at training the musicians in rehearsals, experienced in making good personnel decisions, eager to expand the repertoire and able to bring a greater sense of flexibility and color to the orchestra's sound. Because I had always looked at guest conductors as potential successors, we already had a wealth of known candidates. Starting out, I honestly did not know how I wanted the search to come out and was committed to letting the process inform the decision. I had full confidence in the committee and knew, because it was so focused on the *what* of the position, it would make reasoned and intelligent judgments about candidates based on agreed-upon criteria.

Austrian Franz Welser-Möst emerged as the leading contender. He made his Cleveland debut in 1993, and since 1995 he had guest-conducted the orchestra for multiple weeks annually, leading a total of more than 50 concerts by the time of the search.

As part of the process, we organized a structured job interview of the final candidates led by me and the committee chair. In response to a question to each about what they thought the orchestra needed and what they would bring to it, Welser-Möst was the only one who did not lapse into vague, star-struck generalities about the honor of assuming the position. Strikingly, he made thoughtful comments about the need to instill a more flexible and colorful sound and to push the orchestra stylistically into an even broader repertoire. For me, that willingness to address challenges and not simply be satisfied with the status quo won him the job.

In April 1999, the committee unanimously recommended his appointment to the board. He was offered the job, I negotiated the deal with his manager, and the news was announced in June 1999, exactly two years after the announcement of Dohnányi's departure. Right on the schedule we had planned, he would take over in September 2002, providing the desired seamless transition of leadership from his predecessor, who would become music director laureate.

Dohnányi's final season was to begin on September 13, 2001, in a program of Berg and Wagner with Mahler's Symphony No. 5. Two days before, while sitting in my office in the early morning, I was interrupted by a staff member urging me to turn on the television. In horror, we watched the Twin Towers burn and collapse. As the other two planes crashed in Pennsylvania and Washington, D.C., we were frozen with fear, having no idea what was happening. With the nation on edge, the day's season-opening rehearsal was cancelled. Later in the day, Dohnányi and I decided that, barring another catastrophic event, the best course was to act as normally as possible and proceed with the week's rehearsals and concerts, providing solace to the community through the power of live music. Some patrons and city leaders reached out to suggest we substitute a patriotic program, which Dohnányi and I rejected in favor of the elegant simplicity of no speeches, no national anthem and just the Mahler, a work inspired by the emotional extremes of death, love and life. We were focused on what we were best at.

On Thursday night, Severance Hall was filled to capacity, the audience hungry for the comforting sense of community. I had a simple program insert prepared:

"Tonight's performance is given in memory of those who lost their lives in Tuesday's calamitous events, and in tribute to all those involved in the heroic and ongoing rescue and relief efforts. The Cleveland Orchestra extends thoughts and prayers to the families and friends of those lost or injured. We ask the audience to join the Orchestra in rising at the beginning of the concert to observe a moment of silence in memory of Tuesday's victims. This evening's performance will consist of one work, Gustav Mahler's Symphony No. 5, which will be performed without intermission. Mahler's powerful music provides an expression of human hope, that light can follow the darkness of these tragic days."

At 8 p.m., Dohnányi entered the stage and mounted the podium. As he bowed his head to the crowd, the audience rose to its feet for the moment of silence, which he held to the brink of uneasiness. Then, at exactly the right instant, he raised his head, turned and signaled the opening trumpet fanfare of the solemn funeral march that begins the Mahler. Over the next 70 minutes the piece proceeded to its cathartic celebration of triumph and renewal, turning despair into hope. It was what a concert should be — music at its most powerful. The audience sat riveted until the jubilant ending.

Later in the season, a gala performance of Beethoven's Symphony No. 9 and a formal dinner officially celebrated Dohnányi and his remarkable tenure. Our alternate-year mini-festivals in Carnegie Hall continued shortly thereafter with three celebratory concerts featuring an eclectic range of music: works by Lutosławski, Rihm, Sibelius, Birtwistle and Richard Strauss, paired with Beethoven's Symphonies Nos. 5, 7 and 9 — classic Cleveland-Dohnányi programs marrying the present with the past. It was the best way I could think of for him to bow out in New York.

For his final subscription concerts at Severance Hall in May 2002, he conducted concert performances of Wagner's *Siegfried* — both a spectacular finale to his tenure and a bittersweet coda to the truncated *Ring* project. This made *Götterdämmerung* the only *Ring* opera he never conducted in Cleveland.

Given our attention to building the orchestra's reputation in Europe, Dohnányi's tenure concluded with a two-week tour of European capitals. He would leave the orchestra playing better than ever, with a sharply etched profile for artistic imagination and excellence, its national and international renown never greater.

MANAGING THE MUSICIANS

An important task that dominated our work together for 15 years was personnel management, and our success was one of the key reasons the quality of the orchestra was maintained at such a high level.

NOT NUMBER TWO: CHRISTOPH VON DOHNÁNYI

One of the hardest management tasks anywhere is dealing with underperforming employees and the need to make a change. In the highly unionized orchestra environment, these tasks are even more difficult and complicated. Musicians are tenured under the labor contract, a status granted by the music director after a two-year probationary period. Many think it is impossible to make changes after that. I disagree — it is possible, but the rules are more complicated once tenure is granted. The contract clearly specifies the procedures that must be followed in making any such moves, a process upon which both parties have agreed. This mandates extreme care in granting tenure. To me, the default is no tenure, which means the only question is whether the player is good enough to be granted it, a far easier decision than finding the player bad enough to deny it.

Good personnel policies require maintaining impeccable documentation of any issues. In addition, no matter the reason for making a change, musicians of such distinction always deserve to be treated with the highest respect and dignity.

A critical role in an orchestra is the personnel manager, a curiously hybrid position between players, union and management. The personnel manager is responsible for seeing that the right musicians are in the right place at the right time, ensuring adherence to the labor contract. While technically part of the union bargaining unit, the position functions more like the supervisory role of management.

I was spoiled with extraordinary personnel managers, first in Boston with Bill Moyer and then in Cleveland with David Zauder, who simultaneously played second trumpet.

Zauder was a beloved character who managed his multiple roles with aplomb and style. He was tough but fair; when necessary, he could be a fierce advocate for the musicians or for management. Dohnányi, Zauder and I forged a formidable team bound by a commitment, through constant attention to managing the personnel, to do whatever was necessary to guarantee the highest quality in the orchestra.

In dealing with difficult personnel matters, Zauder, Dohnányi, and I developed a practice we called "good cop, bad cop and really bad cop." Since the labor contract gave the music director final responsibility for personnel decisions, Dohnányi was "really bad cop," but I felt it best to protect the musician from hearing a final negative judgment directly from him, if possible. His necessary role was having the critical earlier discussions with a musician to express concerns about playing. I, as "bad cop," would initiate conversations with the player about the need for a change, and Zauder as "good cop" would act as counselor to or advocate for the player.

INTERLUDE: ORCHESTRAS A AND B

I worked with Bill Moyer for 17 years in Boston. He was great at his job — able, balanced, organized and extremely good at finding unique solutions to thorny issues. In the early 1970s, we started experimenting at Tanglewood with what are called "split-orchestra services" in an effort to ease the busy workload for each musician. The concept means scheduling rehearsals and concerts for only a portion of the orchestra. With three different programs each Tanglewood weekend plus five rehearsals, preparation time was at a premium. We started scheduling one of the weekend concerts for Classical repertoire requiring only half of the orchestra — 50 players — and then another such concert the following weekend with the other half. The result was relief for players over the two weeks with only five different programs for each to prepare. In the initial implementation of the practice, the two half-orchestras were listed on the production schedule as "Orchestra A" and "Orchestra B." Moyer was soon visited by the orchestra committee saying that the members of "Orchestra B" were resentful of what appeared to be secondary status on account of their appellation. They were serious and numerous meetings ensued. The ever-resourceful Moyer came up with a magical solution that made the problem evaporate: we henceforth referred to the two groups in all production schedules as "Orchestra A" and "Orchestra 1."

My initial meeting with a musician involved what I called the "grandfather speech." I reminded the player that, since we are all the worst judges of our own capabilities, it usually takes someone else to tell us when it is time to consider moving on. I would outline three possible reactions from colleagues to one's decision to leave: first is expressing shock and dismay and urging immediate reconsideration; third is saying it's about time; and second is total silence. The player, asked which response was desired, would inevitably say the first. But that requires making the decision to leave just before reaching the peak of effectiveness, not at or over the peak. Reminding the player that the peak was approaching, I would urge taking the initiative to move on.

When the player asked what the music director thought, I immediately offered to arrange a meeting with "really bad cop," so the player could hear his decision directly. But I then asked if the player really wanted to hear what his boss thought, knowing that deep down everyone has a good sense when their time is approaching. No such meeting was ever requested, but Zauder and I knew what "really bad cop" would say if necessary.

In my 15 years working with Dohnányi, the first 10 of which were with Zauder before his retirement in 1997, the orchestra had 62 personnel changes. Thirteen players left for other orchestras, nine to become principals; eight died; two were not granted tenure; twenty-three retired of their own accord; fifteen retired with some form of "help," whether the grandfather speech or a financial incentive; and only one was terminated. That individual fought the decision under the labor contract's provisions, but it was subsequently upheld by the orchestra committee.

After my retirement, two other musicians fought termination, and in both cases, the orchestra committee sided with the decision. Because of their remarkable pride in the orchestra's quality and knowing that personnel matters were always conducted fairly and with dignity, the Cleveland musicians placed the best interests of the institution at the forefront. I usually found them helpful and constructive, although they could act rambunctiously hardline in formal labor negotiations.

CREATIVE PAIRS

Working with a conductor on artistic planning and programming is very much a collaborative process, requiring unfettered exchange of ideas. While messy, the process embraces the truism that two brains are better than one. The ground rules mandate mutual understanding and support as well as acceptance of each party's specific area of accountability. A conductor needs complete enthusiasm for and belief in the music conducted, while management must be comfortable in balancing the practical realities of budgets, schedules and concert production. The absolute requirement is total alignment on artistic objectives and shared values.

Joshua Wolf Shenk's thoughtful book *Powers of Two*[6] is illuminating on such relationships. He analyzes through case studies the numerous stages and characteristics of creative pairs, including the reasons they end. Critical is understanding their multiple interlocking facets. Stress and conflict are inevitable, but they can be minimized by having absolute clarity regarding the individuals' relative spheres of power. These are complex, being both hierarchical and fluid to allow each party to both lead and follow, to both submit and engage.

Shenk's book helped me to understand the real-life experience of what a creative pair is, why it happens, how it must be nurtured and why it is fragile. A key element is the need for face-to-face interaction on a regular basis to foster the easy and ongoing back-and-forth of ideas. Communication by email, memo, phone or even video is simply not the same for inducing lasting collaboration. Dohnányi's and my partnership was the great lesson of my Cleveland years. I had tastes of it with Fiedler and Williams in Boston, with Cosel for *Evening at Pops* and with Boulez in programming, but never before as the centerpiece of running an institution.

For the first ten years, that partnership was predicated on the relative equilibrium of our organizational positions and influence. We each had equal long-term stakes in success and functioned within our mutual space as a team, completely free of ego and hierarchy, constantly challenging each other and forging unified plans around common values and goals. For that, I am grateful and proud of what we accomplished together. It taught me that achieving such an effective partnership always trumps the thrill and power of running a large organization.

Decca's termination of our recording contract in 1995 — and with it the signature *Ring* — devastated Dohnányi, and he reacted with predictable anger. When my last-ditch attempts to rescue the project failed, he held me responsible for the final collapse. A consequence was a serious rupture in our relationship as mutual trust fractured. The results were petty arguments, misunderstandings and tensions. As can happen with two strong-willed people, neither of us behaved at our best, but we kept the disagreements and any unpleasantness in the background so as not to negatively affect the face of the orchestra.

---

6 Shenk, Joshua Wolf, *Powers of Two: Finding the Essence of Innovation in Creative Pairs*, Houghton Mifflin Harcourt, 2014.

All this happened just as we were in the midst of discussions about the transition, which didn't help the matter. When Dohnányi's departure was announced, the equilibrium of our respective positions evaporated as he became a lame duck while I was staying on. As a result, the last five years became unsettled for both of us. I am sure that my evolving friendship with Welser-Möst added fuel to the fire. Even so, we maintained a constructive work ethic as best as we could, but it was extraordinarily difficult personally. I had to remind myself that it was still the longest sustained collaboration I had enjoyed.

Yet there is a happy ending. When I left in 2004, I got an unexpected call from Dohnányi, urging that, even though we had difficult last years together, we should concentrate on and be thankful for what was successful. We both freely admitted that neither of us could have accomplished what we did in Cleveland without the other. The equilibrium of our positions was again in balance — we were now both gone. The bonds were restored, and thankfully we remain close to this day.

The Powers of Two.

CHAPTER 8
A WIDER PERSPECTIVE: JIM COLLINS

The performance business is inherently stressful and all-consuming; the entire organization is on the line at every concert. Any diversion — an ill soloist, a late trombonist, an upset conductor, missing music — demands full and immediate attention so the show can go on at the announced time, beyond which no delays are possible. An orchestra operates in real time with no definitive outcome, so absolute success or failure is subject to judgments which are neither precise nor agreed-upon. The predictable result, given the relentless grind of concert-giving in large institutions, is high stress and preoccupation with short-term thinking. Added to this are the difficulties in being nimble or flexible given the restrictions of intricate and contentiously-arrived-at labor agreements, the repetitive routine of the weekly schedule and the inevitable bureaucratic drag of complex, tradition-bound institutions. And all in a dynamically changing environment — fundamental social changes, the decline of music education, the collapse of the recording business, the rise of digital media, changing consumer habits and financial uncertainty.

These thoughts rolled around in my head as I approached the 21st century reflecting on my orchestra experiences and thinking about how to approach future challenges. Looking at the industry totally from the inside was complicated, given those inherent and recurring stresses. I was finding the business a closed environment that lacked outside voices, which made getting broader perspectives difficult. I yearned for deeper organizational understanding to better comprehend the essence of success and provide context for the work at hand. I was always drawn to views from beyond the orchestra world, certain that there existed fundamental leadership principles that helped define why some organizations were high-performing and others were not.

Vision was a topic that particularly fascinated me. The term had a ring of future vitality but I found little clarity about what it meant and how to apply it. Its application to orchestras was so often smothered in generic statements about being "world-class" and "committed to excellence."[1] This was frustrating and left me with many questions. How to think about vision in a way that was concrete, useful and not full of lofty platitudes? How to provide an intellectual framework to define and measure success? What lessons can be learned from other types of industries? What were the underlying secrets of effective governance and successful management in working with vision to achieve success?

"BUILDING YOUR COMPANY'S VISION"

In 1997, I happened upon an article in the *Harvard Business Review*, "Building Your Company's Vision" by Jim Collins and Jerry Porras,[2] based on their recent bestselling book, *Built to Last,*[3] which examined the successful habits of visionary companies. The article addressed the usually amorphous subject of vision in a way that struck me as elegant and inspiring. I found it refreshingly different from the usual jargon-laden business literature.

The Collins-Porras concept was based on the insight that understanding where you want to go first requires knowing where you are — what they describe as simultaneously "preserving the core and stimulating progress, the yin and yang of vision." The present is defined by core values and core purpose — what you stand for and why you exist. Both are baked into the organization's DNA and are not aspirational; they are statements of what *is*. Set in the context of this present state is a compelling future of 10-to-30-year "BHAGs," or big hairy audacious goals; they are statements of what *will be*. BHAGs must be specific to the organization, galvanizing and bold, but not so far-reaching as to stretch credibility into the realm of bravado.

Applying the model requires deep understanding of the underlying factors driving the organization and distilling them into their most basic truths. The discipline of limiting the resulting vision document to one page forces thinking to a most fundamental level, resulting in a

---

1 Morris, Thomas, "Artistic Vision: True Meaning or Empty Slogan?" *Symphony Magazine,* October-November 2006.

2 Collins, James C., and Porras, Jerry I., *Building Your Company's Vision,* Harvard Business Review, September-October 1996.

3 Collins, James C., and Porras, Jerry I., *Built to Last: Successful Habits of Visionary Companies,* HarperBusiness, 1994.

statement not of things to *do* but of what *is* and what *will be* in the broadest sense. Most strategic planning gets bogged down in endless lists of strategies and action steps. The Collins-Porras model provides the underlying foundation for those things to *do* necessary to realize the vision.

The Collins-Porras model so intrigued me that I immediately wanted to apply it in Cleveland, believing it would be illuminating in charting our future. I initiated a series of senior staff meetings to examine whether it resonated and provided the hoped-for insights. The energy of the discussions was palpable, but the model proved far more complex to apply than its seeming simplicity suggested, requiring more time than anticipated. This was rewarding but hard work.

INTERLUDE: RANDOM BUZZWORD GENERATOR

I was always suspicious of the buzzwords that pepper business and academic literature and tried to avoid using them. The one that bugs me most is "paradigm." It is knowingly tossed around in conversation about big ideas for the future. It sounds great but is stunningly vague. In my seminars, I made a point to ban the word, adding a rule that anyone who allowed it to slip out would contribute $10 into the pot to fund cocktail hour.

Years ago, a friend sent me something called the **Random Buzzword Generator**, a simple chart for producing impressive-sounding jargon that is meaningless. Pick a random three-digit number, then string together the three words corresponding to each digit in the columns (e.g. 0-1-2 = "integrated organizational capability"). The phrases sound terribly erudite but mean absolutely nothing. I took great delight in tossing phrases so generated into my consulting reports just for fun, to see if anyone noticed. No one ever did.

	A	B	C
0	Integrated	Management	Paradigm
1	Total	Organizational	Flexibility
2	Systematized	Monitored	Capability
3	Parallel	Reciprocal	Vision
4	Functional	Digital	Parameter
5	Responsive	Logistical	Synergy
6	Optional	Transitional	Stakeholder
7	Synchronized	Incremental	Projection
8	Compatible	Third-Generation	Hardware
9	Balanced	Policy	Contingency

Our process was iterative, and each new version of our values, purpose and goals was vigorously scrutinized to test credibility and substance, forcing our thinking to ever deeper levels. We discovered numerous surprises along the way, the most jaw-dropping being the realization that the need for money or good financial results are not ends in themselves but in service of something more basic. Fundraising is predicated on what is to be supported, asking *why* the money is needed and framing that need as the pitch. In other words, money is a strategy, not a goal.

Outlining the orchestra's core purpose was also eye-opening. We determined that our reason for being was *not* to put on great concerts — that is *what* orchestras do, not *why* they do it. Our goal, fundamentally, was to create transcendent experiences. In other words, a concert is also a strategy, not a goal.

After 18 months of discussions, a draft vision statement started to emerge, although further work was still needed.

Jim Collins

174

A WIDER PERSPECTIVE: JIM COLLINS

GETTING TO KNOW COLLINS

The exercise prompted me to read more of Collins' writing. I reached out to him, curious to gather greater insights into his work. He immediately engaged, admitting to being intrigued by how his work might apply to the not-for-profit sector. We were suddenly in regular contact, and I shared with him our evolving document.

In 1999, I helped arrange for him to give the keynote address at a League of American Orchestras conference, where we met in person for the first time. He was a mesmerizing presence. Having started his career as a professor at Stanford Business School, he had honed a Socratic style of asking penetrating questions, which he preferred to giving answers. Being around him was energizing — and not for the faint of heart, as he always asked *why* after any statement.

Learning that he was a music lover, I invited him to Cleveland in early 2000 to experience firsthand the creative organization to which I was trying to apply his model. While here, he generously agreed to participate in a working session with the senior staff as we were fine-tuning our vision statement. He pointedly tested the strengths of our thoughts and convictions, challenging us to describe our organization's "economic engine." He explained that such engines can be modeled conceptually as a simple mathematical fraction: so much output or result as the numerator, per input or resource invested as the denominator. The economic outputs are easy to describe — ticket sales and contributions — but defining the inputs and how they leverage outputs proved complicated. As an answer, we devised a generalized sum of the cumulative points of effective contact — concerts, events and points of communication — between the organization and audience-donors that we felt drove both earned and unearned revenues. Collins had provoked a different dimension to our thinking.

Until then, the process had involved just the senior staff. If this was to be a true institutional vision, it needed to have the active endorsement of and ownership by the board. Because that group had already proven to be an effective thought partner in my work, I presented the draft statement to the executive committee to gauge enthusiasm and interest. They were highly responsive and provided perceptive feedback, which we debated and folded into the evolving document. It was then shared with a gradually wider circle of stakeholders — the full board, the musicians, the full staff and volunteers. With each presentation, reactions and suggestions were noted, debated and used to refine the document so that it gradually gained buy-in from the broader organization.

The meetings were not without amusement. One board member suggested, in her first exposure to the term BHAG, that we consider an alternative that did not include the word "hairy." I responded that we had considered "Big Audacious Goals" but reducing the acronym to "BAG" did not inspire.

The final one-page statement was formally adopted by the board shortly thereafter, and became an insightful guidepost for our planning, confirming that the model's initial appeal was validated in its actual application.

Collins' subsequent book, the best-selling *Good to Great: Why Some Companies Make the Leap ... and Others Don't*,[4] came out a year later. Focused on for-profit companies, its success led to inquiries about how the concepts could be applied to the not-for-profit sector. The result was publication of a supplemental monograph, *Good to Great and the Social Sectors*.[5] In it Collins demolished the myth that not-for-profits can be successful only if they are run according to best "business" practices, proposing instead they commit to best "greatness" practices. While he found such principles relevant to both sectors, their applications differed: in for-profits, money is both an input and an output; in social service organizations, money is only an input, and outputs are a combination of results, impact and endurance.

The Cleveland Orchestra was cited several times in the monograph as a case study, most notably the season-opening concert two days after 9/11. Collins characterized the decision to perform only the Mahler symphony without speeches or patriotic trappings a clear example of one of his key principles of greatness — knowing who you are, what you are really good at, sticking to it and knowing the things *not* to do.

MEETING THE FIELD

In 2003 Collins asked me to organize a gathering of 10 orchestra managers at his research laboratory in Boulder. He was fascinated with

---

4 Collins, Jim, *Good to Great; Why Some Companies Make the Leap ... and Others Don't*, HarperBusiness, 2001.
5 Collins, Jim, *Good to Great and the Social Sectors*, Jim Collins, 2005.

MUSICAL ARTS ASSOCIATION VISION STATEMENT
August 7, 2000

MAA CORE IDEOLOGY Core Values
"the essential and enduring tenets of MAA":
- Individual and collective excellence
- Artistic integrity
- Always striving
- A tradition of continuity and stability
- A symbol of community pride

Core Purpose "MAA's very reason for being":
To provide inspirational experience by serving the art of music at the highest levels of artistic excellence

MAA ENVISIONED FUTURE BHAGS
"10- to-30-year Big, Hairy, Audacious Goals":
1. Be the beacon of musical excellence throughout the world
2. Become more famous than the Vienna Philharmonic
3. Create a culture of fanatical concertgoing among the broadest constituency

Vivid Description - "a vibrant, engaging and specific description of what it would be like to achieve the BHAGs"

The Cleveland Orchestra is committed to

1. Be the beacon of musical excellence throughout the world by
- Setting industry benchmarks for excellence through every aspect of what we do
- Becoming the destination of choice for the world's greatest artists
- Having titled players in other major orchestras compete for section positions in Cleveland
- Achieving a collaborative environment through shared core values between and among those who make music and those who support it

2. Become more famous than the Vienna Philharmonic by
- Creating insatiable demand nationally and internationally
- Saturating the airwaves and cyberspace
- Receiving consistent critical acclaim nationally and internationally

3. Create a culture of fanatical concert-going among the broadest constituency with
- Sold-out performances six nights a week, 11 months of the year
- A comprehensive education program that fosters a lifelong involvement with music and The Cleveland Orchestra
- Every Clevelander is touched by The Cleveland Orchestra in some way

orchestras and wanted to gain broader perspectives on the industry. The meeting was billed as a two-day interactive discussion on the brutal facts facing the field. He volunteered to act as provocateur, prodding us to think through processes to bring about change within our organizations; to ponder the differences between "legislative" and "executive" management skills; to understand the allocation of power between the music director, the CEO and the board leader; and to delineate the distinctions between true core values and what were merely ingrained practices and traditions. The discussions were intense, as Collins burrowed into our thinking (or lack thereof), often uncomfortably. The meeting produced a series of working conclusions, among them:

- *Avoid dealing with financial issues in isolation.* All financial decisions have artistic and organizational implications, and vice versa.
- *Work to prevail, not just survive.* Survival is maintaining the status quo.
- *Distinguish between being in the "content" and the "process" business.* An orchestra is not just about what is played but about how, why and where the music is performed.
- *Distinguish between the quality of the music and the quality of the experience.* Playing really well is necessary for success but not sufficient if it doesn't create positive experience.
- *An orchestra requires more legislative than executive leadership skills.* Legislative leadership power is distributed — in this case, between the board chair, the music director and the CEO.
- *Right decisions are more important than consensus decisions.* Moving toward consensus often results in finding the least objectionable path forward, which by definition is more convenient than necessarily right.
- *Someone must assume the burden of decision-making.* The process of decision-making by groups is different from the actual making of a decision, an act that must be individual.
- *The brutal facts need to be understood and confronted.* Issue avoidance is not a solution.
- *A culture of discipline is essential to address immense challenges successfully.* The necessary hard work is the result of structured thinking over time that is embedded in the organization's culture.[6]

---

6 From the author's notes of the meeting.

Rereading my notes of the session, I am amazed by how pro-
phetic the conclusions were. It is striking how the field's challenges
today remain at least as relevant, and as elusive, in our changed educational, technological, financial and social environment. Of interest
is that none of us in attendance are still in the field today — turnover
that illustrates another of the industry's critical challenges, lack of
leadership continuity.

LEAVING CLEVELAND

By 2001, The Cleveland Orchestra had met the three big goals I set
out to the board leadership in 1997 — exceeding the $100 million
fundraising goal, completing the hall renovation on time and on budget, and implementing the music director transition seamlessly. The
question for me again became how long to stay, knowing that addressing challenges in the context of a rapidly changing landscape would
require a commitment for another extended period. Having already
been in the position for 15 years, this was not something I was prepared to do, and I feared that staying would preclude doing something
else, a dream still undefined but tantalizing.

Knowing I had to remain through Dohnányi's finale and preside
over the first seasons of Welser-Möst, I made the decision to leave on
my 60th birthday in 2004. I privately informed Ward Smith and Dick
Bogomolny in order to give them three years to address succession in
an orderly manner. After reviewing the field of potential candidates,
they ultimately found a successor under their noses — Gary Hanson,
a loyal colleague for 16 years and my number-two. His appointment
and my retirement were simultaneously announced in July 2003. I left
in March 2004, midway through Welser-Möst's second season, with
Hanson prepared to take over the day I left and a new board president
in place as Bogomolny handed off the position to James D. Ireland
III, a civic-minded and music-loving Cleveland native who had built
several private equity firms. Managing these three transitions without
ripples is among my proudest achievements.

The most difficult consequence of my decision was not having
the enticing opportunity of collaborating artistically with Welser-Möst
over a longer period. I had, after all, brought him to Cleveland as a
guest conductor, and then hired and trained him in the role of music
director. He was a close and treasured friend, and we had already de-

179

veloped a wonderfully productive partnership. When first arriving, he had been impressed by the vision statement and was especially taken by the BHAG to "Become More Famous than the Vienna Philharmonic," a goal that particularly appealed to his Austrian sensibilities.

I did leave him with long-term artistic initiatives in place including biennial residencies at Vienna's Musikverein and the Lucerne Festival, the initial seeds of the orchestra's innovative yearly residency in Miami, annual staged and semi-staged opera performances in Severance Hall, a five-year project for Mitsuko Uchida to lead and play all the Mozart piano concertos and a continuation of the long relationship with Pierre Boulez.

Welser-Möst remains music director to this day, although it was announced in January 2024 that he would relinquish the position in 2027, after 25 years. He enjoys wide and well-deserved recognition for his over-two-decade leadership of the orchestra. I always viewed his appointment as a long-term one, and the widespread acknowledgment of his achievements today pleases me greatly.

BEYOND CLEVELAND

When I decided to leave the orchestra, I had no idea what to do next, although I was certain it was neither running another institution nor doing just one thing. I was content to let matters develop of their own accord, just as they had after I left Boston.

Through all my deliberations, Collins was a trusted advisor and coach, urging me to follow my instincts and calling. As he had found in leaving academia, the very acts of change and self-renewal are to be embraced as opportunity. And sure enough, opportunities came knocking, some tempting me before I left and some later. My principal obligation would be as artistic director of the Ojai Music Festival, which provided an outlet for my artistic passions. As it was not full-time, I could simultaneously pursue additional paths in teaching, consulting and joining boards.

I started leading management seminars for the League of American Orchestras in 1999. This work forced me to better structure my thinking and improve my presentation skills — performances, if you will. Over time, the subjects addressed were increasingly focused on artistic goals, strategy and governance. To broaden the perspectives, I often brought in experts from other fields to enrich the discussion, rather than relying only on a faculty of orchestra leaders. Through it all, Collins' concepts were always at the forefront and I eagerly incorporated into the curriculum his ideas, none more powerful than vision. As the work had been so valuable in Cleveland, I was anxious to help others apply the concepts.

In 2004, I created a seminar for the League specifically addressing institutional vision. Individual orchestras applied for participation in a six-day intensive workshop. But I soon discovered that, while the gathering successfully conveyed the ideas and engaged the participants, applying the learning back home was less successful; attendees, returning to their jobs, were overrun by the press of day-to-day business and crises.

Over the next five years, I continued to adjust the format to counteract this discouraging pattern. We began requiring the CEO, a board leader and artistic leader from each participating institution to attend in order to impose cross-functional collaboration and interaction within the legislative leadership team. Most acknowledged that this was the first time the three institutional leaders had spent extended time together on major issues, a disturbing reality. Then each participating orchestra was asked to devise a follow-up project applying the seminar learning, with requirements for formal progress reports and evaluation visits by seminar faculty over the following year. That period was subsequently extended to two years in order to monitor results over a longer term.

While there was progress, the impact of the work was still slow. I discovered a major impediment to be frequent turnover in board and management leadership. The need to bring changing leadership and culture up to speed made focus on long-term issues difficult to nurture and maintain. The resulting organizational instability and lack of continuity thwarted any accumulating sense of accomplishment, undermining extended institutional progress. Addressing major change would clearly take more than teaching current leaders the tools to apply. The results were discouraging after all the effort, so the seminar ended in 2009. Through it all, 63 geographically diverse orchestras of all sizes participated; many of them included some form of consulting in the subsequent project period to monitor progress. I got to know the field well.

Two organizational principles became clear through this work. First was the primacy of boards. They have not only fiduciary responsibility but a direct role in fundraising. This gives them an operating stake in financial success or failure, unlike for-profit boards who have only fiduciary responsibilities, with operational leadership being the sole responsibility of the CEO. Effectiveness in philanthropy, whether in giving or getting others to give, mandates that boards thoroughly understand, and are excited by, the organization's vision. Such ownership cannot be abdicated to the CEO and music director. Organizationally, most problems, whether leadership or financial, originate with the board, which is responsible for hiring the right CEO and music director. This is why, in discussing case studies in the seminars, I repeatedly asked, "Where was the board?" — a question whose importance cannot be overstated.

Second was the critical importance of the people, a principle Collins calls "first the who,"[7] the absolute prerequisite to deciding direction. He writes about "having the right people on the bus and in the right seats before deciding where to drive it." This requires active people management and recognizing that some just don't fit the culture or can't keep up with the pace, which he describes as "getting the wrong people off the bus." His useful template for hiring — competence, character and chemistry — mandates finding individuals not just with the necessary skills but a sound ethical compass and behavioral style that are in sync with the values of the institution. Reflecting on my years of hiring decisions and watching auditions in Cleveland, I saw that serious problems occur more often because of faulty character or mis-aligned chemistry than lack of skills.

As soon as I left the orchestra, I unexpectedly found myself in high demand as a consultant. Initially it was exciting and stimulating, keeping me in touch with the field to which I had devoted 35 years. I was more experienced than 15 years earlier, and because consulting was to be only one of my endeavors, I was less concerned about a recurrence of disenchantment. What's more, my exposure to Collins had given me new perspectives and tools, the most frequently used of which was advising on vision.

I became disciplined in choosing which engagements to accept. Years earlier, my Amsterdam partner had taught me to ask two questions in considering an assignment: who is the client, and is it empowered to implement recommendations? If the answer to the first is anything less than crystal-clear, the assignment is a no-go. If the answer

---

7 Collins, Jim, *Good to Great*, HarperBusiness, 2001.

to the second is not an unequivocal yes, the consulting assignment is also a no-go.

For vision projects, I made sure my client was always the board (through the board leader). As I had learned from Collins, articulating the foundational principles of what an organization stood for, why it existed, and where it wanted to go requires effective board ownership; good management alone cannot do it. Having learned through the League seminars that CEOs, board leaders and music directors hardly ever spent time together, I was not surprised at the lack of clear and shared vision that appeared to be prevalent in the field.

My work was not restricted to vision. I mediated labor disputes, advised on governance practices, helped with artistic and strategic planning, guided leadership searches and served as an executive coach. From 2004 to 2009, I undertook consulting projects for 20 orchestras, festivals, large and small ensembles and presenters — from the contemporary music group Eighth Blackbird to Kentucky's Paducah Symphony, Carnegie Hall, The Philadelphia Orchestra and the New York Philharmonic. I found Collins right about there being a fundamental set of best-practice axioms around leadership, structure, governance, vision and operating practices — unchanging principles, regardless of size, complexity or type of business. How they were applied, of course, varied with circumstances. I found that adapting to change was easier for midsize and smaller organizations, less strangled by size, inertia, tradition and self-importance.

Over time, I became increasingly disillusioned that so many clients seemed unwilling to acknowledge underlying challenges and commit to solving them. In my own assessment, over 80 percent wanted to avoid the hard work, more often preoccupied with fixing blame on others or circumstance rather than accepting responsibility themselves. Collins confirmed that this pattern was not unusual. Most clients' true motivation in engaging consultants is affirmation of their own beliefs and actions, not identifying and solving critical issues. Finding that my experience was not so different from those in the for-profit world at least allowed me not to take it personally.

I was soon discovering again that consulting was not for me. I had never set out to build such a business; my impulse was simply to help where I could. If frank and painful advice was needed, I tried to deliver it with tactful yet unambiguous clarity, which I am sure did not always endear me to clients. As I earlier learned, I preferred having my hands on the actual work as opposed to diagnosis, analysis and advice from the outside. The result was a gradual withdrawal from consulting, so that by 2009 I was through. Collins was not surprised, noting his own preference for studying and writing over consulting.

Having studied and taught governance, I felt the need for direct experience as a board member and quickly discovered that being on boards differed from talking about them — not unlike the difference between learning about how to do something and actually doing it. In the late 2000s, I joined three not-for-profit boards: the American Music Center, the Curtis Institute of Music (as a member of the board of overseers and later its chair), and Interlochen Center for the Arts. Each was fascinating in its own way and presented me with differing experiences.

The issue facing the American Music Center, an organization that promoted and supported contemporary music and composers, was singular and clear — duplication of function with other organizations. The board led a merger with one of those to form a new entity, stronger and more effective than the sum of the two parts. When the original board was merged out of existence, my involvement ended.

Philadelphia's Curtis Institute of Music, one of the premier music conservatories, was beginning to face the evolving realities of the 21st-century musical landscape, in which genres were fragmenting, boundaries were blurring and the possibilities of a career in music were infinitely expanding, demanding the rethinking of its educational program. These were interesting and meaningful challenges to be part of. For a while, it was enthralling, thanks to an exceptionally gifted board leader in H.F. "Gerry" Lenfest. A telecommunications pioneer and major community philanthropist who gave away most of his considerable wealth before he died in 2018, Lenfest masterminded building new facilities and opening Curtis to new thinking and resources. Alas, when he retired, the organization drifted back into a self-satisfied embrace of its history, not wanting the benefit of outside perspectives. With its future not grounded in the changing realities of society or music, I ended my involvement.

In 2008, I joined the board of Interlochen Center for the Arts in northern Michigan, where my eyes had been opened to the magical possibilities of music during my one summer there in 1959. I found its seduction much the same, although its scope of activities had vastly expanded, with the addition in 1963 of a boarding school for almost 600 students and a wide embrace of multiple disciplines — music, dance, visual arts, theater, film and new media, creative writing and interdisciplinary arts. I was attracted because the institution was beginning to rethink its future, having thrived for decades on its sterling reputation. Particularly attractive to me was its multi-disciplinary nature and focus on high school or younger students, for whom idealism was at its highest and anxieties about finding a job, as happens in conservatories, had yet to taint enthusiasm. This intrigued me and I wanted to be part of it.

At an early meeting to discuss a possible endowment campaign, the board was unable to answer why it was necessary, other than the need for money — not a compelling case for fundraising. Interlochen's vision for the future seemed vague and squishy, insufficient as a basis around which to raise considerable funds. A case must outline a galvanizing future that will convince prospects to invest in making that future a reality. I led the group in a vision process with board colleague Bruce Coppock, with whom I had consulted earlier on similar work for the Saint Paul Chamber Orchestra, where he was CEO. The process took a year-and-a-half and totally engaged the Interlochen board. It culminated in a one-page statement, modeled after the Collins-Porras template, that remains in place to this day.

The most illuminating element was determining Interlochen's underlying purpose, its true reason for being. The one cited most often had been training young artists, which its public relations trumpeted by highlighting famous performer graduates. But the vast majority of its more than 125,000 alumni were not active artists. They became illustrious business leaders, lawyers, doctors and teachers, and went on to serve the arts as supporters and patrons. We concluded that if Interlochen's reason for being was to train artists, as exemplified by those who were famous, it was not doing such a great job. The board realized its purpose was rather sparking enthusiasm for the arts, a goal that could be manifested in many ways beyond performing. By this measure, Interlochen was a vast success. Our resulting statement of purpose became "to ignite lifelong passion for the arts" — simple, direct and energizing. As it did in Cleveland, the work demonstrated how deep and disciplined thinking can change understanding and provide clarity and direction — Collins' ideas in action.

I remain on the Interlochen board today and have been involved with a transition of executive leadership, completion of the campus master plan, substantive increases in fundraising, and a reexamination of its educational program in light of the changing environment. It has been deeply satisfying to be involved with an organization that is concentrated on charting its future rather than looking backwards to polish its heritage. My experience has been a graduate education in how boards should and can function, an achievement enhanced by exceptionally strong executive leadership in President Trey Devey.

I maintain a close friendship with Collins, visiting him in Boulder every six to eight months. He has visited Cleveland to hear the orchestra and Ojai for the festival several times. Always the curious music lover with an inquisitive mind, he would pointedly ask about what he was going to hear and why it was programmed. We ended visits with lively post-mortems of frank feedback. Each time I am with him, we talk about our lives and projects, and he grills me, as only he can, on why I think about things the way I do. He is my private recharging station.

Collins is another person who entered my life at an opportune moment, just as I was searching for broader perspectives on why organizations worked. He brought clarity to my transition from orchestras. His encouragement and guidance helped prepare me to enter and then leave the world of consulting. More recently, he urged me to write this book.

His recurring theme is renewal — how organizations go about it, what the challenges are, what pitfalls need to be avoided and what elements are to be preserved. Through the years, as part of his own journey, he realized that those same elements apply to individuals — how we develop, how we grow, how we reinvent ourselves. I now see my own journey as one of constant renewal. At the core, I have always been a passionate music lover, but how I expressed it evolved. Collins gave me the tools and encouragement to address transformation without fear and to understand my own yin and yang of purpose — to simultaneously preserve my core value of passion for music and stimulate progress in finding ways to give it life.

CHAPTER 9
AN IDEALIZED LABORATORY:
SPRING FOR MUSIC

I am unequivocally convinced that a fundamental imperative of an orchestra is to lead taste, not follow it, and to do so in the context of an overarching artistic philosophy. That means intentionally embracing risk, not just in individual programs and activities but as a basic pillar of institutional philosophy. Great concerts are not ends in themselves — they embody a dynamic that creates connections with audiences by provoking reactions, whether positive or negative. What is unacceptable is eliciting no response.

Throughout my years with the Boston Symphony and Cleveland Orchestra, I was obsessed with programming, becoming ever more convinced that putting music squarely at the center of institutional planning and thinking was the key to success. I was constantly tinkering with, agonizing over and thinking about programs. Over time, I developed strong views about what worked, what didn't and why, and I found conventional thinking ill-informed and based more on fear than conviction. I was encouraged by how keeping concerts fresh resulted in increasingly invigorated audiences. But there was always resistance from the old guard, not wanting to stray from the familiar, believing this was the only way to attract people like them. Existing audiences do need to be retained, but more important is enticing a new and youthful public who will crowd tomorrow's concerts. Every piece of data I have ever seen validates the positive correlation between adventurous programming and a younger turnout. Consistent and unyielding dedication to the new and unusual is the key to achieving this goal.

The central tool in invigorating concerts is programming, and experience has taught me how making imaginative choices is the prime ingredient in forging a distinctive and meaningful artistic profile. I witnessed how Fiedler deliberately and painstakingly calibrated the emotional arc of each concert. I saw how Williams expanded the range of music performed at the Boston Pops, stamping his beliefs on it while never diluting the premise that at heart it was a symphony orchestra. I watched how Boulez redefined the repertoire through his tireless advocacy for 20th-century works, at the same time expanding the possibilities of concert formats. I saw how Dohnányi, building on the Classical heritage of The Cleveland Orchestra, established a distinctive and provocative artistic profile, drawing on both a broader range of pieces and unusual program structures, never clouding the central tenet of Cleveland being at heart a classical ensemble. And I saw how Spring for Music and the Ojai Music Festival attracted engaged audiences while remaining unyielding about artistic adventure.

In today's market-driven economy, it is accepted orchestra dogma that selling tickets is a dominant measure of success, and doing so requires choosing programs that are "popular" with the public. The problem is that "popular" gets defined by what sold well in the past, which is not necessarily determinative of what will sell in the future. Popular acceptance of composers and repertoire is not fixed over time; it ebbs and flows, depending on changing tastes, evolving times, and advocacy by performers and media. Mahler was largely unknown in 1960 but, thanks primarily to sustained propagation by Leonard Bernstein, is now popular. Likewise, the music of Sibelius, performed often in the 1940s and 1950s, fell from favor and has only in recent decades regained its footing.

Trying to predict what sells and what does not is complex. It depends not just on individual pieces but the whole program. There are infinite opinions on which individual pieces really help sell a concert and which ones don't. Being well-known does not mean automatic sellouts — Mahler's Symphony No. 2, Tchaikovsky's Symphony No. 5 and Brahms's Symphony No. 1 come to mind. I find that only 10 classical favorites are assured box-office hits: Beethoven's Symphonies Nos. 5 and 9, Rachmaninoff's Piano Concertos Nos. 2 and 3, Tchaikovsky's *1812 Overture*, Gershwin's *Rhapsody in Blue*, Handel's *Messiah*, Orff's *Carmina Burana*, Vivaldi's *Four Seasons*, and Ravel's *Bolero*. Building a season around just these works is not a formula for artistic vitality. Such a strategy not only restricts the repertoire but runs the risk of wearing out the appeal of those pieces. In the 1970s, Tanglewood's annual Beethoven weekend was so consistently successful that management's only concern was finding the least expensive conductor to lead it, believing that the idea's past popularity made it magically impervious to poor sales. Through mindless repetition and mediocre conducting, the public caught on, sales sagged, and the event was discontinued. The lesson is to never treat popular composers or repertoire as mere commodities — a strategy that never fails to deplete their appeal, much as failing to rotate crops decimates the soil's life.

Additionally, there is the question of desired audience profile. Everyone yearns for new and younger listeners, but they are not necessarily attracted by the familiar war horses so beloved by older and wealthier patrons on whom institutions are fixated. I am reminded of the New York Philharmonic's experience in music director Alan Gilbert's first season, when he bravely and smartly programmed concert performances of Ligeti's challenging *Le Grand Macabre* in an attempt to enliven the orchestra's profile. The board and management panicked when the traditional subscription audiences balked at buying tickets, even though the performances were sold out to a new, younger and hipper public through non-traditional marketing at discounted prices. By not following up in succeeding seasons with similar ideas, the experience became a one-shot success and did not build lasting change. Achieving that result is only possible through consistent actions and strategies that touch everything the orchestra does — and which are maintained and refined over time.

The industry programming norm is predicated on 19th-century warhorses — the so-called "canon" — in unchanging three-piece structures of opening work, concerto and masterwork. Contemporary music is seen as a necessary curse to be included from time to time, safely nestled within the insulating comfort of greatest hits. Name-brand soloists are positioned as the drivers of ticket sales and, together with the warhorses, dominate marketing headlines in brochures and ads. Think of the mythical program Knussen and I jokingly devised — three works of Elliott Carter followed by *Bolero* —and what the misleading ad headline would inevitably be, to the consternation of both Carter and *Bolero* fans.

This kind of thinking is the opposite of leading taste — a self-defeating strategy that contracts the range of repertoire and strangles artistic vitality. Such strategies justified by historic sales data are, by definition, following taste. How much better to schedule only pieces about which artists have something distinctive to say or perform them in interesting juxtapositions with other works. This provides audiences with the opportunity to experience them differently as changing the context always alters impact.

And above all, the necessary long-term strategy for leading taste is building enthusiasm around the institution itself, not specific pieces programmed or artists performing. These principles became ingrained in me over my Boston and Cleveland years.

THE IDEA

Having willingly left orchestra management in 2004, I still found myself in despair from afar over what I saw were death-spiral programming practices. Understanding that I was no longer in a position to lead change from inside, the question was what, if anything, I could do about it from outside.

In 2006 I got a call from David Foster, then-president of Opus 3 Artists, the largest American artist management agency for classical music. I had known him since the early 1970s, when he worked for another company and handled touring for the Boston Symphony and Boston Pops. I had hired him to represent The Cleveland Orchestra for touring when I got there. He was very good at his job, with down-to-earth professionalism coupled with an ability to laugh at himself and the music business.

Foster proposed to me establishing a new orchestra series to be presented at Carnegie Hall. He noticed that the hall was engaging an ever-narrower circle of North American orchestras, concentrating on the biggest and flashiest — Boston, Chicago, Cleveland, Philadelphia, San Francisco and the MET Orchestra. The focus on name-brands had narrowed the range of opportunities for others to perform there at a time when their technical and musical excellence was increasingly acknowledged.[1] Foster wanted to create a new series of concerts showcasing the breadth of American orchestras, in essence

---

1 Carnegie Hall data confirms Foster's concerns: in 1985, the Hall presented 15 North American orchestras other than the brand names; in 1995 the number declined to seven and in 2005 to six. In addition, programs were becoming dominated by big-name soloists and greatest-hits repertoire. The only two off-brand orchestras presented in 2015 were part of Carnegie Perspectives concerts featuring Meredith Monk and Anne-Sophie Mutter — those performers, not the orchestras themselves, being the drivers of invitation as the orchestras were reduced to being vehicles for the soloists.

establishing an alternative to being presented by Carnegie. While he expressed genuine concern about the narrowing opportunities at the venue, it was not lost on me that reversing this trend would be good business for him, given the many conductors, artists and orchestras he represented.

He explained that he had initially shared the idea with Mary Lou Falcone, who ran her own PR agency and was the acknowledged master of her craft. I knew her but we had never worked together. She represented a who's who of artists and orchestras — including Carnegie itself, a relationship Foster understood would be helpful in achieving success in New York's busy classical music market. Both knew that they needed an additional partner with knowledge and experience in orchestras, repertoire and programming. That was the reason for the call, and I was immediately intrigued and signed on.

The three of us began meeting to refine the concept. As we talked, the idea broadened into a competition, with the sole determining factor for securing an invitation to participate being the creativity of the proposed program. We conceived an annual festival of six to seven concerts at Carnegie Hall, focused purely on the music, with tickets at affordable prices in order to attract new audiences. The event would

The Trio: me, Mary Lou Falcone and David Foster

take place in May, when most orchestra seasons were ending and before summer seasons began. We came up with the name Spring for Music, a takeoff on the successful Fall for Dance festival of ballet and modern dance presented every autumn by New York's City Center.

We formulated a manifesto outlining the artistic principles on which the project was to be based:

> Spring for Music believes that an orchestra's fundamental obligation is to lead taste, not follow it, and that imaginative programming will advance, and not just satisfy, expectations. Accordingly, Spring for Music provides an idealized laboratory, free of the usual marketing and financial constraints, for an orchestra to be truly creative with interesting, provocative and stimulating programs reflecting its beliefs, its standards and its vision. Creative programs reflect each orchestra's particular characteristics of sound, ensemble and style, as determined by its musicians, its music director and its tradition. Spring for Music's philosophy comes from the belief that an artistic point of view must infuse everything an orchestra does, and that its programs not only illustrate but validate that viewpoint. Great programs have imaginative, meaningful and deliberate thought behind the selection of pieces, their sequence and their presentation. This does not mandate a rigid program "theme" or simply a healthy dose of contemporary music; rather it reflects a stimulating mix of pieces, styles, artists and composers that engages the listener in an absorbing adventure — a journey of seduction, intellect and emotion, where the program's totality becomes greater than the sum of the individual pieces. A great program provokes gasps, sighs, tears or smiles and, above all, creates a sense of the unexpected — the listener can never predict how it will actually turn out; it is imbued with the inherent risk of uncertainty.

THE DETAILS

Our first job was clear definition of the project, an essential step for any start-up. We formed a not-for profit corporation to enable receiving philanthropic funds, with a small board of industry leaders to give the project visibility and credibility. These steps were necessary before approaching funders, as we needed to secure some portion of financing prior to any public announcement. From an organizational standpoint, Foster and his Opus 3 colleagues would produce the concerts, Falcone would handle marketing and PR, and I would be the artistic director, responsible for selecting the participating orchestras and programs. We wrote a detailed business plan and assembled an eight-person management team from across the country built around the key operational skills we needed — marketing, public relations, digital media, production, finance, and writing. It was a lean group with maximal flexibility and minimal overhead, infused with energy. We had no office, meeting monthly in whatever space we could find in New York.

The underlying driver of the concept was orchestras' desperate desire to perform in Carnegie Hall, unquestioningly thinking it the ultimate in reputational validation, with exposure before national critics and opinion leaders. Such is the power of Carnegie's commanding brand position in New York. The other main presenting venue, David Geffen Hall at Lincoln Center, is the home of the New York Philharmonic and has few available dates to offer, given the Philharmonic's unyielding schedule, leaving the market to Carnegie.

The reality is that invitations to be presented by Carnegie, while coveted, are scarce. Even so, their added value, financially and artistically, is not the bonanza it seems. In engaging an orchestra, Carnegie pays a negotiated fee, provides the hall, markets the tickets and keeps all ticket proceeds, taking on the full financial risk of the event. Given Carnegie's market dominance, its fees are smaller than elsewhere, as demand far outstrips supply. They are never enough to fund an orchestra's full costs, not only of the players, conductor and soloist but also travel, hotel, per diem and instrument cartage. Subsidies are always needed. Artistically, given the glut of orchestra concerts in New York, Carnegie, as the party at risk, demands safe programming and the inclusion of name soloists whenever possible so as to ensure strong ticket sales. Only rarely is an ensemble given the freedom to perform a distinctive program that truly reflects its artistic beliefs.

Before Spring for Music, the only real option to a Carnegie invitation to perform there was self-presentation, in which the orchestra rents the hall at a significant fee, pays for promotion and marketing but keeps all the ticket receipts, thus assuming the financial risk for the concert. It still has to finance performers' fees and all of the travel expenses. The aggregate costs are in the hundreds of thousands of dollars, and even with capacity ticket receipts, the net is significantly smaller than in a Carnegie presentation. What's more, such an event does not benefit from the hall's considerable marketing machine; the orchestra itself must promote the concert in a market in which it has no experience, with the result that a full house is far from guaranteed. Additionally, in the declining reality of critical coverage for classical music, reviews — good, bad, or any — cannot be assured. Hearing frequently, in my consulting, of orchestras' eagerness to consider such self-presentation, such was the desperation to appear there, I consistently recommended against it because of the enormous financial resources for questionable return, beyond the psychic reward of playing there. Some listened; many did not.

Spring for Music would be positioned as a third option for performing at Carnegie, one that was not materially worse financially than being presented by the hall and far better than self-presentation — while at the same time being an opportunity to make a bold artistic statement with high visibility that would likely assure press attention.

We would produce and market the concerts. We decided to keep the operation at arm's length from Carnegie in order to maintain control, so we rented the hall. The rental contract was specific about operating rules and regulations and covered use of just the basic stage configuration, with required variations, such as risers or special lighting, triggering extra costs to be borne by the orchestra. Spring for Music, as the presenter, would sign contracts with the various orchestras for each of the concerts. Our media partner, WQXR, would provide live and delayed radio broadcasts plus simultaneous and archival streaming of each concert. For the six or seven concerts annually, the budget for the orchestra costs, marketing, hall rental, broadcasting and administration was about $1.3 million.

As this was to be a competition for participation, it was essential that the pool of eligible orchestras be clearly defined, broad enough to attract a wide range of ensembles but not so broad as to make the selection process unwieldy. We unilaterally defined eligibility as orchestras with annual budgets from about $2.5 million up, a criterion which encompassed about 65 groups and one that generally embraced fully professional ensembles. Each eligible orchestra would be asked to submit a program proposal reflecting its artistic vision and unique character. We stated explicitly that the sole criterion for selection would be the imagination, structure and creativity of the proposed program and its consistency with stated artistic vision and practices. These last points turned out to be prophetic, demonstrating the absence, in many orchestras, of clear and compelling vision.

As artistic director, I would be the sole judge of submissions, and once accepted, there would be no change in a program without mutual agreement. I reserved the right to suggest a change to improve or to provide better balance across the full festival, but it was clear that if the orchestra insisted on maintaining its submitted program, that was acceptable. This flexibility was to prove helpful in a few instances.

Each selected ensemble, regardless of size or reputation, would receive the same fee — a substantial advance against 100 percent of the ticket revenues for its concert, plus a stipend toward travel and preparation costs. These amounts included no extra fee for the specified electronic media rights required under our partnership with WQXR, a central provision of the deal. This was new for touring American orchestras, which were used to treating such matters as options subject to additional negotiation.

Central to our thinking was transparency in all respects — schedule, finances, contracts and sales. Requests-for-proposals, sent annually to the eligible orchestras, included details about the application process, program submission, criteria and schedule for selection, the financial deal and electronic media needs. Each one submitting a proposal was required to warrant understanding and acceptance of all terms of the financial deal in advance. Since every orchestra was treated equally, this approach precluded any later renegotiation of terms.

All seats, including boxes, were priced at $25. Given the low ticket price, we established a no-discount, no-complimentary ticket policy that was novel in New York's classical concert culture, where discounts and comps were widespread. Since a critical element in Spring for Music was encouraging orchestras to leverage appearances in their local communities, we developed a "hometown fan" strategy. Each orchestra could purchase blocks of tickets in priority locations at $25 each to bring groups of local supporters to the concert. Falcone came up with the brilliant idea of giving different colored scarves to each of the groups, to be worn or waved at the concert, creating an atmosphere of shameless, boisterous boosterism.

Central to our vision was enlivening the concert presentation experience itself to purge what have become stale and predictable rituals. Part of the challenges were the inherent limitations imposed by the formality of concert halls themselves. While we could not change the design and layout of the hall, we could change how orchestras presented themselves within the given strictures of Carnegie Hall.

We asked each orchestra not to wear tails or tuxedos, urging it instead to be creative in what was worn — an attempt to rid the concerts of what, for me, is a sartorial anachronism that conveys an aura of antiquity and distance. Our goals were enhancing the visceral connection between performer and audience and making the experience less intimidating.

We reimagined the start of the concerts, asking each orchestra to adopt a "European entrance," in which the public enters the hall to an empty and darkened stage. A few minutes before concert time, the house lights dim and the stage lights brighten as the orchestra enters the stage together, triggering instant applause. After the orchestra tunes, a WQXR announcer takes the stage with a representative of the ensemble — a board member or prominent community leader — to greet the crowd with a scripted introduction lasting no more than five minutes and not repeating information in the program book. To discourage incoherent ramblings, we insisted that the talk be both fully scripted and rehearsed. The colored handkerchiefs were introduced and given an initial wave by the audience, and often by the orchestra from the stage, creating an atmosphere of instant and palpable energy. The WQXR announcer introduced the conductor, and the concert would begin. In the tradition-bound world of orchestras, such baby-steps toward change were seen as earth-shattering.

Our initial phase was to produce four seasons, to begin in May 2011. The overall funding need was $5 million. I contacted my long-time friend Daniel R. Lewis, who had been a major donor to The Cleveland Orchestra and was supportive of projects with which I was involved. Intrigued, he enthusiastically agreed to be an early and generous financial backer and to be board chair. In addition, I had a long relationship with The Andrew W. Mellon Foundation and its then-president, Don Randel, whom I had first met years earlier as a fellow member of the Princeton marching band. Thanks to Randel's advocacy, Mellon made an early multi-year, seven-figure commitment, giving us confidence in the viability of the project plus enormous credibility in the field.

With these major gifts in hand and the operational details worked out, we announced Spring for Music publicly in the spring of 2008. The plan was to use the momentum of the enthusiastic press response, as well the public excitement generated by the later announcements of the 2011 and 2012 seasons, to support raising the remaining money. Effective fundraising requires an exciting idea, a compelling case for support, and persuasive cultivation and solicitation. Personal relationships never hurt, and thanks to Falcone's with Philadelphia's Gerry and Marguerite Lenfest and mine with Chicago's Joan Harris and Philadelphia's Joseph Neubauer, plus a host of other individual and foundation gifts, the project was ultimately fully financed. We felt it a great achievement for a start-up conceived and initiated amid the economic meltdown of 2009-10.

Spring for Music was intentionally idealistic, about which the team was deeply excited. But it was not without significant risks:

- Would orchestras actually apply and be engaged in the requirement to be creative in programming?
- Would orchestras commit to the considerable financial and logistical obligations of a trip to New York?
- Would the range of orchestras applying be representative of the range of those eligible?
- Would audiences buy tickets, even at the low price, to a series of concerts in New York with non-brand-name orchestras presenting unusual and atypical programs?
- Would Spring for Music attract new and younger audiences to orchestra concerts?
- Would Spring for Music create impact in New York's glutted musical season, and would the press notice?
- Would we be financially successful in controlling expenses and keeping the budget balanced?

Adding to our anxieties was a unique reality of the orchestra business; three-year lead times are necessary for planning. This meant

Waving the scarves at Carnegie Hall

the application process for the first Spring for Music, scheduled for May 2011, needed to occur in fall 2008. Following a similar pattern for future festivals, the processes for the 2012 and 2013 events would take place in fall 2009 and 2010, all still before the first festival had even been produced. Given the inherent phenomenon of orchestras being reluctant to innovate until they see someone else do so successfully, this required a leap of faith for those submitting proposals for these first three seasons. The first application process to occur after a festival had been produced would happen in fall 2011, which would be for the fourth festival in 2014. Additionally, it would not be until planning for that fourth festival that we would have hard empirical data on the results of the first. The project was not a slam-dunk.

PHASE I

Requests-for-proposals for the first season, seven concerts in 2011, were sent to the eligible orchestras in September 2008. We anxiously awaited the response; to our delight, 25 applied, a terrific cross-section of orchestras in size and location. None of the largest submitted applications, but we expected them to pass, content with possible invitations to appear directly from Carnegie.[2] On the whole, I found the proposed programs a remarkable validation that orchestras were hungry to be artistically creative.

The seven groups selected were highly varied — the Orpheus Chamber Orchestra (New York); the Toledo, Albany, Dallas, Oregon and Montreal Symphonies; and the Saint Paul Chamber Orchestra. All distinguished themselves programmatically: Orpheus's six commissions inspired by Bach's "Brandenburg" Concertos; Toledo's unique pairing of Shostakovich's moody Symphony No. 6 with the Russian-flavored André Previn-Tom Stoppard theatrical collaboration *Every Good Boy Deserves Favor*; the Albany Symphony's realizations of American spirituals by contemporary composers; the Dallas Symphony's performance of a commissioned oratorio by Steven Stucky based on the August 4, 1964 discovery of three murdered civil rights workers in Mississippi; and the Saint Paul Chamber Orchestra's commission to genre-crossing Maria Schneider.

Montreal's four-century survey of the symphony stood out — an imaginative sequence of works by Gabrieli, Webern and Stravinsky interspersed with Three-Part Inventions ("Sinfonias") by Bach played on the piano, and all followed by Beethoven's Symphony No. 5. Here was a perfect example of the thoughtful and unexpected programming we had hoped to generate, featuring the most standard of masterworks but positioned in a context that showcased it in a new light. As *The New Yorker*'s Alex Ross commented, "The sequence seemed mysteriously fluid and logical. Such programming forces you to lean in rather than sit back: it demanded alertness."[3]

The story of Oregon's intriguing "Music in a Time of War" illustrates how Spring for Music worked. The orchestra had never in its 100-year history appeared in New York, or even east of the Mississippi. It grabbed at the opportunity as a way not only to appear at Carnegie but to do so with a typical example of the programming inventiveness it had become known for under its then-music director, Carlos Kalmar. Its submission started with Britten's pacifist lament,

---

2 One such large orchestra haughtily declined to apply, thinking itself worthy of nothing less than a direct invitation from Carnegie — a curious stance since it was hardly a regular presence there. Its executive director told me that Spring for Music, while a wonderful project, was really for "less important" orchestras. How sweet it was when, seeing the initial year's success three years later, the orchestra applied for 2014.

3 Ross, Alex, "Mix and Match: Spring for Music, at Carnegie Hall," *The New Yorker*, June 6, 2011.

Sinfonia da Requiem, followed by John Adams' gripping song cycle *The Wound-Dresser*, based on Walt Whitman texts about injured Civil War soldiers, and closing with Vaughan Williams' violent and intense Symphony No. 4. This easily won Oregon an invitation. Exercising my prerogative as artistic director, I subsequently suggested to Kalmar a small change to the first half to give it even greater impact: start with Charles Ives' *The Unanswered Question*, followed by the Adams and Britten, all performed *attacca*. Kalmar agreed, so the seamless musical journey of the first half — the Ives question of existence leading right into the heartfelt requiems by Adams and Britten — perfectly set up the Vaughan Williams in the second half. Here was a program of relatively unknown music, put together in a way that made a cohesive statement. If the Vaughan Williams or Adams or Britten had been programmed independently and paired with a popular concerto or masterwork, the impact would have been blunted, heard as something odd in an ordinary context. Placing these pieces together forced audiences to listen differently and to judge the works in relationship to each other rather than to something familiar. As Alex Ross said of the performance, "The Oregonians' furious rendition of [the Vaughan Williams] would have been impressive in any context, but as the capstone to a brilliantly worked-out program, it had shattering force."[4]

The 2011 season looked wonderful, and we were mightily encouraged. But there were still two seasons to plan before the first note was to be performed. The 2009-2010 economic gloom pervaded the application processes for 2012 and 2013, and applications declined by half. Still, we were pleased with the submissions' quality and range. We decided to reduce the number of concerts, starting in 2012, to six to be held on consecutive days within one week. The orchestras selected were again highly varied: Birmingham (Alabama), Edmonton (Alberta), Houston, Milwaukee, Nashville and New Jersey in 2012; and Albany, Baltimore, Buffalo, Detroit, Oregon and Washington, D.C. in 2013. One of the submission rules was that, while an orchestra could not apply in successive years, it could do so after a one-year hiatus, which is how Albany and Oregon earned their second invitations in 2013.

With the first three seasons planned, Spring for Music debuted in May 2011. When tickets went on sale, we watched anxiously to see if our own enthusiasm was matched by that of the ticket-purchasing

4 Ross, Alex, "Mix and Match: Spring for Music, at Carnegie Hall," *The New Yorker*, June 6, 2011.

public. We had high hopes and were blessed with terrific and constant press that actively cheered us on.

My optimism was slightly muted by the reality that ticket sales reached only 54 percent of capacity that first year, less than I had hoped for. But the enthusiasm for and the energy of the concerts were deeply encouraging, as was data showing we were already attracting a new and younger public to orchestra concerts. But it was clear that it would take time to build an audience for a new venture with non-brand-name orchestras without recognized soloists and performing unusual programs, even at $25 a ticket at Carnegie Hall.

Artistically, the concerts were outstanding. Each orchestra, hungry to show off, was at the top of its game. Critical coverage was substantial and positive, and totally captured what we were trying to achieve. With the favorable reaction and enthusiastic word-of-mouth for that first season, we anxiously watched the 2014 application process three months later. Sure enough, the number of applications jumped to 20, and the inventiveness of the proposed programs was even higher than in prior years. We saw the orchestra field's "lemming" principle — avoid new initiatives in favor of following others' successful ideas — on full display; among the applicants were the New York Philharmonic and the Pittsburgh and Cincinnati Symphonies. Once they saw Spring for Music in action, they didn't want to be left out.

PHASE II

We faced a major decision in 2011, soon after the first Spring for Music festival was produced. Funding was only secure through 2014, so if there was to be a 2015 festival (and beyond), we would have to commence the selection process in the fall of 2012, only a year from then. While we were pleased with the first season's success, that was an exceedingly short time span in which to figure out how it could continue, how long we would need to plan for, how much funding was necessary, where it would come from, and what kind of infrastructure would be needed to sustain the project. It was a daunting set of questions, particularly with only one year of experience and hard data to draw from.

We already knew that despite our success in funding the first four years, a few of the initial investors who had been thrilled to help launch the project were not prepared to continue. This is a philanthropic pattern that afflicts many such start-up enterprises — seed funding is precisely that, money to get the activity off the ground until it can become self-supporting and/or get continuing grants from elsewhere. The theory goes that if a new project is successful, those who are engaged with it should participate in keeping it going through their own philanthropic support, an understandable and logical argument.

I had learned that the key to funding success is an effective board which owns the vision of the institution. And here was our real challenge: we were basically a group of outsiders who had conceived a project that was *in* New York but not yet developed into an entity that was *of* New York. I knew that continuing would require establishing a degree of ownership by its New York constituency, which meant reimagining a board to encompass those New York enthusiasts. The reality was this would take at least another four or five years, perhaps as long as 10, which would be beyond our small organization's ability to sustain itself financially.

Our solution was to consider a hybrid Phase II, in which Spring for Music would establish a partnership with an existing musical institution, in essence piggybacking on the partner to create a joint venture with mutual responsibilities for management, operations and funding. Remaining at Carnegie Hall was our goal since it was the key driver of orchestras' intense desire to participate. While the conservative culture of Carnegie was somewhat antithetical to the spirit of Spring for Music, and while we were, therefore, not against moving to Lincoln Center or, more intriguingly, the Park Avenue Armory, we were mindful of the risk of a diminished draw for orchestra applications, given the mystical allure of Carnegie.

We considered five possible partners: Carnegie Hall, Lincoln Center, the Park Avenue Armory, the New York Philharmonic and, as a long-shot, Washington's Kennedy Center, then under the leadership of Michael Kaiser, thinking it might want to expand its brand into New York by producing concerts there. Through early 2012, we held conversations with them all, knowing that while each could start up its own orchestra series without us, we owned the name and an established brand. All the discussions came to naught: Carnegie Hall was interested only in a scaled-down version that it could produce completely on its own and ultimately declined; Lincoln Center would have difficulty finding a period of available successive dates around the New York Philharmonic's busy schedule; the Armory's priorities did not include producing orchestra concerts; the New York Philharmonic, though initially interested in presiding over the presentation of American orchestras in New York to supplement its own concerts, declined for financial and operational reasons; and the Kennedy Center was ultimately not interested in producing concerts in New York and thought that such programming in Washington would not attract audiences.

It was all discouraging, but I did not see a way forward without a partner. Our only course was to declare victory and discontinue Spring for Music after the 2014 season. Limping into an uncertain future beyond that was not an option. In mid-2012, we reluctantly announced that 2014 would be our last. It was the right decision, if a sad one.

FINALE

In the meantime, we still had three festivals to produce. The 2012 and 2013 programs were distinguished: Houston's pairing of Shostakovich's little-known *Anti-Formalist Rayok* with the explosive Symphony No. 11; Edmonton's presentation of works by three of its composers-in-residence; New Jersey's performance of my old favorite, Busoni's Piano Concerto; Nashville's pairing of Ives' incomplete *Universe Symphony* with Percy Grainger's "music to an imaginary ballet" *The Warriors*; Albany's New York premiere of the original 1948 version of Morton Gould's Third Symphony; and Buffalo's performance of Glière's uncut *Ilya Muromets* Symphony.

The Detroit Symphony outdid itself, performing two concerts in 2013. The second was a last-minute substitution for the Oregon Symphony, which unceremoniously pulled out, citing financial and internal issues. Detroit's music director, Leonard Slatkin, graciously took over Oregon's inclusion of Kurt Weill's *Seven Deadly Sins* with the magnificent and colorful Storm Large as vocalist. Detroit's other program was an all-time great — the four numbered symphonies of Charles Ives, a continuous portrait of the composer's musical journey from the European symphonic tradition as embodied in his First Symphony (1898-1908) to the American maverick experimentation of his Fourth (1912-25).

For the 2014 finale, we were particularly pleased with the range of orchestras and repertoire included. The New York Philharmonic performed the local premiere of Christopher Rouse's Requiem, a mammoth work which the orchestra had decided not to put on its own series at Lincoln Center despite Rouse being its composer-in-residence. It clearly felt that Spring for Music provided the right context and a complementary outlet for the work. The Seattle Symphony played, in another New York premiere, its commissioned *Become Ocean* by John Luther Adams. The Winnipeg Symphony featured music by the dean of Canadian composers, R. Murray Schafer, plus a concerto for Inuit throat singer. And the Pittsburgh Symphony presented a realization of Mozart's Requiem, reimagined by music director Manfred Honeck as if performed at Mozart's own funeral, with texts by Mozart read by actor F. Murray Abraham.

Shortly after the Rochester Philharmonic had been selected three years earlier, its music director resigned, leaving it conductor-less and rendering its proposal moot. Wanting very much to retain my hometown orchestra's spot, I suggested as an alternative a performance of *Merry Mount*, the lone opera by Howard Hanson, longtime director of Rochester's Eastman School of Music. This forgotten work, given a wildly successful premiere at the Metropolitan Opera 80 years before, had not been heard in New York since. The orchestra happily agreed and hired the wonderful young American conductor Michael Christie to lead the performance.

The centerpiece of the concert by the Cincinnati Symphony, joined by the Cincinnati May Festival Chorus, was Nathaniel Dett's oratorio *The Ordering of Moses*. Written as Dett's graduation thesis for the Eastman School in 1932, the work remained unperformed until 1937 when these same forces gave the world premiere in Cincinnati, a performance broadcast nationally by NBC Radio. At the time, it was bold to provide such a prominent platform for a piece by a Black composer. The broadcast, however, was inexplicably interrupted two-thirds of the way through by an announcement that "due to previous commitments, we are unable to remain for the closing moments of this excellent performance."[5] Over the years, there has been much conjecture about the real reasons for the sudden pre-empting of such a major broadcast. The result was nationwide audiences hearing only a portion of the work, and other than one subsequent performance at the Juilliard School in 1938, the complete score remained unheard in New

---

5 Transcribed from a recording of the performance.

York. Its inclusion that final year was therefore a major event. The performance was preceded by playing the original radio introduction over the PA system. At the moment of interruption, the performance was halted and the actual radio announcement about "previous commitments" was played, after which the rest of the piece was performed. It made for a powerful re-creation of the oratorio's troubled premiere.

Spring for Music went out in style.[6] The four festivals were packed with unusual and stimulating repertoire, program structures and contextual flow that were very different from standard concerts — precisely the results we had hoped for and proving the enormous pent-up creativity across the range of orchestras. Seventy percent of eligible ensembles applied over the four years, a heartwarming validation of the concept.

While it took time to catch on with audiences, even at $25 a ticket, the percentage of capacity sold grew steadily from 54 to 73 percent over the four years. Those results — remarkable considering the number of orchestra concerts in New York and Spring for Music's predominance of lesser-known orchestras and unusual repertoire — totally debunked any fear that a public would not turn up for unusual and creative programs. I was not surprised as it was consistent with my own experience in Cleveland — audiences will respond to creativity if applied in a consistent contextual framework over time.

As encouraging as the audience numbers was its makeup. Half were new to Carnegie Hall, half were under 55 and a quarter were under 44, striking statistics proving that Spring for Music succeeded in drawing new and younger audiences to orchestra concerts.[7] Our encouraging hometown fans to accompany each orchestra gave the concerts an energized buzz by providing a built-in cheerleading squad of proud local supporters. The Toledo Symphony took the prize in 2011, bringing an astounding 1,500 hometown fans with it.

The project was on budget throughout and fully funded so that when we closed it down, total expenses were exactly balanced by revenues.

---

6 In 2014 Deborah Rutter, Michael Kaiser's successor as head of the Kennedy Center and formerly the president of the Chicago Symphony, teamed up with the Washington Performing Arts Society to create its own version of Spring for Music, SHIFT, declining to acquire the Spring for Music brand. I was happy to see them take up the goal of presenting the wide range of American orchestras and in the nation's capital. SHIFT debuted in 2017, with strong encouragement and major funding from the Mellon Foundation, and continued for a few years, eventually moving to an alternate-year pattern. Its future after the pandemic is uncertain.
7 Spring for Music internal marketing analysis.

We did succeed in making changes to enliven concert-opening protocols, and even the most conservative orchestras were pleased to experience the European entrance of their nattily dressed musicians before an audience laced with hometown fans, all waving their colored scarves enthusiastically and generating huge and energetic ovations before the music even started. Even so, the inherent resistance to altering the concert experience — both for the orchestras and for Carnegie Hall — proved frustrating. Seemingly simple matters, like concert dress and those opening protocols, baffled orchestras and produced endless discussions, as did securing understanding that streaming and broadcasting were part of the deal and not subject to further fees and negotiation (as had been specifically agreed to as a pre-condition for applying). Changing standard lighting or stage setups at Carnegie triggered exorbitant extra costs under its rigid work rules and traditions. Most discouraging was having to rebut claims for extra payments to stagehands for use of a click track in John Luther Adams' *Become Ocean* in order to coordinate the widely separated musician groupings on stage, and, because the concerts were deemed "broadcasts," for allowing live tweeting by designated journalists from the hall during the concerts.

Generating permanent change in this industry proved elusive. While we were successful in energizing calcified programming practices for the project itself, that impact proved short-lived as almost all orchestras reverted to prior staid habits as soon as Spring for Music was over. Change gets instilled permanently if its value is truly internalized by organizations. Trying to do so through external leverage, such as the powerful incentive of appearing at Carnegie Hall and our imposed requirements of program creativity, were not enough. It was perhaps naive to think that the project could force permanent change from the outside, and I certainly underestimated the length of time needed for the project to build a sufficient audience.

Regardless, it was a heady experiment professionally and personally. Spring for Music was the first time I had ever been involved in creating a project from scratch, building an organization around it and then carrying it off. Until then my entire career had been confined to serving and leading existing institutions. This was a new kind of experience, with a geographically diverse team without hierarchy or offices, built around pure competencies and a deeply held and clearly articulated common vision. It was nimble, efficient and effective. That itself was a crucial lesson. The spirited cohesion of our eight-member team was palpable, and we had enormous fun. Even today, we still merrily gather for an annual holiday dinner in New York, an event that has already lasted more than four times longer than the project itself did.

The experience gave me a totally new lens through which to view orchestras; I saw how they appear to their presenting partners from outside as a "buyer" rather than from inside as a "seller." I experienced first-hand how risk-averse and reluctant they are to take chances unless they see others taking those chances before them and succeeding. I found that those that benefited most were precisely the ones with clear vision and effective leadership. Those without stumbled badly, not knowing how to leverage the festival to the long-term advantage of their institutions.

Most important, I learned that making change requires persistence and energy over time — one-shot efforts, no matter how effective, get frittered away without constant follow-up. That is why Spring for Music could not succeed in providing systemic change in concert-going, either in New York or in the orchestras' hometowns. I learned a lot about institutions and the need for them to belong to and be nurtured by the communities in which they live — to be *of* them, not just *in* them.

Though sad Spring for Music could not continue, I had deep satisfaction giving it my all, learning what I could and, when the time came, moving on. I was committed to testing whether there was a way to encourage and unleash creativity, and to prove that there were audiences for adventurous repertoire not predicated on name-brand orchestras and artists. The fulfilling answers to both questions were a resounding "yes" and "yes." I then left it to others to carry on the work of baking change into the system. It was a fulfilling project, but one that finally got working with orchestras out of my system.

CHAPTER 10
THE POWER OF TWOS:
OJAI MUSIC FESTIVAL

The Ojai Music Festival was founded in 1947, and from the very start, programming concentrated on the new. Even so, the range of repertoire through its history has been extraordinarily broad: from Monteverdi's 1610 Vespers in 1955; to Stravinsky's *Les Noces* in 1956, conducted by the composer; and to Mark-Anthony Turnage's genre-busting *Blood on the Floor* in 2000. Ojai interprets "contemporary" as looking at all music from the standpoint of today. Nothing seems out of bounds. The festival takes place over one long weekend in early June — compact and concise. It has an unusual leadership structure; a multi-year artistic director who annually chooses a different chief curator, or music director as it is called, with whom to fashion each festival.

Ojai seemed to hover over my entire career even before it was first injected into my musical consciousness. I had not appreciated how central it was to become when Michael Tilson Thomas first told me about it as we both started working for the Boston Symphony. He had come to the attention of Ojai's longtime artistic director, Lawrence Morton, who appointed him as part of music-director troikas in 1968 and 1969, his first big breaks. Tilson Thomas was rhapsodic about the festival's musical idealism and the place's wondrous beauty. I was fascinated, but Ojai remained vague in my awareness until later, when Pierre Boulez rapturously sang its praises. Based on his unrelenting enthusiasm, I first visited in 1996, when he was music director for his sixth time. I returned in 2001, when Esa-Pekka Salonen was music director, and then again in 2003 for Boulez's seventh and final time leading it, more than any other in the festival's history.

Those first visits swept me under Ojai's magic spell. Located 80 miles northwest of Los Angeles in a gorgeous valley ringed with high mountains and smothered with the scent of its plentiful citrus trees, it had a spiritual aura, no doubt from the years philosopher-teacher Jiddu Krishnamurti lived and taught there.

In 1996, Boulez was joined by the Los Angeles Philharmonic, pianist Mitsuko Uchida and the Juilliard Quartet. The broad repertoire included a healthy dose of Stravinsky and Schoenberg, plus Elliott Carter and an entire evening devoted to Boulez himself. Mahler, Ravel and Schubert provided a counterbalance. It was serious stuff, and I was hooked.

The artistic director at the time was Ara Guzelimian, formerly a member of the Los Angeles Philharmonic staff but by then head of artistic operations for the Aspen Music Festival. In 1998, he was succeeded in Ojai by Ernest Fleischmann, the legendary executive director of the Philharmonic, who had just retired after a 29-year run. When I returned in 2001, Salonen led a festival concentrating on music from Latin America, again with the Philharmonic, of which he was music director. Featured were the Messiaen's *From the Canyons to the Stars* and Revueltas' *La Noche de los Mayas*, two rarely performed major works I had never heard.

Concerts took place in the Libbey Bowl, a 1,000-seat open-air facility beneath glorious sycamore trees, in the town's central Libbey Park. The 1957 structure could best be described as "run-down rustic" with its years of wear and tear vividly on display. The small stage had minimal backstage facilities and technical capabilities. A rotting wooden floor backstage was overlaid with discarded metal road signs to counteract the steady water rot from the small creek below — when walked on, it undulated like a slow-motion trampoline. The electric supply was insufficient to power sound and lights, requiring a supplemental generator, whose annoying noise in turn required acoustic isolation from the performing space. While the stage was somewhat covered by the Bowl's arched roof, natural acoustics were minimal and sound had to be amplified. The audience seats, gorgeously situated in the soft shade of those miraculous trees, consisted of splintery wooden benches, charming to look at but mercilessly rugged to sit on and poorly raked, making sightlines difficult.

Being outside with limited stage facilities, amplified sound and uncomfortable seats usually added up to a compromised musical experience. But despite these, the Ojai Festival's stellar musical reputation was impressive, as was its history of extraordinary luminaries gracing that stage — John Adams, Aaron Copland, Peter Maxwell Davies, Lukas Foss, Olivier Messiaen, Kent Nagano, Simon Rattle, Esa-Pekka Salonen, Ravi Shankar, Igor Stravinsky and Mitsuko Uchida, in addition to Tilson Thomas and Boulez.

And the festival had a robust and committed audience.

THE CALL

Out of the blue in 2001, I received a call from Guzelimian, asking whether I might be interested in becoming Ojai's artistic director to succeed Fleischmann. Unaware that I had already decided to leave Cleveland in 2004, Guzelimian thought it doable to lead Ojai concurrently with running the orchestra, as he had done years earlier working full-time at Aspen while occupying the post. I remained mum about my Cleveland decision but was privately captivated by the possibility.

But there was a problem — I had not heard officially that Fleischmann was leaving. Guzelimian explained the board had made the decision for a change but was still in the process of working out details with him. The inquiry felt awkward because Fleischmann was a close friend. I responded that I could not seriously entertain the idea until that situation was resolved and announced. As I was to be on the West Coast a few weeks later on other business, I did agree, at Guzelimian's urging, to a confidential meeting with three members of the Ojai board, but only on the condition that the potential job opening not be discussed.

I found them unfocused about where they wanted to take the festival and unclear about what leadership was required. It seemed that serious strategic work was needed before the board could start a search. They agreed and expressed the need for outside help. As I was already drifting back into this work, they hired me as the consultant. The engagement was predicated on not discussing the artistic director job until there was an official opening and the consulting assignment was completed. I figured this was a no-risk win-win, providing me with a clear sense of the board and its commitment to the future, and giving them a chance to know me.

Over the next year, I led three encouraging board retreats, finding the group eager to do the hard work of charting the festival's future. At the same time, the details of Fleischmann's retirement were completed, to take place after the 2003 festival. It was not an easy decision for him — and there was an unintended consequence. He was furious on learning I had been hired as a consultant without the board or me informing him in advance and before details of his departure were finalized. He conflated the two decisions, blaming me for engineering his departure, irreparably damaging our relationship. Nothing I could do or say would assuage his anger before he died in 2010. It was a sad and unnecessary end to a friendship I had cherished.

With the consulting completed and the artistic director opening announced, the board offered me the position, which I happily accepted, to take effect with the 2004 festival. They were comfortable with my doing the job concurrently with the Cleveland position, not yet knowing I would be leaving just prior to that first festival. For me, the timing could not have been better. And because the job was not full-time, I could continue living in Cleveland and have plenty of time to pursue other ventures.

The new role appealed to me greatly, offering a definitive shift from the executive to the artistic side. I loved the idea of hiring a different musical partner every year with whom to fashion a festival, a dynamic model that ensured variety and vitality across seasons. I loved the concentrated context of one long weekend in which everything mattered. I loved the commitment to cutting-edge music. I loved the festival's venerability. And I loved the setting — Ojai is one of the most sublimely beautiful places in the world. The scale was totally different from what I had been accustomed to, with a budget of only $1 million as opposed to $35 million in Cleveland. I was impressed with the stature of artists attracted and what was able to be produced for so little, clearly because they loved to perform there. This was an artistic gig, not one for money.

The job of artistic director involved three responsibilities: first, to engage a music director annually; second, to conceive a festival with each that reflects their artistic personality; and third, to build programs consistent with the overall aesthetics and heritage of the festival. It seemed irresistible — a job I was destined for. Yet there were aspects that scared me to death. In Boston and Cleveland, I had always been deeply engaged in artistic planning, but my role had been, by necessity, of a stealth nature, behind the public shield of the music director. In Ojai, I would be the visible and accountable artistic leader, a switch from an interior to an exterior role that I was not used to, and one to which I would need some time to adjust.

With orchestras, all concerts include that ensemble as a given artistic element. While orchestral repertoire was one of the possibilities in Ojai, so were chamber music, contemporary music, solo music, world music, jazz, opera, music theater, and multimedia productions. I had familiarity with and interest in some of those, but no real experience. Furthermore, with an orchestra, given the immovable realities of a schedule defined in minute detail by a labor agreement, much of the planning work amounts to filling the weekly and annual grids of concerts and rehearsals with artists and programs. Ojai's schedule was defined not by agreements but evolved through practice. When I started, the festival consisted of five concerts, with performances on Friday evening, Saturday morning (a "family concert"), Saturday evening, Sunday morning and late Sunday afternoon, allowing Los Angeles ticket buyers, who constituted over half the audience, to return home before dark. As I soon learned, only habit prohibited changing the pattern.

Everything about the job was broader, more flexible and fundamentally organic —each planning cycle starting with a totally blank page. By contrast, my past work was much more prescribed — working with one kind of music, in a rigidly defined schedule, with a concert season that lasted throughout the year, having responsibility for an entire organization, working in a place I was living, and at a scale of operation huge and complicated. I was privately worried — was I up to the Ojai opportunity?

GETTING STARTED

Given the demand for artists and ensembles and as with orchestras, key commitments were necessary at least three years in advance. Fleischmann had already selected Kent Nagano to lead 2004, an appointment I welcomed. He and I had happily worked together in Boston. He had a long Ojai history, having already served in the role three times. Among his several posts, he was then music director of the Los Angeles Opera and well-known in southern California. As I pondered how to approach planning with him, I understood the defining importance of the music director appointment not only in shaping the programming but in establishing the basic artistic premise on which to construct a festival.

The necessary lead-time gave sudden urgency to appointing music directors and beginning the planning for 2005 and 2006, decisions I would have to make two years before producing my first festival. Ojai's history of such appointments consisted primarily of conductors or composer-conductors, a vast majority with strong ties to southern California. As the first artistic director not from that area, I arrived with a wide geographic circle of artist friends and acquaintances, a perspective I immediately called upon in making these first appointments.

I made an obvious choice for 2005 by inviting Oliver Knussen. Seeing the need to broaden a repertoire I found heavily Eurocentric, for 2006 I reached for a younger American voice — Robert Spano, then-music director of the Atlanta Symphony. While both continued in the conductor or composer-conductor tradition, they were decidedly without southern California roots. Spano would come with his own Atlanta Symphony and Chorus, further breaking what had become an over-reliance on Los Angeles ensembles. To me, Ojai was not a regional, but a national and international festival, and that needed to be reflected in the choice of artists.

With the leadership settled through 2006, I concentrated on programming 2004 with Nagano and immediately felt my lack of experience, as well as the yawning lack of pre-existing schedule or performer parameters I had been used to. While we scheduled some unusual works — Carl Orff's rare opera *Die Kluge* and a commissioned work by Unsuk Chin — the festival, with hindsight, looked neither adventurous nor cohesive, but rather a collection of unrelated concerts. The one innovation I did institute was gingerly breaking the Friday-through-Sunday pattern by adding a "pre-festival concert" on Thursday evening, a change that by 2009 evolved into the official opening event of a four-day festival.

My initial tentativeness was repeated with Knussen in planning 2005, a festival further marred by his cancellation due to ill health a month before opening, necessitating last-minute changes and substitutions. I was still grounded in my orchestral roots of filling predetermined slots, and yet to understand the need to construct narrative coherence across not just individual programs but through the weekend as a whole. Still not having produced my first festival when planning these two, I did not have the benefit of incorporating what I learned from actual results. There is no substitute for experiencing what might look compelling on paper but ends up very different when put in front of an audience. It all made for a difficult and unsettled start.

Looking back, I am not proud of either of those first two seasons, but at least they started to give me feedback as to what worked and what didn't. I began to feel more confident as I started planning 2006 with Spano. We featured music by Osvaldo Golijov, an important new voice from Argentina about whom I was very enthusiastic. A highlight was his recently premiered opera *Ainadamar*. Eight months before the festival, I attended a performance of his riveting song cycle *Ayre* with the soprano Dawn Upshaw and the emerging contemporary-music sextet Eighth Blackbird. I was so enthusiastic that I added it at the last minute since Upshaw was already scheduled to sing in *Ainadamar*. Spano invited jazz singer and composer Luciana Souza for the solo role in Golijov's cantata *Oceana* and a concert of Brazilian folk songs with guitar. For the "pre-festival" Thursday night, we devised a surreal program of Conlon Nancarrow's Studies for Player Piano, a particular favorite of mine. The works were realized on a performer-less piano onto which was clamped a laptop rigged by a "contraption" designed and built by the unique sound artist-composer and close friend of Nancarrow, Trimpin. To start the concert, Spano performed John Cage's spoken *Lecture on Nothing*, a weird theater piece in which the text gradually reduces itself to literally nothing — the delivery slows, finally stopping completely for a good five minutes.

I felt pleased with this festival's cohesiveness and adventurousness. It seriously stretched traditions with the concentration on Golijov, the broader range of genres and the interlacing of artists across multiple concerts, resulting in a festival that introduced a world of non-European music to Ojai and drew new ticket-buyers. And it created controversy — the extended silences of the Cage made some members of the audience nervously uncomfortable, triggering several yells of "Enough!" While a huge hit with the public and bringing record ticket sales, that year's program generated backlash from the festival's die-hard Boulez-Stravinsky partisans, who had trouble with composers like Golijov, Nancarrow and Cage, as well as with Brazilian music. I considered the furor a positive sign and was energized to experiment more.

For 2007, I selected pianist Pierre-Laurent Aimard as music director, and for 2008, conductor David Robertson, both appointed before the exhilaration of the 2006 festival. While Robertson reverted to the conductor-as-music-director tradition, Aimard was a total departure — the first pianist as sole director in the festival's history.[1] I had worked with him frequently in Cleveland and deeply admired his forward-looking musical instincts. I initiated free bonus events in venues other than the Libbey Bowl to provide greater texture and connectivity across the festival. Featured were the Saint Paul Chamber Orchestra, with whom Aimard had an ongoing relationship, and the legendary percussion ensemble Nexus, whose members I had known at the Eastman School during my student days in Rochester. They asked me to join them in the performance of Stravinsky's *Les Noces*. What a thrill to play this masterpiece with those old friends on the very stage on which Stravinsky had conducted the piece in 1956.

INTERLUDE: LIGETI'S METRONOMES

In 2007, we presented Ligeti's notorious *Poème symphonique*, a work for 100 metronomes. All of the devices are set off at the beginning and keep ticking until their mechanisms wind down and then stop. The initial sound, like the cacophony of 100 woodpeckers, gradually thins out, in the process spawning unexpected, random cross-rhythms. We set up the 100 metronomes surrounding the Libbey Bowl audience. We had learned that winding six half-turns generally led each to last about 17 minutes, give or take five. The piece came at the end of an evening program, so it was dark. To maintain surprise, the metronomes were covered from view by black cloths until the start, when they were ceremoniously unveiled. The sound of all 100 chattering was remarkable, initially causing giggles, a reaction that gradually calmed down. By the five-minute mark, delight gave way to perplexity, then to annoyance with the unchanging racket. By the eight-minute mark, annoyance gave way to outright hostility. None of the metronomes had yet stopped. Around the 10-minute mark, several individuals shouted out in anger. A few stormed the metronome tables to stop the noise. At 12 minutes, some metronomes started to peter out, and the sound changed and thinned, with cross-rhythms materializing out of the din. As if by magic, everyone realized what was happening and shifted into rapt silence. That concentrated attention held until the last one finished, about five long minutes later. At the end, the truly engaged audience rose in cheers.

In 2008, Robertson conducted a live orchestral soundtrack to a projection of Charlie Chaplin's silent film *Modern Times*, with the score

---

1 Pianist Emanuel Ax had shared the music director position with conductor Daniel Harding in 1997, and pianist Uchida had done the same with conductor David Zinman in 1998.

by Chaplin himself. The music of Steve Reich was featured, including his 1971 percussion masterpiece *Drumming*, with Reich himself, the emerging ensemble Sō Percussion and again Nexus, some of whom were among the original players for whom Reich wrote the piece. With all those percussionists in residence, Robertson conducted Varèse's iconic *Ionisation* for 13 players, asking me to join in.

Over these first five festivals, I found myself pushing into new musical styles, new composers and new patterns of concert structure. Given the explosion of creative talent available and my own expanding familiarity with the new, I was already opening the festival to unfamiliar artists, repertoire and energy. I resolved to avoid repeating music directors, as had been the festival's practice, and to apply my best thinking to future choices — both the who and the sequence. To be honest, my music director selections were not the result of intentional multi-year design but occurred organically as I followed my instincts and curiosity about composers and performers who intrigued me.

I was learning how to conceive of each festival as an artistic entity, with intense attention to relationships within programs and the sequence of individual events from beginning to end. Given how audiences interacted with the festival, this was essential. Ojai was remote — an hour-and-a-half's drive from Los Angeles. With 75 percent of ticket sales from outside the town, audiences stayed there once they made the trip, making it efficient for them to experience multiple events. The essence of the audience transaction was thus not with individual concerts or artists but rather with the festival as a whole — buying the *idea* of Ojai in a manner not dissimilar to what I had found with the Boston Pops years earlier.

The different music directors each year and the resulting variety of musical focus across festivals mandated marketing the festival's overarching idea: standing for adventure, surprise and the unexpected. Audiences were promised to hear each year music that they didn't know, some of which they might like and some they might not — giving them overt license *not* to like certain things. Inherent in the transaction, however, was trying everything. The result was an engaged audience that was not shy about telling us, the artists and everyone else what they thought; that dialogue became a vital part of the overall festival experience. Over the years, all artists commented positively on the audience's attentiveness, calling it the best in the world.

This built trust. When tickets were put on sale at each festival for the next one, audiences were told only the sketchiest details about programs and artists, and nothing about the schedule. Still, almost 50 percent of the tickets were sold before the final details of the full festival were announced six months later, absolute validation of audiences' total embrace of the idea of Ojai.

At the same time, there were challenges beyond the music. I was still adjusting to working on a smaller scale. The board was small, consisting mostly of town residents, a constituency that had historically founded, nurtured and supported the festival. I was beginning to struggle with whether this was sufficient for the future and if a larger, regional or even national board was required.

The professional staff was minimal when I arrived, and its first executive director from outside Ojai, Jeff Haydon, had just been hired. The seasonal staff was mostly local, with many functions handled by volunteers. Over these initial years, I built a professional production team to cope with the increasingly dense and complex schedule and to ratchet up the sophistication of concert production. I was fixated on not just "putting on" concerts but "producing" them — paying attention to the look of the stage, the lighting, and the sound and to minimizing the distractions of stage changes.

Haydon and I needed to build trust in the institution by not only producing exciting festivals but keeping the finances in balance. Fleischmann had left the organization with a considerable deficit, primarily by excessive spending for his final festival. Since I was experienced at finance going back to my early years in Boston, I had no problem mastering planning within the context of approved budgets, a process that involved allocating the ever-declining balances of uncommitted funds among potential projects. Balanced budgets achieved through 2006 gave the board such confidence that it conducted a special fund-raising campaign to erase the inherited deficit so that by 2007, the institution was out of debt and its balance sheet clean.

LIBBEY BOWL

The consuming focus that materialized in 2007 was the ever-deteriorating condition of the 50-year-old Libbey Bowl. Over the years, wood rot and termites had caused so much damage that when the city engineer inspected the building, he easily pushed an eight-inch screwdriver almost its full length into the base of the main wooden arch supporting the roof — not a good sign. For the safety of performers and audiences, to say nothing of the future of the festival, a total rebuilding was in order. It seemed unlikely that the city of Ojai, which owned the Bowl, would initiate and finance the reconstruction alone, so the festival — its most visible user, even though occupying it only 10 days a year — raised $1 million from major donors, asking the city to match it. The offer triggered urgency and the city agreed. The festival and city would then jointly solicit any remaining funding needs from the broader community.

A local architect was hired to create a design for the new structure, with a mandate that it be slightly larger, with more adequate backstage facilities and better power and lighting capability. The audience area was to have improved sightlines and more comfortable seating than the old, splinter-rich wooden benches. The goal was a building that would not make an architectural statement in itself, consistent with the town's self-effacing vibe. The dominant impression needed to be made by what was on the stage.

The existing bowl would be demolished after the 2010 festival and the new facility opened for the 2011 festival, a tight timetable that Ojai's year-round good weather made feasible. For the estimated costs of $4.3 million, the festival, together with the city, raised the additional $2.3 million needed. The community rallied around the project, and a third of the city's 3,000 households contributed. As I remained concentrated on artistic planning, this amazing fundraising achievement was due primarily to the extraordinary efforts of Haydon and the festival's board chair at the time, Esther Wachtell. Demolition and construction took place on schedule and on budget.

BREAKTHROUGH

A pivotal moment occurred at the closing party after the final concert in 2006. Flush with excitement over the just-concluded festival and feeling the adrenalin rush of its energy, I took a brave step in inviting Eighth Blackbird, who had performed Golijov's *Ayre* so brilliantly, to be music director for the next open season in 2009. The group had become one of the most dynamic purveyors of contemporary music, playing from memory to enliven performances by allowing freedom for movement and drama. This totally broke with tradition and en-

Ojai's "new" Libbey Bowl

abled a festival truly different in repertoire, format and energy from anything before. Eighth Blackbird invited 30 young musicians to join them, mixed and matched across repertoire, making the whole event feel like a four-day jam session of friends. We commissioned a major theater piece from the composer and electric-guitar virtuoso Steven Mackey. Most of the repertoire was by young American composers never heard there before, along with serious doses of George Crumb, Reich and Ives, topped off with two golden oldies, Schoenberg's *Pierrot Lunaire* performed by Eighth Blackbird and Bach's *Goldberg Variations* performed by then-emerging pianist Jeremy Denk in his Ojai debut.

The most striking departure was the final Sunday concert, a four-hour marathon of 20 pieces by 14 mostly living composers, performed without break by various permutations of performers. It ended with Louis Andriessen's *Workers Union*, an extraordinary piece for "any loud-sounding group of instruments," written with no key or defined melodies, only guidelines for lowered or raised pitches, but all with very precise, driving rhythms. What results are waves of ascending or descending sounds in unison rhythmic patterns over the work's 20-minute span. The six Eighth Blackbird players started the piece, joined one-by-one by all the remaining players-in-residence, building to a truly raucous ending that even I joined on glockenspiel. It was rock-and-roll, bringing down the house to lusty cheers.

THE POWER OF TWOS: OJAI MUSIC FESTIVAL

That festival again created heated controversy among the old guard, who still pined for all-Boulez concerts. I was summoned to lunch by two board members, who unsubtly told me I had gone too far. They feared patrons would flee in the future, despite the new and younger audience that had turned out. I reassured them that each year would be different to reflect the differing profiles of the various music directors, and that range was widening. As such, the next years might be more to their liking, for I had already engaged composer-conductor George Benjamin for 2010, a festival that would by design be more Eurocentric, and the well-known soprano Dawn Upshaw for 2011. Change is difficult, even in Ojai.

But the experience with Eighth Blackbird was totally freeing, and it reconfirmed my instinct to let my imagination run wild, leading to an even wider range of music director appointments and further broadening of events. I selected pianist Leif Ove Andsnes for 2012, choreographer Mark Morris for 2013 and, based on his success in 2009, pianist Jeremy Denk for 2014. I was now far away from the tradition of conductors or composer-conductors as music directors.

Festivals showed increasing adventure as I constantly experimented with the schedule, the programs and the production, incorporating lessons from each festival and unashamedly trying out new ideas, stimulated by the ever-changing music directors. I reveled in the creative back-and-forth with each one, hardly able to contain my boundless enthusiasm for the new and unusual. Those discussions always opened surprising paths to other artists and music, all of which I gleefully pursued so that the process became an organic network of unexpected discoveries, all ultimately linked with an underlying web of connections. This was the same period I was immersed in Spring for Music, so between that and Ojai, I was having tremendous fun creatively.

With George Benjamin, 2009 reverted to what had been traditional Ojai fare — Stravinsky, Schoenberg, Boulez, Ligeti and Messiaen, Benjamin's beloved teacher. This was a natural reflection of his musical world, but these were framed with other dimensions of his eclectic tastes, which were not so well-known. We featured a concert of music by Frank Zappa, who, in addition to being a serious rock musician, was a composer of considerable note and a friend of none other than Boulez. Not only was Benjamin fond of Zappa, but Frankfurt's Ensemble Modern, in residence for the festival, had made a specialty of his music. Benjamin was fascinated with Indian music, so we included three mini-concerts of ragas. Another secret passion of his was improvising piano accompaniments to silent movies, so I prevailed on him to do so one night at the town movie theater. His spontaneous take on Carl T. Dreyer's classic *Vampyr* was an amazing amalgamation of Debussy, Messiaen and Benjamin himself.

This was the year of a major innovation. To reach audiences beyond the Bowl and place Ojai on a national stage, we began live-streaming concerts, starting modestly with just a single camera feed. The transmissions evolved technologically over the years and to this day remain a regular part of what the festival does.

In 2011, Dawn Upshaw became the first sole female music director in Ojai history.[2] On the weekend prior to the festival, we presented a gala concert celebrating the opening of the new Libbey Bowl. Upshaw sang the Shaker song "Simple Gifts" *a cappella* as a touching invocation for the new facility, and then repeated her 2006 performance of Golijov's *Ayre*. For the festival itself, the big event was Peter Sellars' staging of George Crumb's *The Winds of Destiny*, a cycle of American Civil War songs as realized for soprano, four percussionists and amplified piano. The production took advantage of the expanded technical capabilities of the new facility.

Ojai seemed a natural for artists with multiple talents, all of which could be displayed over the festival's span, thereby providing audiences with a picture of artistry in totality. To showcase Upshaw's career as a teacher, we produced a recital with six of her vocal students from Bard College, staged as an informal musicale with the singers performing solos and duets. One young soprano, Julia Bullock, was to make a momentous return in 2016 and has now become a major star.

With Leif Ove Andsnes in 2012, I initiated the immersion concept — instead of six major events with a few extras, the festival expanded to more than 20, still within the four-day period, with added late-night and early-morning concerts, community events, special performances for donors, film screenings and expanded symposia. It made the festival a continuous tapestry of activities that used the whole

---

2 Conductor Diane Wittry was co-music director with Peter Maxwell Davies and Nicholas McGegan in 1988, and Mitsuko Uchida was co-music director with David Zinman in 1998.

town as its stage, becoming truly *of* and not just *in* Ojai. The concept grew organically from participating artists wanting to perform more with each other. Critical was making sure no concerts overlapped so that the most committed patrons could attend everything from morning to late night, as many did. The one later experiment with overlap in 2013 created howls of protest from the regulars, so we never did it again — Ojai audiences don't want to miss a thing.

This 2012 festival introduced audiences to the music of John Luther Adams. I had become entranced with his unique spatial works honed by his living in the vast natural vistas of Alaska. Adding significantly to the festival's broadening sense of community, his *Inuksuit* was given a free performance in Libbey Park. Forty-eight percussionists and wind players, starting in the center, gradually fanned out as the work progressed through its 80-minute span, reaching the outer perimeters before slowly closing back into the center for the quiet conclusion, with piccolo players sitting in trees (of their own volition) and playing quiet birdlike patterns, creating a surreal marriage of nature and music. The audience was free to wander informally among the musicians, forging an intense conjoint experience of audience, performer and space.

Strange and Sacred Noise *on a hilltop with John Luther Adams in foreground.*

INTERLUDE: CLOWN NOSES

The two-piano concert with Leif Ove Andsnes and Marc-André Hamelin that closed the 2012 Festival featured Stravinsky's four-hand piano version of *The Rite of Spring*. Andsnes and Hamelin played it on separate instruments, so they could add musical lines and harmonies that Stravinsky omitted in his arrangement. Their performance triggered an encore, Stravinsky's uproarious *Circus Polka*. Backstage, before the concert, I impishly handed both pianists lime-green foam-rubber clown noses, suggesting not too subtly that, if they felt so moved, donning them for *Circus Polka* would be a *coup de théâtre*. Both chuckled, saying nice idea but probably not. But in the heat of the ovation for *The Rite*, Andsnes suddenly reached into his pocket and pulled out the nose, moving Hamelin to do the same. They theatrically put them on, sat down and played *Circus Polka*, leaving everyone with a picture-perfect ending to the festival, two great pianists at the height of their powers wearing round green schnozzles.

What attracted me to Mark Morris for 2013 was not his choreography but his musical passion and knowledge. His tastes are deep and broad, with particular affection for American maverick composers such as John Cage, Henry Cowell and Lou Harrison, all of whose music had been scandalously scarce in Ojai. While some dance was inevitable, we agreed to limit it to just one evening, as his role was specifically as musical curator. Since he no longer danced with the company, creating a festival without his performing was an intriguing challenge, although he did conduct one piece. It turned out not to be a problem; his artistic presence was forcefully apparent through the imagination of his ideas, the kinetic energy he created and his outsized personality.

Having unleashed the immersion concept a year earlier, I found it hard to contain as the number of events expanded to over 30, with free morning exercise classes in Libbey Park led by some of the dancers, two unannounced march-through appearances in the park by the Nordhoff High School Marching Band (which I termed "random acts of marching band") and an evening of social dancing for patrons led by Morris and his dancers. A touching highlight was a presentation of "Dance for PD®," Morris' national program to help people with Parkinson's disease benefit from the insights and techniques used by dancers to increase coordination, balance, flexibility and strength through music. One of my favorite events featured Cage's music for toy piano, performed by six-foot pianist Yegor Shevtsov looming over the miniature instrument in the Libbey Park playground. We experimented with dividing evening concerts into two parts, each programmed independently with expanded breaks rather than intermissions, thereby creating more and shorter events. The festival merged challenging new music unfamiliar to Ojai with Morris' whimsy, curiosity and theatricality, all of which was made widely available with expanded multi-camera live-streaming.

At my first creative meeting with Jeremy Denk to plan 2014, he admitted a secret dream to write an opera libretto based on Charles Rosen's seminal musical treatise, *The Classical Style*. He felt that the harmonic drama inherent in tonal classical music was ripe with stage drama. He envisioned a mini-opera with a cast consisting of Rosen himself; the three basic chords in tonal music, the Tonic, the Dominant and the Subdominant; Haydn, Mozart and Beethoven; various characters from Mozart's *Don Giovanni*; a musicologist; and a chorus of skeptical conservatory students.

That was all I needed; I immediately agreed to commission it. A little stunned but happy with my reaction, he later confessed to freaking out, knowing he was now committed to turning what had been merely a fantasy into reality. I introduced him to Steven Stucky, a composer with wide-ranging musical knowledge and with a puckish sense of humor, to whom I knew Denk would respond. Initially resistant,

citing numerous commissions, Stucky became more and more attracted to the idea with each discussion, finally relenting with unabashed
enthusiasm. Denk's libretto was brilliant — erudite, funny and touching — and Stucky responded with a winning score combining period
pastiche and contemporary flavor. It was interlaced with musical quotations, some obvious, many hidden — the ultimate musical insider's
parlor game. The staged work, entitled *The Classical Style: An Opera (of
Sorts)*, formed the centerpiece of the festival.

Surrounding it were Ligeti's complete Études for piano, a
20th-century classic and Denk specialty; a wacky evening of Mahler
realized by the jazz pianist and composer Uri Caine; Weill's *Seven Deadly Sins* with the amazing Storm Large re-creating a role from Spring for
Music a year earlier; and a concert of American hymns sung in-the-
round at Ojai's mystical Meditation Mount at sunup.

Over those years, the dramatic expansion of events, the addition of new performance venues, the creation of special projects and
the constant need for more sophisticated production all had budgetary consequences. Despite these pressures, I was able to keep annual
increases in artistic costs to barely above inflation thanks to two strategies. First, most presenters engage artists for individual performances of previously prepared touring programs or specific repertoire. In
Ojai, I was against presenting programs available elsewhere, wanting
unique events and repertoire that could be heard first only there — an
idealistic but expensive principle that required everything be specifically created and prepared just for the festival. Therefore, artist agreements had to be based not on numbers of performances but periods
of time that included multiple performances plus necessary rehearsals.
Adding additional events within those periods was easy, with little or
no additional cost in either fees or housing expense.

Second, special staged projects, such as *The Classical Style*, are
expensive because they require longer rehearsal time and more elaborate production. As I added more such events, starting with Peter
Sellars' *The Winds of Destiny*, I turned to co-production partnerships,
in which each partner, in addition to paying its own performance
costs, shares the costs incurred for the creation of the production itself
— commissioning fees for the composer and librettist, artist fees and
housing for the rehearsal period. In the case of engaging an artist from
abroad, partners also share the costs of travel to the U.S. and back.

Without such collaborations, all of those costs reside with the initiating promoter, making projects unaffordable.

In 2011, I initiated an ongoing co-production partnership with Cal Performances in Berkeley, one of the preeminent classical presenters in the country. An old friend, Matias Tarnopolsky, had just taken over there and was looking for new projects. Together we concocted Ojai North, with four or five programs repeated in Berkeley immediately after Ojai. Sharing preparation, commissioning and major travel costs not only allowed us to do more without increased artistic expense but exported our brand of programming geographically. Tarnopolsky is inherently creative, so the partnership gave me someone with whom to bounce around ideas. It was he who initially suggested Mark Morris as a compelling music director. The partnership would last until 2018, when he left Berkeley to become president of The Philadelphia Orchestra.

I created additional co-production deals around certain individual projects, such as *The Classical Style*, which ultimately became a three-way co-commission and co-production with Carnegie Hall alongside Ojai and Berkeley. That made the project financially feasible and kept us in the driver's seat with the premiere.

REACHING A CRESCENDO

I was loving this job. The adventure of working with various music directors was enthralling, the breadth of programming was truly reflective of everything I believed, and full and enthusiastic audiences validated my commitment to leading taste. The continual urge to push myself and the festival further did not abate. I was now increasingly afar from the musical world of my past experiences. With the 75th anniversary looming in 2021, I felt the festival community deserved a longer horizon on the selection and announcement of music directors, providing a deeper sense of forward direction across seasons. The performance industry's anachronistic practice of keeping future plans secret from its supporters until tickets go on sale always puzzled me. Why not provide a greater window into future planning to keep audiences engaged? This seemed particularly crucial for Ojai since, unlike orchestras, which have the reassuring continuity of musicians and a music director over multiple years, each festival was distinctive, with totally different artists, repertoire and concept.

Having already invited percussionist-conductor Steven Schick for 2015 and opera director Peter Sellars for 2016, and wanting to complete the selection through the upcoming anniversary, I invited pianist-composer Vijay Iyer for 2017, conductor Esa-Pekka Salonen for 2018, soprano-conductor Barbara Hannigan for 2019, violinist Patricia Kopatchinskaja for 2020 and pianist Mitsuko Uchida for 2021. These appointments were all announced as a group to create momentum and continuity through the anniversary celebration. When Salonen canceled because of schedule complications, I moved Kopatchinskaja two years earlier to 2018 and appointed composer-conductor Matthias Pintscher for 2020. It was a distinguished and diverse group.

Steve Schick is a conductor, teacher and performance artist. It is his very multiplicity of talents that attracted me, and we went wild for 2015, expanding the immersion concept to what turned out to be unreasonable lengths. We added a special pre-festival event on Wednesday night, a multi-media presentation created by the Chicago Symphony's "Beyond the Score" series to celebrate Boulez's imminent 90th birthday. It seemed appropriate given our long friendship and his 50-year association with Ojai, and Schick was happy to feature his music.

Along with remarkable displays of percussion virtuosity, Schick conducted and performed as actor and speaker in Kurt Schwitters' unique (not to say bizarre) sound poem *Ursonate*. Morton Feldman's *For Philip Guston*, a hypnotic work for piano, percussion and flute that lasts four-and-a-half hours, was played starting at 5 a.m. in the intimate Ojai Art Center. In all, works by 45 composers, a majority of them living, were presented. The indefatigable Schick was so omnipresent that *The New Yorker*'s Alex Ross called him "one of the supreme living virtuosos, not only of percussion but of any instrument."[3]

Given the intensity of the festival experience, I learned the serious lesson that adding a fifth day, Wednesday, plus an even richer panoply of extra events led to a schedule too overwhelming for even the most hard-core fans. From then on, we kept it to four days and thinned out the schedule to fewer than 30 events.

I had known Peter Sellars since he was a student at Harvard in the 1970s and just starting his career. We had talked for years about

---

3 Ross, Alex, "Outsiders," *The New Yorker*, July 6, 2015.

working together in Ojai. In 2016, he returned for the third time but his first as music director.[4] We created a complicated and diverse program that included three staged productions — Kaija Saariaho's *La Passion de Simone* with Julia Bullock; a portrait of the singer Josephine Baker, composed by Tyshawn Sorey, again with Bullock; and Claude Vivier's rare *Kopernikus*. The festival was rounded out with evenings of Indian music and Egyptian popular music, as well as a free concert with the Youth Orchestra of Los Angeles. As with Mark Morris, Sellars did not perform on stage but was ever present, reflecting on music and current social issues in talks and concert introductions. Though not consciously planned, all the music in the festival, with two exceptions, was composed by women, a fact that we deliberately did not trumpet but left to the critics and audiences to discover.

The most visible change was moving the final Sunday evening event to the neighboring town of Santa Paula, where we produced a free street party with all the artists plus two Mexican bands of community workers and musicians from Los Angeles. The town, just 20 minutes away, is a center of citrus farming and the exact opposite in demographics of Ojai's upscale and predominantly white profile. The original idea was having the event in Ojai, a plan foiled by municipal red tape, so we went to Santa Paula, which enthusiastically embraced it and helped it happen effortlessly. The event engendered surprising controversy on our board, several members feeling strongly that the festival belonged in Ojai. I disagreed, advocating the need to reach out occasionally with events in neighboring communities. As it turned out, with this festival's strong emphasis on community, diversity and social issues, Santa Paula was the perfect place for the closing event. The experience was a sobering reality check on how cloistered within Ojai the festival had become with some supporters.

What initially led me to Vijay Iyer for 2017 was the breadth and depth of his musical gifts and the tempting prospect that he could provide a transformational broadening of the Ojai experience. I was fascinated with him as an artist and a human being, and I knew he would bring something totally new to the festival, deeply challenging its and my conventions. Multi-talented as pianist, improviser, composer, thinker, writer, collaborator and teacher, Iyer is often referred to as

4 He appeared in 1992, directing Stravinsky's *L'Histoire du soldat* conducted by Boulez, and in 2011, directing Crumb's *The Winds of Destiny* with Upshaw.

a "jazz pianist," a description he firmly disavows as misleading and confining. I learned that it is not what he does that really defines him, but rather who he is and what he stands for. He has been called a "social conscience, multimedia collaborator, system builder, rhapsodist, historical thinker and multicultural gateway."[5] Deeply committed to the idea of art as community, he is a leader in reimagining the role of the musician in the 21st century. He is held in high regard, as witness a MacArthur Fellowship in 2013 and a faculty appointment to the Harvard music department in 2014.

My world had been "classical music," and while I dabbled from time to time in world music and jazz, I entered a different galaxy with Iyer. I had to struggle to keep up, as I was totally unfamiliar with his musical constellation. After each meeting, I frantically researched the artists and composers he suggested, searching out recordings; it was a crash course in worlds totally foreign to me. His own performances were unlike anything I was familiar with, their sounds and shapes so different from the stereotype of traditional four-to-the-bar jazz. Here was music with a high degree of improvisation, paralleled in the harmonic complexity, organic shape and metrical intricacies of his piano-playing. What at first sounded formless and unstructured began, with greater familiarization, to speak deeply to me.

Even with this completely different kind of music director, one committed to musical styles and composers never before heard there, we designed a festival consistent with the fundamental traditions of Ojai. Our goal was to showcase Iyer's multiple dimensions as performer, composer, thinker and advocate, wanting the festival to embody these ideals in the musical, ethnic, racial and generational diversity of artists and music presented. The festival's breadth, never restricted historically to "contemporary" or "classical" music, gave us license to experiment broadly.

What was ultimately meaningful was not just the new world of music presented but placing that music in a historical and social context, a far broader framework than had happened in Ojai before. At this festival's intellectual core was the Association for the Advancement of Creative Musicians (AACM), the organization founded in Chicago in 1965 by a progressive group of African-American performers and still active today. This represented an important chapter of American

5 Pareles, Jon, "Conscience of a Composer," *The New York Times*, December 19, 2014.

musical history that, embarrassingly, I had not even been aware of. At its 50th anniversary, in 2015, *The New York Times* said, "The AACM has been one of this country's great engines of experimental art, producing work with an irreducible breadth of scope and style."[6]

The festival's centerpiece was the West Coast premiere of *Afterword*, an opera by composer and trombonist George Lewis, a work based on the AACM's history, with texts drawn from quotations by early members. Lewis had written the definitive history of the organization, *A Power Stronger Than Itself: The AACM and American Experimental Music*.[7] On Sunday morning was that otherworldly concert by Muhal Richard Abrams, Roscoe Mitchell and George Lewis — the very embodiment of AACM — that became the indelible musical event of my life.

The 2017 Concert: George Lewis, Roscoe Mitchell and Muhal Richard Abrams

We presented several of Iyer's compositions, including the premiere of a violin concerto, jointly commissioned with Cal Performances and Tanglewood, and *Radhe Radhe*, a multimedia project he

---

6 Chinen, Nate, "50 Years On, Association for Advancement of Creative Musicians Influences Jazz," *The New York Times*, March 6, 2015.
7 Lewis, George, *A Power Stronger Than Itself: The AACM and American Experimental Music*, The University of Chicago Press, 2008.

conceived with filmmaker Prashant Bhargava for a 2013 centennial celebration of Stravinsky's *Rite of Spring*. Iyer composed his score to accompany a 35-minute Bhargava film of the festival of Holi, India's joyous, chaotic and colorful celebration of spring. His concept was to reconsider the aspects of ritual and transformation represented by both Holi and *The Rite*.

As improviser, Iyer performed with his trio and sextet, and in a historic coming-together with master tabla player Zakir Hussain, vocalist Aruna Sairam (who had captivated Ojai audiences in 2016), and saxophonist Rudresh Mahanthappa, four great artists making music together for the first time. Sorey, whose *Josephine Baker: A Portrait* had enthralled Ojai in 2016,[8] was prominently featured with the International Contemporary Ensemble in *Conduction®*, using a language of physical gestures to construct a musical composition in real time.

The assembled community of composers, performers and audience could not have been more relevant to our fractured times. As Iyer has written, "If I choose to belong to a coalition, a community, an 'us,' it must mean we who remember the past; we who care about the future; we who are compassionate, generous, patient and committed deeply to the welfare of others; we who agree that naming ourselves as an 'us' is not an end, but a beginning."[9]

Throughout this festival, a personal issue was gnawing at me — when I should leave Ojai. I did not want to become "boring," as Ken Haas had warned me about years earlier. I was under contract through 2021, but the idea of departing on the occasion of the 75th anniversary concerned me. It felt better for Ojai to appoint a successor to start in 2020, allowing for continuity of new leadership through the anniversary and into the future.

I announced my decision to retire after 16 years, effective in 2019, two years earlier than planned and fifty years from starting my career in Boston. Having recently had a second heart stent installed (my first was in 1996) and increasingly fatigued by the many trips to and from Ohio, I simply felt it was time. I was ever mindful of my own advice to Cleveland Orchestra musicians to take leave while on the upswing and just before peaking. Hannigan, not only a fabulous artist but a dear friend, seemed the perfect partner with whom to end my

---

8 Sorey reworked and revised the piece as *Perle Noire: Meditations for Joséphine*.
9 Iyer, Vijay, *Our Complicity With Excess*, Yale Asian-American Alumni Symposium, May 7, 2014.

tenure in 2019. My successor could start with the assurance of music directors in place for 2020 and 2021, Pintscher and Uchida. It seemed the natural and appropriate time to pass the baton. With the decision made, I wanted to hit it out of the park for my last two festivals, and with Kopatchinskaja and Hannigan, how could I not?

A violinist, actress and performance artist, Kopatchinskaja gives performances infused with explosive energy and mischievous charm. The 2018 festival showcased her fiddle virtuosity in music by Beethoven, György Kurtág, Luigi Nono and Pauline Oliveros. The centerpieces were two fully-staged concerts that she conceived and directed: "Bye Bye Beethoven," a theatrical takedown of the rituals of classical concerts; and "Dies Irae," a dramatic musical commentary on the horrors of climate change. Collaborators ranged from the JACK Quartet, in Ojai for the first time, to the amazing Mahler Chamber Orchestra, a touring ensemble, which chooses to have no home base, of virtuosos playing chamber as well as orchestral music. A major dramatic cantata for two sopranos and ensemble was commissioned from Michael Hersch, a serious and uncompromising composer whom Kopatchinskaja champions. She was joined for two concerts of works by Galina Ustvolskaya by the pianist Markus Hinterhäuser, artistic director of the Salzburg Festival and a leading proponent of the composer. His performance of her six powerful and fiendishly difficult piano sonatas had shattering impact in the Libbey Bowl, enhanced by the blazing afternoon sun bearing down on the audience and performer.

The dominant musical mood of 2018 was serious and dark, except for a program of Moldavian folk music reflecting Kopatchinskaja's roots. Her father and mother joined on cimbalom and violin. The festival concluded with Ligeti's Violin Concerto, for which, in keeping with her sense of whimsy and flair, helium balloons were released into the air, timed to the *sforzando-diminuendo* of the winds' final flutter-tongued chord.

I inaugurated a second co-production partnership with England's Aldeburgh Festival, founded by Benjamin Britten on the coast northeast of London. Its director, Roger Wright, had worked with me in my early Cleveland Orchestra years before moving on to become head of Deutsche Grammophon and then controller of music at BBC Radio 3. Right after Ojai and Berkeley, four programs were presented in Aldeburgh, further extending our brand.

Barbara Hannigan is another artist of multiple talents — soprano, conductor, mentor and curator. I first met her in 2010, when she sang Gérard Grisey's *Quatre chants pour franchir le seuil* with the New York Philharmonic. I had never heard such assured technique, purity of pitch and tone, and ease in delivering textual meaning. The piece knocked me out with its overlapping polyrhythms, microtonal tunings and evocative sound world. Right then I committed myself to presenting it with her in Ojai, and it became a centerpiece of the 2019 festival. As that would be my final one, we both resolved to design programs infused with challenge, provocation and celebration.

Demonstrating her commitment to helping emerging artists, Hannigan had founded Equilibrium, a mentoring initiative for young professional musicians in which she leads master classes, training sessions and collaborative performances. Eight Equilibrium artists joined her in Ojai, performing in various events and providing the cast for a fully-staged production of Stravinsky's *The Rake's Progress* conducted by Hannigan. My partnership efforts necessarily went into overdrive for this massive project, and it ended up a co-production by Ojai, the Gothenburg Symphony in Sweden, the Klara Festival in Brussels, the Munich Philharmonic and the Aldeburgh Festival.

There were two concerts focusing on John Zorn, another major American composer previously ignored by the festival. Hannigan sang his mind-boggling *Jumalattaret*. She had thought it unsingable when first encountering it several years earlier, but her laser-like persistence and discipline ultimately conquered it. Most meaningful to me, and to Hannigan who had collaborated frequently with Knussen early in her career, was including a musical tribute to my dear friend who had suddenly died 11 months before.

The Ludwig Ballroom Band — members of Amsterdam's orchestral collective Ludwig in residence for the festival — added lightness, playing for a late-night dance party. In keeping with my vow to end with a bang, the final Sunday featured Walton's *Façade*, an "entertainment" for chamber ensemble and narration based on nonsense texts by Edith Sitwell. It was spoken in high camp style by Hannigan and most of the festival artists, and she roped me into it as well. Terry Riley's *In C* followed, performed as a communal jam session. My tenure closed with her conducting and singing music from Gershwin's *Girl Crazy* arranged by her and Bill Elliott — a joyous rocket launch of an ending.

INTERLUDE: TOP 10 THINGS TO SAY BACKSTAGE
One of my least favorite parts of the music business was going backstage after concerts, an occasion where everyone stands around while the artists bask in the glories of the performance just completed. What to say in such situations is always a challenge, particularly after a less-than-inspiring performance. Needed are phrases totally honest yet noncommittal or vaguely laudatory yet blandly damning. I put together the "Top 10 Things to Say to a Conductor Backstage" after a lackluster performance — all items that I have either heard, read about or said. I shared this with Hannigan, and to this day, we greet each other gleefully backstage after a concert with one of the phrases, our favorite being "Wow!"

Top 10 things to say to a conductor backstage
10. Fascinating!
9. Now I understand.
8. You did it again.
7. I really loved the last note.
6. I'm speechless.
5. I heard things in that performance I didn't even know were in the score.
4. Leonard Bernstein never did it like that.
3. Wow!
2. Superb is not the word.
1. You should have been in the audience.

Because one of my goals was showcasing the totality of a music director's talents, Hannigan agreed to a daunting schedule of appearances, demonstrating her astonishing artistry as singer, conductor and mentor. Such a schedule is particularly challenging for a singer, given the need to protect the voice. At a post-festival dinner in Aldeburgh to debrief, she admitted being initially concerned, but with rigorous daily discipline that took my breath away, she got through it with astonishing energy and even temper. While acknowledging physical and emotional exhaustion by the end, she confessed that, to her surprise, she was not aware of bouncing between singing and conducting while going through the festival. Rather, her overwhelming sensation was of doing only one thing — showing her true self as a total artist. This is the best testament I can think of to what we achieved.

Hannigan and I became fast friends, particularly bonded around programming as she expands her conducting career. As I originally saw in Ojai, her work ethic and commitment to new music are inspirations. She is incapable of doing anything halfway and embodies to me what a great artist must always stand for — extraordinary artistry, hard work, unending curiosity and a healthy sense of humor.

UNDERSTANDING THE FLYWHEEL

Working with these 16 incredible musical partners was where the power of Joshua Wolf Shenk's creative duos[10] reached its fullest and most satisfying realization — a veritable "power of twos." My Cleveland collaboration with Christoph von Dohnányi was rich, but Ojai was different and more intense in having a changing partner each year. These individuals each had an extraordinarily different style, bringing a variety of differing musical offerings, all with infectious energy. Each collaboration, while intense, was relatively short-lived; given the advance time needed for planning, I was continually working with three or four at once, a completely different creative process in depth and complexity than in my orchestra days. It was addictive and thrilling. The energy from each stimulated the next in a swirling, self-reinforcing cosmos of ideas and music.

Festival planning was an iterative and interactive process, and to my surprise, I found the shape of each cycle remarkably similar from year to year. The music director and I always started with a list of possible artists with whom to collaborate and ideas for anchor projects around which the festival could be built. I produced notes on each meeting so we could ponder and reflect on our work to date. As time went on, we filled in more and more details, a process similar to painting-by-numbers — a picture becomes increasingly clear with the addition of subtle colorations. These multiyear processes meandered as we agonized over the smallest details, a program gradually congealing into a cohesive shape. Then suddenly, about a year before each festival, that shape would miraculously spring into focus.

I found that almost all music directors, while very good at repertoire ideas, were variable in actually building programs and being able to structure them into a coherent entity with shape and logic across the

---

10 Shenk, Joshua Wolf, *Powers of Two: Finding the Essence of Innovation in Creative Pairs*, Houghton Mifflin Harcourt, 2014.

four days. This should not be surprising given that most artists rarely get the chance to devise a festival as a whole. With each in Ojai for only one season, none had the opportunity of building earlier experience into later festivals. But I myself did build such experience across festivals and, having spent an entire career working on programming, continually refined and expanded these skills. Thus the talents we each brought to the table were complementary. Music directors provided ideas, artists and performance skills. My role was to make certain each festival had coherence, an artistic profile and relevance to the brand and was held to a consistent standard of excellence. My insistence on a variety of voices, styles and viewpoints in music directors ensured a rich and multidimensional artistic tapestry over time.

The selection of a music director was my defining decision each year, a choice that would set the festival's very tone and focus. It was this responsibility that gave me the most reward. Over my 16 years, I intentionally diversified my choices, which finally included only three conductors and two conductor-composers, plus four pianists, two sopranos, a violinist, a choreographer, a percussionist, a chamber ensemble and a stage director — a variety affording whole new worlds of repertoire that kept me grounded in the dynamic vitality of today's music and artists. And the appointments and music expanded over time in terms of race and gender diversity, of which I am proud. With hindsight, there is a certain cumulative logic to the sequence, with each festival leading mysteriously and magically to the next — it is hard to envision the Iyer year without the Sellars year, or the Kopatchinskaja one without Iyer.

My imagination intensified as time went along, so those last five — Schick, Sellars, Iyer, Kopatchinskaja and Hannigan — were far more daring than what had come before, going further in breadth of repertoire, sophistication of programming, complexity of production, variety of venues and social context.

I wanted to understand better why I felt this crescendo of intensity, beyond the obvious fact of being able over time to do the job better and better. It was Jim Collins who provided the needed perspective. In 2019 he published a second monograph, *Turning the Flywheel*,[11] expanding on his "flywheel effect" from *Good to Great*. The concept is based on his observation that success can be best explained not as resulting from a linear sequence of events and decisions but from re-

---

11 Collins, Jim, *Turning the Flywheel*, HarperCollins, 2019.

peating and self-reinforcing cycles of compounding energy. The visual representation is a giant flywheel that takes enormous energy to get moving, is ultimately energized by its own momentum and requires less energy to maintain but steady concentration to keep from slowing down. Allowing that energy to wane runs the risk of reverse momentum, which in turn takes superhuman effort to counteract. Along the flywheel are discrete, recurring steps, each requiring attention and action to keep the wheel moving forward and at a gradually faster and faster pace. It is a fascinating visual.

Collins wanted to use the festival as a prominent case study in his monograph. What ensued were extended discussions as he challenged me to create a model that graphically outlined the dynamics of how Ojai worked. The final version compellingly describes the festival's essence — how it builds upon itself in ever-repeating cycles, always with the need for critical decisions at particular points in each cycle.

This clarified to me the gradually accelerating momentum in the expansion of my own musical knowledge, fertile imagination and broadening taste. This is why those last five years seemed so different from those prior — why I had selected as music directors a percussionist, a theater director, a jazz pianist-composer, a violinist-producer, and a singer-conductor as music directors, all far beyond the breadth of choices I had made earlier and light-years different from the conductor or composer-conductor model of the festival I inherited. That is why I was constantly experimenting with the non-musical variables of concert production — the festival layout, schedule, numbers of events, venues, stage décor and lighting, curtain times, concert durations, program formats and ticket prices. I made constant renewal of the experience, which reflected my own personal reinvention, a defining value of the festival.

Even so, at the center of the concept was the unchanging and compelling essence of what Ojai stood for — adventure and unpredictability, the known and the unknown, challenge and flair. That aesthetic was the guidepost. Asked by enthusiastic patrons at the end of a festival how I could "top that," I always answered that topping what had come before was never a consideration; all I could promise was that next year would be different, and that each season was deliberately designed to be unlike its predecessor.

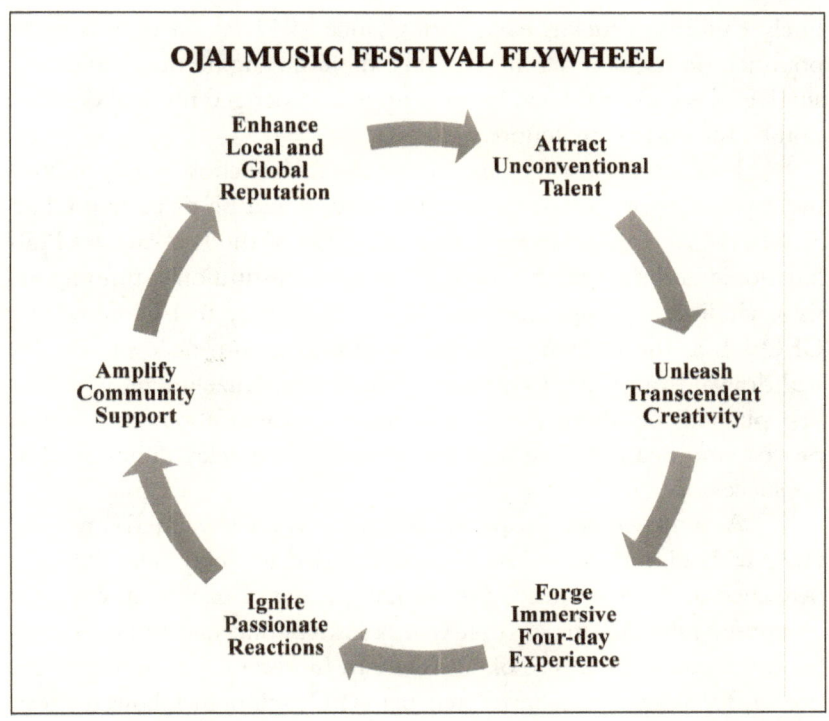

OJAI MUSIC FESTIVAL FLYWHEEL

Enhance Local and Global Reputation → Attract Unconventional Talent → Unleash Transcendent Creativity → Forge Immersive Four-day Experience → Ignite Passionate Reactions → Amplify Community Support → Enhance Local and Global Reputation

A critical element of Ojai's flywheel was converting success into growing reputation; the festival gradually became more than a local or regional event, developing genuine national and international impact. This did not happen solely because of the music and artists being presented. It took specific strategies to make Ojai a musical destination not only for audiences but for journalists and opinion leaders in the music business from around the world. My long career gave me a particularly powerful Rolodex, and each year I personally invited key individuals to be present, people who would not only enjoy the festival but spread the word back home. It was a practice I dubbed the "Big Mouth Strategy."

Because of the festival's distinctive programming, it garnered more national and international coverage and attention than organizations many times its size. In the words of the *Los Angeles Times'* Mark Swed, "An incomparable international event ... and still the quirkiest major music festival in America, and possibly anywhere,"[12] and of *The New Yorker*'s Alex Ross, "The Ojai Music Festival has been raising a

12 Swed, Mark, "How Thomas Morris brought the Ojai Music Festival to the big time," *Los Angeles Times*, May 30, 2019.

finely calibrated ruckus each spring since 1947."[13] All of this compounded on itself over time and, like the little engine that could, this small and compact festival became an acknowledged musical destination by the end of my tenure.

I was exceptionally pleased that the festival chose wisely in finding my successor so that its arc of success could be extended. Chad Smith, the vice president for artistic planning of the Los Angeles Philharmonic and the creative force behind that institution's stunning artistic vitality, was appointed in March 2018, only to be offered the CEO job at the Philharmonic 18 months later and necessitating his withdrawal from Ojai. In an odd twist of fate, Guzelimian, who had first pitched me about the Ojai position and was about to retire as provost and dean of The Juilliard School, was quickly announced as his successor.

As it turned out, the pandemic shutdown necessitated canceling 2020 with Pintscher, and as Uchida decided to delay her 2021 appearance to 2024 because of scheduling issues, Guzelimian engaged composer John Adams for that year, a festival that had to be delayed for three months because of COVID. In hindsight, my timing to retire in 2019 could not have been better! Guzelimian followed up in 2022 and 2023 by appointing the American Modern Opera Company ("AMOC") and Rhiannon Giddens respectively. The Ojai Music Festival appears to be in great hands.

Even though I had given up the heady responsibility and habits of having final executive responsibility and was working in an organization a fraction of the scale I had been used to, I was totally content in Ojai being focused on working with artists, producing concerts and learning more music. While technically outside my responsibilities, I was not unaware of the infrastructural and organizational challenges around me. The festival was, in effect, two separate organizations that were not totally conjoined. The artistic team, nonresident and international in scope, had wholly different perspectives from an infrastructure based in Ojai. This was often frustrating, but as a non-resident artistic director, I could never be present enough to help reconcile this tension and always felt somewhat outside the institution. To this day, the paradoxes inherent in being at once a local, regional, national and

---

13 Ross, Alex, "Outsiders," *The New Yorker,* July 6, 2015.

international institution based in a small town are a work-in-progress, a challenge with serious implications for governance, leadership, budget, audience and funding.

I finally see clearly that my work in Ojai was a summation of my previous experience — a gathering of strands, a weaving-together of everything I had learned. In hindsight, this insight clarified why I found it such a satisfying and unquestionable pinnacle of a long journey. It was a place where, with the musical passion Vic Firth instilled in me years earlier, I still performed percussion on several notable occasions, including with mentors such as Nexus, whom I had idolized while still in high school and college. I refined the basic principles that I learned from Arthur Fiedler years earlier of constructing programs as emotional arcs; those at Ojai were very different musically from those of the Pops but had the same reasoned foundation. I advocated music of our time and showcased an expanding enthusiasm for and knowledge of contemporary music that Oliver Knussen opened my eyes to. I undertook a total change of career with complete determination, much as I had helped John Williams do in coming to the Boston Pops in 1980. I exhibited total fearlessness in standing up for what I believed in artistically with the stubborn persistence I had seen in Pierre Boulez. I embraced the absolute necessity for clarity of purpose and always putting the music first that I learned from Ward Smith. I refined the building of successive artistic partnerships over an extended time, modeled on the creative duo I perfected with Christoph von Dohnányi. I gleefully adopted renewal and reinvention, both organizationally and personally, as Jim Collins instilled in me. And my work was infused with the idealism, innovation, and risk that were at the center of Spring for Music.

It is no wonder these last five years of Ojai felt like such a compelling and powerful whole — my own personal flywheel at work. It was a long and at times arduous journey, but with such glorious teachers and partners, how could I fail?

CHAPTER 11
ORCHESTRAS REDUX

I am deeply worried about the future of orchestras. They exist to-day in a dynamic environment that challenges the very structural model they have embodied for over a century. Complicating cyclical economic swings have been fundamental evolutions in technology, education, communications, philanthropy, musical tastes, audience habits and social priorities. While some of these dynamics were al-ready evident when I left orchestras, their pace is accelerating, cre-ating a world that today can seem unrecognizable. Even so, they cling to traditional practices and structures with no real change in the way business is conducted. They are stuck in unchanging concert rituals, governed by the rigidity of inflexible work rules that guarantee routine, fixated on crafting image and reputation around star music directors, and they remain addicted to a repertoire centered on the Romantic war horses of the 19th century that are receding into the past. Questions abound about their very relevance.

Orchestras are what first attracted me to music, and even now nothing thrills me like the visceral sound of 100 energized players in a live performance of Mahler's Symphony No. 1, Ravel's *Daphnis and Chloe* or Birtwistle's *Earth Dances*. But my journey has taken me to mu-sical realms way beyond orchestras, providing not only creative stim-ulation but broader insights from inside as well as outside on how to address their future. I passionately want them to flourish.

A CLASSIC TENSION
American orchestras were founded to provide European validation of their communities' emerging cultural and social status. From the start, they were infused with Eurocentric repertoire and conductors; only in

243

the 1960s did they emerge as institutions distinctly shaped by American funding structures, cultural norms and audience habits. They were initially creatures of entrenched founders, powerful board chairs or long-serving music directors. Being successful was much simpler before year-round seasons, jet-setting maestros, and the need for sophisticated marketing and fundraising strategies.[1]

With the establishment of the National Endowment for the Arts and the Ford Foundation's unprecedented funding of $85 million (adjusted for inflation, over $800 million today) in the mid-1960s, orchestras became enshrined as a national industry. Ford's goals were to stimulate expansion of seasons, improve musicians' pay and build endowments. PBS soon emerged as a major presenter of classical programming as commercial television edged away from its earlier interest in cultural broadcasting. Powerful European record labels began investing heavily in making discs in the United States.

Ford sparked a period of substantial growth towards year-round musician employment. As a consequence, orchestras became increasingly institutionalized; beliefs, norms and values were ingrained not only in the culture of how they behaved but in written rules and practices as enshrined in labor contracts and seasonal structures. The result was a growing tension between the vitality of musical creativity and the bureaucratic infrastructure necessary to support it.

I wrestled, with varying success throughout my career, with trying to reconcile these forces. In Boston, preoccupied with the sheer wonder of the BSO and the prestige of my position, I ignored managing that tension and failed to build the alliances necessary to shape a shared institutional vision. In Cleveland, with greater experience and perspective, I forged critical strategic relationships with the board, the music director, the musicians and the staff around common goals. Yet the incessant imperative of selling yet more tickets and raising additional money to support an ever-increasing budget became numbing.

After Cleveland, I struggled to balance the unconventional and idealistic idea of Spring for Music with the inherent inflexibility of orchestras and presenting institutions while needing to build a lasting philanthropic and audience base. But the inbred inertia of the classical music machine proved implacable, and despite critical and artistic success, the project was abandoned after four seasons. That was my last brush with the orchestra business.

---

1 The Boston Symphony did not hire its first development director until the early 1970s.

MUSICAL CREATIVITY

Today we are experiencing a golden age of creativity as boundaries between musical genres blur — a phenomenon that has burgeoned over the last two decades and one in which I was directly immersed at Ojai. Artists today are not necessarily pigeonholed by genre; many forge individual voices across styles and cultures.

Consider flutist Claire Chase, who has embarked on a commissioning project extending to 2035 to create new music for flute from composers of all types, not only stretching the technical boundaries of the instrument but adding new dimensions through staging, collaboration and technology. Or singer and multi-instrumentalist Rhiannon Giddens, who, with formal operatic training from Oberlin, is composing ballets and theater pieces and has taken over artistic leadership of Silkroad (formerly the Silk Road Project) from Yo-Yo Ma. Or multi-talented Tyshawn Sorey, equally at home playing drums in far-out improvisations with Vijay Iyer, performing formal percussion concertos by the likes of the Austrian composer Olga Neuwirth or composing a theater piece based on the life of Josephine Baker.

This creative energy encompasses not just individual artists but ensembles and presenters. For example, multi-genre, multi-disciplinary groups like Eighth Blackbird who pioneered musical performance as theater. Or the International Contemporary Ensemble, which redefined an ensemble as a free-form collective, constituted around not a labor agreement but artistic projects and like-minded musicians. A new world of presenters has emerged, such as Knoxville's Big Ears Festival with more than 250 events across all genres over its four days. Or the Prototype Festival in New York, a crucible for the creation and performance of experimental opera that brokers production partnerships with presenters across the country. Or hybrids like the American Modern Opera Company in Cambridge, Massachusetts, a loose confederation of artists, directors and composers to create new works. Or The Industry in Los Angeles, an experimental opera company offering innovative productions of new works that upset any traditional sense of place or time and blur the relationships between artists and audience.

These innovative organizations are small-scale, nimble and visionary, and built around the creative intersections of composers, directors, performers and presenters. Creativity has shifted from being generated *within* boundaries to being forged *at* boundaries, in collisions of styles and genres. Such intersections in turn create new intersections, which themselves become generative. As Frans Johansson writes, "When you step into an intersection of fields, disciplines and cultures, you can combine existing concepts into a large number of extraordinary new ideas."[2]

With the Internet, this bustling activity is accessible to anyone anytime. It has changed how music is performed and consumed, as well as how and how often people interact with each other in person. A concert today must be more compelling than ever just to be heard through the welter of live and virtual alternatives.

What musicians do in preparing a piece or putting together a performance defines them as entrepreneurs — organizing activities embracing considerable initiative and risk. Subjugating all that to an institution which employs them seems conflicted by its nature. It is no wonder so many today bypass institutions and forge their own ways. "Classical music" has become diffuse — it is all just "music," and many artists are happy with the lack of clear definitions since their work cannot be categorized.

MUSICAL INSTITUTIONS

Viewed against this free-flowing outburst of creativity, traditional organizations seem trapped in the inflexibility of large infrastructures, the inertia of fixed costs, generous employment agreements, an insistence on making and enforcing rules, narrow repertoire and the repetitive grid of a performance schedule. In contrast, the new world is chaotic, messy and full of experimentation with its anything-goes spirit, making rigid adherence to both narrow definitions of the musical canon and prescribed rules seem starkly out of touch.

The organizational theorist Karl Weick's work on coupled systems provides context for thinking about the internal dynamics of today's orchestras.[3] By studying the levels of interdependence between an organization's many working parts, Weick distinguishes between tightly coupled and loosely coupled systems. Tightly coupled systems have inseparable parts that affect each other continuously, constantly,

---

2 Johansson, Frans, *The Medici Effect*, Harvard Business Review Press, 2017.
3 Weick, Karl, "Educational Organizations as Loosely Coupled Systems," *Administrative Science Quarterly*, Vol. 21, No. 1, March 1976, and Karl Weick and J. Douglas Orton, "Loosely Coupled Systems: A Reconceptualization," *Academy of Management Review*, Vol. 15, No. 2, April 1990.

directly and immediately. Loosely coupled systems have parts that work independently, affecting each other suddenly, occasionally, indirectly and eventually. On the surface, tightly coupled systems are attractive, as they seem efficient, predictable and stable. But they are also notoriously rigid and vulnerable to external shock — anything that happens to any individual part immediately affects every other. Because loosely coupled systems are less rigidly interlocked, they are more immune to external shocks and therefore better able to adapt to a changing environment.

Orchestra institutions are tightly coupled systems in the extreme. Every part directly affects all others: performances are scheduled consistent with the minutiae of labor agreements, using the same personnel, all dressed the same and performing on the same days of the week at the same time in the same program format with the same music, before audiences sitting in the same seats through a whole season and obeying the same concert rituals. It is no surprise that external shocks, such as an economic downturn or pandemic shutdown, are convulsive to their tight and inflexible cultures.

On the other hand, the digital revolution and the explosion of creativity across genres and styles are perfect examples of loosely coupled systems that adjust to external shocks far more easily. The differences in deep-rooted dynamic structures between orchestras and new digital spaces help explain the fundamental disconnect between them today.

In addition, orchestras have a long history of evolving along a particular and singular direction. Their institutional histories have consistently defined growth as "bigger" and "more," with self-reinforcing cycles of getting ever larger, doing more, paying more, raising more money and, in the process, becoming more complex. The result is becoming not only averse to change but increasingly unable to consider it, due to being bound to the single, rigid direction of growth. It is no wonder change is so difficult; orchestras get weighed down by the very bureaucracies and behaviors created to support them while stubbornly clinging to a one-way view of the future.

Despite the far-reaching changes and frequent warnings of crises, little has actually changed in leadership structure, seasonal patterns or internal cultures in over 50 years. Perhaps this is not surprising, since the very term "institutionalization" can pejoratively conjure blandness, drabness, uniformity and lack of individual voice.

MONEY

Today's orchestras are not financially healthy. Most of the largest are seriously undercapitalized, with annual expenses exceeding revenues and inadequate endowments. Even before the pandemic, most had substantial structural deficits, even though balanced budgets were regularly reported thanks to excessive draws from endowments and/or non-recurring bridge funding to mask what are fundamental financial imbalances.

Since the beginning of the orchestra business in America, the subscription system, in which patrons buy tickets to multiple concerts across the season, has been a foundational pillar of the business model. This has both the financial advantage of producing multi-concert revenue from a single transaction, providing cash in the bank in advance, and the marketing advantage of not having to fret about selling lots of tickets to individual concerts. But traditional subscriptions have steadily declined as audience habits have changed, leading to greater dependence on single ticket sales, which are inherently more volatile because of their dependence on the perceived popularity of each program or artist. Single ticket revenues have increased but not enough to make up for declines in subscriptions, and even with rising ticket prices, total income has not kept up with the inexorable increase in costs.

When I started my career, orchestras generally covered more than 50 percent of their budgets with earned revenues.[4] Today, earned revenues have shrunk to half of that. Conversely, the percentage of budgets funded annually through contributions and endowment draws has had to increase dramatically — a challenge as competition for philanthropy has grown across the not-for-profit sector. Orchestras' economic engines are now significantly more predicated on fundraising than ticket revenues.

On top of these fiscal realities, the pandemic shutdown disrupted financial trends and business structures. Historically, financial crises have tended to be cyclical. The 2008 recession was a temporary disruption after which most institutions reverted to where they were before it hit. The pandemic shutdown was different, causing complete disruption of live concerts and ticket income, lasting longer and having deeper impact than merely financial. It upended habits and long-established behaviors — how and where people worked, how and

---

4 In 1970, my first year with the Boston Symphony, total earned revenues from ticket sales, tour fees and record royalties amounted to 70% of the total budget.

where they bought goods and services, how and where they consumed entertainment, how they interacted and how they lived.

Business professor and author Scott Galloway postulates that one of the pandemic's most enduring effects was as an accelerant,[5] meaning positive or negative trends in evidence before the shutdown become disproportionately better or worse by its end. This is confirmed by current ticket sales trends in which income, which was declining before the pandemic, is significantly reduced and not bouncing back[6] as music lovers have grown used to experiencing inexpensive and instantaneous digital access. Re-establishing a sales base for live events is so far proving stubbornly difficult. And because classical music audiences tend to be older, many still hesitate to gather inside crowded venues. The landscape has been forever altered and it is unrealistic to assume a reversion to the pre-shutdown state, not that it was financially stable to begin with.

Orchestras weathered the shutdown with serious budget cuts, varying degrees of shared pay reductions for musicians and staff, extraordinary generosity from donors, and, most critically, unprecedented governmental COVID relief support. Most emerged with cash surpluses and in surprisingly better financial shape than before.

But a financial reckoning is coming as government largesse is depleted, expense reductions are eliminated and the urgency of the pandemic wanes as a fundraising pitch. The pressing danger is sliding unthinkingly back into comfortable business as usual, mistaking positive cash balances for long-term financial health. Philanthropy to fund pressing social issues rather than the performing arts is proving to have greater appeal to donors. Building a future around a few angel benefactors is risky in the long run and seriously weakens the case for an institution's relevance to the broader community. Financial market volatility is a continuing certainty, mandating greater prudence in investment management and more conservative endowment draws to preserve asset values. Assuming perpetual growth in endowment market values is unrealistic.

My inescapable conclusion is that operating budgets must be smaller in the future, on top of already tight pre-pandemic budgets

---

5 Galloway, Scott, *Post Corona: From Crisis to Opportunity*, Portfolio/Penguin, 2020.
6 A 2022 study by Alan Brown of WolfBrown shows that 15%-20% of prior regular attendees may be unwilling to return. Brown, Alan, *Audience Outlook Monitor*, WolfBrown, Executive Briefing, June 27, 2022.

that allocated far too little for increasingly necessary innovation and experimentation. And playing it safe by not investing in the future represents a doom loop of failure for an artistic institution. One prescient orchestra executive recently said, "The status quo is an existential threat, brilliantly disguised as stability."[7]

PRE-EXISTING CONDITIONS

As serious as the money pressures are, it is simplistic and misleading to paint the current predicament as purely financial. Orchestras are suffering from deeper systemic issues predating the pandemic that were acknowledged and raised repeatedly over the years but persist today.

In 1998, The Andrew W. Mellon Foundation conducted an assessment of the orchestral field through a structured process of input and perspectives from performing-arts managers, educators, funders, composers and musicians.[8] Mellon's findings on critical issues were far-reaching and significant: deterioration in institutional leadership; absence of artistic leadership; predictable programming; too many uninteresting concerts; alienation and hostility of musicians; lack of alignment between the institutions' intrinsic artistic interests and community expectations; failure to involve creators in the artistic life of the institution; lack of audience trust to encourage experimentation; and lack of disciplined and strategic thinking about such challenges. The study concluded that orchestras do not have a clear sense of their own artistic individuality, that current organizational structures and cultures do not encourage or reward leadership, and that they do not understand what constitutes success. It was a depressing assessment.

Wanting to help, Mellon's response was to invest an astounding $120 million in the field over the next 20 years in a funding program that initiated cross-constituency and cross-orchestra dialogue. Even with this substantial investment and effort, its earlier assessment, to which must be added the critical issues of diversity, equity and inclusion, still rings true, and the situation today looks much the same with few exceptions. One is The Saint Paul Chamber Orchestra, which was reconstituted in the early 2000s into a smaller, flexible ensemble under a rotating group of artist partners rather than a single music director. Another is the embrace by the Detroit Symphony in 2011 of

---

7 Quote from Jon Limbacher, President of the Saint Paul Chamber Orchestra, at a memorial service for Bruce Coppock on January 27, 2023.
8 Wichterman, Catherine, *The Orchestra Forum: A Discussion of Symphony Orchestras in the U.S*, The Andrew W. Mellon Foundation, November 23, 1998.

live-streaming of all its concerts to expand the broader community's access to the orchestra.

Despite 25 years of studies and assessments reaching similar conclusions, orchestras on the whole appear resistant to fundamental change. New initiatives masquerading as reinventions typically address symptoms, not causes — selling more tickets, raising more money, playing more movie scores or concerts for the community. These are Band-Aids and do not address the root causes of dysfunction.

The world today is drastically different from that of 100, 50 or even 25 years ago, and orchestras ignore societal shifts at their peril. As Heidi Waleson succinctly summarized in her frightening book on the demise of New York City Opera: "The historical business model — the repertory system, the enormous theaters, the labor requirements, the balance of earned and contributed income — is being challenged by profound shifts in audience habits and donor behavior. The symphony orchestra and the opera company are simply no longer the default choice for a large swath of the population."[9]

What is required is unambiguous focus on the underlying factors threatening these institutions in light of the changing environment around them. Let's start by admitting that the old model is out of date and in desperate need of reinvention. Dabbling around the edges through incremental changes to labor agreements or vague commitments to improve communications and work collegially will not suffice. To flourish, orchestras will ultimately be forced to become smaller in scale, more expansive in what they produce, more locally focused and differently organized.

A PIVOTAL MOMENT

Extrapolating the future from the present is a naive and doomed strategy. Orchestras today face a monumental crisis, making this a tantalizing moment for revitalizing their future. Incrementally addressing the magnitude of issues that go way beyond finance will mean limping into the future with declining relevance. It is time for new ideas from multiple and nonstandard viewpoints that leap in unexpected directions, and for existing practices of organizational culture, leadership and purpose to be questioned and sharpened. Included in the conversation must be composers, performers and thinkers from outside the orchestra world

---

9 Waleson, Heidi, *Mad Scenes and Exit Arias: The Death of the New York City Opera and the Future of Opera in America*, Metropolitan Books, 2018.

— experts in digital technology and media, pioneers in organization-al design and representatives from different sectors of the community. Critical breakthroughs start with the collision of differing opinions and points of view, and active rejection of comfortably and unthinkingly slipping back into the status quo. Make no mistake, orchestras will in-evitably change — they will be forced to, if necessary, in which case the process will be convulsive. How much better to seize the initiative and trigger such thinking in constructive and cathartic, not destructive, ways, and then persist in making change happen over time.

So what to do? Addressing systemic change is difficult and takes leadership, persistence and patience. From my own experience, shared vision is the glue that enables success — understanding why the insti-tution exists, what it stands for and where it is going. Vision comes alive and is made real by what institutions do and how they act, not just by what they say.

On becoming music director of the San Francisco Sympho-ny in 2019, Esa-Pekka Salonen announced the bold step of asking eight young and diverse artists from beyond the world of traditional symphonic music to join him as partners in rethinking the role of an orchestra.[10] I applauded the move, but some viewed it with skepticism, claiming it lacked structure and focus. But its value would have been unambiguously validated if the institution, with these partners embed-ded in its very fabric, had profoundly redefined what it does, how, and for whom. Alas, the question was made moot by Salonen's surprising announcement after four years that he would not renew his initial con-tract because he did "not share the same goals for the future of the in-stitution as the Board of Governors does."[11] Simultaneously, the board disbanded the partners.

Core purpose is a principle around which institutions must become galvanized. Some think orchestras exist to provide entertain-ment, to provide employment, to sell tickets, to ensure financial sus-tainability or to lead social change. These are all important, but at

---

10 The group includes the film composer and pianist Nicholas Britell; the soprano and curator Julia Bullock; the flutist and performance artist Claire Chase; the composer and guitarist Bryce Dessner; the violinist and artistic trailblazer Pekka Kuusisto; the composer and collaborator Nico Muhly; the artificial intelligence entrepreneur and roboticist Carol Reiley; and the jazz bassist and vocalist Esperanza Spalding.
11 Hernández, Javier, "San Francisco Symphony's Maestro to Step Down, Citing Split With Board", *The New York Times*, March 14, 2024.

its heart, an orchestra must be about creating profound experience. Putting transcendence, as experienced through music, explicitly at the center of the organization's purpose will go a long way toward establishing a framework for addressing the future. It is ultimately why musicians join orchestras, why audiences buy tickets, what motivates board members to serve, what inspires patrons to contribute and what makes orchestras valued in their communities.

To effectuate real change, to shake up the status quo and to face foundational assumptions that are out of date require attacking the old model head-on rather than dabbling around the periphery by addressing symptoms. Here are three ideas to rejuvenate the vitality and creativity of programming, season structure and artistic leadership — all at the heart of how orchestras must fundamentally recalibrate their futures.

1. Enliven Programming

The vast majority of orchestra concerts have become parades of similarly structured and conceived events. Programs are calcified. Today, two-thirds of them are built around the so-called canonic European masterworks and half of those are structured as opening work, concerto and a large-scale symphony. This means less than half of programs show genuine imagination and creativity in repertoire or structure rather than formulaic repetition.[12] Yes, special events with artistic vitality — an exceptional soloist, an unusual piece of repertoire, or a special production — surface from time to time, but I am talking about the majority of concerts that constitutes the core of the season. The goal must be to make each program uniquely energized and avoid even a whiff of casual routine.

Great concerts must provoke reaction, and that means understanding the fine line between audience comfort and discomfort. Programming should aim slightly below that threshold of comfort so there is always some unexpected grit in the result; key is calibrating enough of that grit to register attention but not so much as to engender resistance. In 2019, I was quoted in *The New York Times*, in response to a question

---

12 Data is from the announced 2018-19, 2019-20, 2020-21 and 2021-22 seasons of the seven largest orchestras in the U.S. Because of the pandemic shutdown, the last third of the 2019-20 and the entirety of 2020-21seasons were canceled, but analyzing the announced programs still gives an accurate picture of the orchestras' artistic intentions.

about amplified sound levels, in a line that also succinctly describes this principle: "It shouldn't hurt too much. But it should hurt a little."[13]

Sports provides an unlikely model for how to engage audiences. Fans flock to games or watch them on live television because they don't know how they will turn out — unpredictability motivates participation. Concerts must provoke the adrenalin of uncertainty, whether from what artists have to say about familiar music, the inclusion of unknown or new pieces, the surprise of unusual program structures or the imagination of the concert production itself.

While it is encouraging that recent seasons are starting to recognize music by composers who had been neglected due to ethnicity or gender, program structures are still conventionally predictable, with vast stretches of the repertoire ignored. Why is most of the music so deadly serious? What about the lighter classical repertoire? What about ballet music? What about early music? Where are the Haydn symphonies? Why so few 20th- and 21st-century works? Where are the chamber and contemporary works that can shed perspective on major pieces? If orchestras genuinely want each concert to really matter, it is not enough to be just purveyors of 19th-century potboilers. Orchestral music will remain at the center of the repertoire, but how much better to place it in a broader musical and historical context. Above all, demonstrate that music of today is a fervent belief and priority, a practice that not only connects with the messy creativity that surrounds orchestras but forces listeners to experience old favorites in different ways.

Concert structures offer opportunities for greater variety — venues, times, lengths and formats should be changed to suit the programming, with each event painstakingly produced for maximum impact. Why must so many begin at 7:30 or 8:00 p.m. and last two hours with a 20-minute intermission? Why are most concerts performed in the same space when some are more appropriate in venues of different configurations or in different locations for different audiences? How much more interesting to vary all these factors.

One orchestra that has been paying attention to deep-seated artistic vitality is the Los Angeles Philharmonic. Its programs are continually less reflective of the default masterwork model. Programming is consistently imaginative, embracing contemporary music as rule,

---

13 Woolfe, Zachary, "Ojai Will Never Be the Same, Thanks to His Musical Imagination", *The New York Times*, June 5, 2019.

not exception. Included within the season are multiple mini-festivals that embrace wider perspectives — concerts of contemporary music, opera, jazz, world music, chamber music and other genres, often with guest ensembles. Programming shows a cohesive artistic point of view embedded in the institution as a whole, and one that is not just talked about but made real by what it does. This achievement is due to strong and creative leadership over time from engaged music directors and imaginative CEOs, both paying attention across the entire season and supported by a committed board. I am watching the organization with interest as it undergoes transitions in executive and artistic leadership, changes that will conclusively demonstrate the degree to which its healthy artistic culture continues to be ingrained in the institution.

2. Reinvent the Season Structure

The weekly subscription grid structure is broken. Audiences are no longer buying packages of concerts stretching months into the future — that is not how they live their lives — and are purchasing shorter series or switching to single events. With easy digital access, consumers increasingly demand control of not only what they see but how and when they see it. Orchestras' seasonal subscription structure is no longer successful at either retaining existing or attracting new audiences.

Artistically, the rigid grind of preparing and performing a different program each week lends an assembly-line aura to the season, creating routine for the audience and tedium for artists, amplifying the soporific effect of dull programming. Salonen, decrying the immutable structure as an impediment to creativity, has said, "We are presented with a grid, and then you kind of fill it with content, and the content can be interesting, good and imaginative, but it still has to fit into the grid."[14]

Institutions should instead consider constructing some, if not all, of their seasons around multi-week blocks of thematically coherent programs and activities, each curated by a conductor, soloist or composer. These would be conceived as mini-festivals, with orchestra concerts, chamber music, guest ensembles, educational activities and community outreach all mixed together, and with variety in the concert rituals themselves to avoid predictability. Digital media should no

---

14 Tommasini, Anthony, "Esa-Pekka Salonen Says Tweak the Orchestra, Don't Blow It Up," *The New York Times*, March 7, 2019.

longer be just a way to deliver live events to a broader public but treated as an integral element of special projects predicated on technology. In abandoning a routinized grid, such a flexible structure would stimulate risk-taking and mandate greater attentiveness. Moving away from the seasonal spread of individual concerts into the more compact modular format allows audiences to experience the context of closely adjacent and complementary events.

The roles of conductors and solo artists should be redefined as extended partnerships, in which they perform not a singular function but several within each block, ridding the system of the one-week gig mentality. Most artists I know are more interested in developing deeper relationships with an ensemble and audience than a one-week booking can provide, welcoming multiple weeks in residence in one place with different programs and the option of participating in chamber and contemporary music, giving master classes and serving the community.

I envision a season ultimately constructed around six to eight such modules, with perhaps three or four curated and led by the music director, and the rest by different artists-in-residence, whether conductors, composers, soloists or even innovators from other fields. Imagine having multiple artists-in-residence on staggered three-year terms, each taking charge of different modules. Think of the opportunities to connect substantively with the artists of today and plug into the musical excitement that surrounds us. Think of the opportunities to involve orchestra musicians in artistic planning of some modules. They represent a vast untapped resource of ideas, and their participation would provide a broader sense of ownership and stimulate greater job satisfaction — a win-win.

Implementation could be phased in over several years, as long as the initial shift is bold and substantive. To transition, such curated modules could be interspersed with periods of the conventional weekly structure as at present. Multiple concert subscriptions for performances spread across a season could still be maintained for those diminishing numbers who want to buy them as other opportunities for marketing multiple-concert packages become possible, either by selling modules as self-contained mini-festivals or selling memberships that include a bank of tickets to be used across the season for desired concerts. Because of the complexity of such overlapping sales pitches, the sacred cow of subscribers having the same seat for all concerts needs to be challenged, although I suspect this is a serious deal-breaker for very few. The necessary overarching goal is to produce contagious vitality and thereby attract new and repeat ticket buyers. The reality is that exclusively continuing the subscription grid structure across the whole season for both planning and sales purposes is no longer viable socially, financially or artistically.

3. Make Artistic Direction Explicit

Artistic leadership in the old model is, and has been, vested publicly and contractually in music directors. They are deemed responsible for everything artistic, including the orchestra's musical vision — what it stands for, what it does and with whom. This includes setting programming philosophy, conducting more concerts than others do, approving guest conductors and their programs, hiring other titled artist positions, and managing the musicians. More crucially, the music director is supposed to be the orchestra's public face and at the center of broader conversations about institutional direction and priorities — crucial leadership responsibilities that are in addition to leading concerts and tours. The music director is defined as an all-powerful community deity — the "Maestro Syndrome."

Yet there is a significant disconnect; music directors are present for only a fraction of the year. In the biggest orchestras, they conduct on average 11 subscription weeks annually and are rarely in the community beyond those, an occasional week for administrative work notwithstanding. Even after adding additional weeks for touring and special projects, they average just over one-third of the 42 performing weeks of a year-round orchestra,[15] which means that for a large majority of the year, the "boss" is not present, not listening and not leading.[16]

In addition, many music directors concurrently hold other posts, often, in today's global marketplace, with competing organizations, resulting in further dilution of an orchestra's distinctive identity. What organization anywhere would sanction its leader simultaneously running another in the same field that competed for joint brand identity with that leader?

---

15 Most year-round orchestras have roughly 10 weeks of paid vacation included in labor agreements.
16 Data is from the announced 2018-19, 2019-20, 2020-21 and 2021-22 seasons of the seven largest U.S. orchestras.

The resulting lack of consistent artistic leadership across all activities means that responsibilities are, by default, either ignored or implicitly devolved to directors of artistic planning or chief executives, some of whom are far better equipped to assume them than others.[17] Even so, responsibility without authority creates organizational suspicion and distrust.

The solution is not complicated and has been implemented by theater, dance and opera companies, and by orchestras abroad — American orchestras need full-time non-conducting artistic directors. They need to be fully present and vested explicitly with responsibility and accountability for the overall artistic activities of the institution, including hiring conductors and soloists, setting programming and managing musicians as prescribed in the labor contract, along with monitoring levels of artistic excellence and consistency.

The advantages are obvious: first, responsibility will match accountability, eliminating artistic authority being usurped by individuals not held accountable; second, the leader will visibly oversee all activities, experiencing personally what works and what does not; and third, leadership will have continuity across all activities, ensuring standards are aligned with overall artistic vision. The myth of music directors being artistically responsible for the institution, which they really have never been, must be replaced by putting an artistic director formally in charge.

There are plenty of qualified candidates both within and outside the orchestra field. Unlike the European model of combining the chief executive and artistic director into a single "intendant," two individuals are required, given the vast operating and funding responsibilities inherent in the American system. In addition, having an artistic director and chief executive present all the time provides opportunity for a well-functioning creative duo.

---

17 One of the most renowned among such executives was Ernest Fleischmann of the Los Angeles Philharmonic, who was a trained musician. He exercised singular control over everything at the Philharmonic, including artistic matters formally vested not in him but in the various music directors. This system worked with Zubin Mehta and Carlo Maria Giulini, who happily deferred the wider responsibilities to him, but André Previn had different views and wanted to preserve his contractual prerogatives. In 1989, after a classic clash, Previn resigned his post prematurely, saying pointedly, "In the current structure of the Los Angeles Philharmonic, it has become obvious to me there is no room for a music director." Bernheimer, Martin, "Previn Wanted to Run the Philharmonic – So Does Fleischmann," *Los Angeles Times*, April 26, 1989.

"Music directors" would continue to function in much the same way as they actually have — leading more regular-season concerts than other conductors do as well as special projects and tours, having priority on choice of repertoire and implicitly exerting the dominant artistic imprint on the orchestra. But let us be honest — they are really part-time leaders functioning as "principal conductors." The job's scope should be reduced and formal artistic authority moved to the artistic director, to whom the "principal conductor" or "music director" (the title is really irrelevant) would report.

The artistic opportunities afforded by this are tantalizing — and necessary, as the subscription grid gives way to multi-week modules. Think of the possibilities of engaging the complementary curatorial presences of different conductors, artists and composers across the modules for performance, education and community engagement activities — all in sync with the vision of a singular artistic director. This plethora of voices enriches and broadens an orchestra's artistic scope, much as Ojai's annual rotation of music directors under the overarching vision of a multi-year artistic director has shown.

To make this work, the artistic director must have the people skills to balance multiple planning ideas and opinions, whether from conductors, artists, composers or players, combined with the toughness required to make timely decisions. To be avoided is collaborative *decision-making* where choices are made by consensus, resulting in adoption of least-objectionable options, a path that neuters risk and saps energy. Different and desirable is a collaborative *culture* of rich and varied input, which is empowering but not inconsistent with vesting final responsibility in a single leader — who must engender trust and respect throughout the organization in exercising that authority.

Does such a structure present downside risks? Of course, particularly if the artistic director is the wrong fit in competence, character or chemistry, but that is a risk in any critical hire. The upside potential is providing leadership continuity over time, the ability to shape a cohesive artistic vision that embraces everything the orchestra does and in allowing far greater diversification of artistic voices in the overall fabric of activities.

INTERNAL CULTURE
Pursuing any of these ideas sets up conflict with historical traditions,

contractual relationships and behavioral norms of the current model. They cannot be implemented without serious implications for labor agreements with musicians. Fundamental modifications will be necessary to provide for responsibility over the musicians shifting from the music director to artistic director; to rethink working conditions and schedule provisions from a season built around the rigid subscription grid to one predicated on flexible modules; to reinvent scheduling and compensation provisions to allow for variable participation by individual musicians in orchestral, contemporary and chamber music activities within the fabric of the agreement; and to reimagine electronic media as central in the content mix and not as supplementary delivery vehicles for existing concerts, bringing such provisions inside the labor agreement as opposed to the current practice of separate bargaining with the national union.

Beyond these challenges is an urgent need to address, in the context of ongoing structural deficits, the post-shutdown financial realities of declining ticket sales and a challenging fundraising environment. These will no doubt require reductions in the overall scale of operation and numbers of concerts performed, expansion in the breadth of what is presented and reallocation of financial resources to support greater innovation and risk-taking. The consequence will be changes in the structures and amounts of compensation not just for the musicians but throughout the organization. Taken together, these are industry-shattering adjustments and implementing them will extend well beyond incremental contract modifications. Necessary will be wholesale rethinking of agreements and confronting the current longstanding collective bargaining culture.

Relationships between musicians and orchestra institutions have been historically defined by labor agreements. Before 1960, orchestra musicians were paid so poorly that they had to hold additional part-time jobs. Job security was subject to the whims of tyrannical music directors with unchecked power — Fritz Reiner in Chicago and George Szell in Cleveland being notable examples. Their deaths coincided with the emergence of orchestra musicians' collective labor power through the American Federation of Musicians. In 1962, the International Conference of Symphony and Opera Musicians was created as a forum for orchestra musicians to trade information and formulate labor strategies as they formally earned the right from the national union to ratify their agreements.

Against a history of meager salaries and job insecurity, bargaining grew more aggressive and adversarial, a process a member of the Boston Symphony once colorfully described as "ritual fang-baring."[18] The resulting gains in pay, benefits and job security were necessary — musicians deserve a living wage and job protections and fought long and hard for them. The ensuing trends towards year-round employment created longer seasons, a goal explicitly encouraged by the Ford Foundation. Growing seasons meant more concerts — pops, outdoor summer seasons, community outreach and education programs and tours — to fill the expanded weeks. But there were unintended consequences; most expanded activities, apart from tours, involved under-rehearsed performances of less serious repertoire led by someone other than the music director, and these were not the meaningful artistic experiences orchestral musicians signed up for.

As a consequence, a plethora of time-off provisions have been bargained into contracts: those with pay such as vacation, leaves for personal reasons, parental leave, jury duty and sabbaticals at reduced pay; and also those without pay like "optional weeks" that players individually request. Creating this relief for musicians to recharge emotionally, musically and physically from the relentless year-round grind of expanded seasons is helpful. But it had the unintended consequence of requiring substitute musicians to fill critical positions vacated by those away, further diluting the artistic cohesion a year-round ensemble was meant to ensure. The result, despite generous compensation, benefits, job security and working conditions, was a paradox of widespread job dissatisfaction because of endless routine and variable artistic standards across myriad activities.

Orchestra labor relations today are dominated by classic we-they, deadline-driven adversarial bargaining. The process is based on dueling lists of self-interested demands. Negotiations are lengthy and often lead to an urgent crisis around a deadline, usually when the current agreement expires, that serves to stimulate the parties to resolve the most intractable disagreements. Every issue must be painstakingly negotiated and codified in the agreement, from the largest ques-

---

18 I personally heard the comment made during a 1971 labor negotiation session by longtime BSO bassist Leslie "Tiny" Martin. He was an immense character (both literally and figuratively), with both orchestra and union leadership experience and known for being a forceful advocate, practical problem-solver, and wry commentator on any subject.

tions of compensation levels to the smallest details of whether tuning on stage is considered to be before the concert or part of its defined length. The result is the need for long and complex agreements, which I wryly describe as inventories of compromises for ameliorating past transgressions. It is a practice honed over the years that has become ingrained in and defines institutional cultures of not just musicians but board and management as well.

In the 2000s, orchestras nationally took steps to improve stage demeanor, with most, including Cleveland, adopting the stunningly simple step of having the players turn and face the audience during ovations. Though not a radical change, it demonstrates how far orchestra culture had strayed from the common-sense goal of encouraging genuine contact with audiences across the footlights. Soon after leaving The Cleveland Orchestra, I attended a concert that concluded the first half with Ravel's Piano Concerto for the Left Hand. The audience stood and cheered the work's bravura conclusion. Noticing that the musicians did not turn to face the audience but stood glumly facing the conductor, I asked my successor why, since I knew of the new practice. He responded that the agreement made with the musicians required them to turn and face the audience only at the end of concerts and not at the end of individual pieces within a concert. There, in a nutshell, is everything wrong with the bargaining culture of orchestras.

Robert Mnookin, an expert in conflict resolution at the Harvard Law School, describes the behavior this traditional approach engenders, citing characteristics not normally associated with artistic institutions: viewing the other side as evil and the enemy, casting the other side as being at fault, seeing the process as a competition with only winners and losers, succumbing to inherent knee-jerk reactions, and mobilizing your side as being on a righteous mission.[19]

I question whether traditional adversarial collective bargaining is an appropriate and workable process for dealing with today's overwhelming financial, artistic and organizational crises. I doubt it. What is required is a pivot from the directional thinking that has informed the bargaining culture defining the relationship between the institution and the musicians.

Collective bargaining is an effective process for resolving conflicts, but it can be conducted in different ways. One alternative to adversarial bargaining is interest-based bargaining, in which the par-

---

19 Mnookin, Robert, *Bargaining With the Devil*, Simon & Schuster, 2010.

ties mutually identify each other's interests and work together to find common ground. The practice is loudly excoriated by unions. In the words of longtime union labor attorney Leonard Leibowitz: "Collective bargaining is by its very nature adversarial. And sad to say, it has to be. They have, we want, they don't want to give. That's adversarial. Adversaries in this sense don't have to be hostile or confrontational, but they must acknowledge that they are coming to the table with different, often opposite, interests."[20] But today, better artistic satisfaction and assuring a vital future are not opposite interests, and in light of the rapidly changing environment, they need to be at the center of orchestras' internal relationships.

Despite protestations, interest-based bargaining has been shown to work to positive effect — for example, at the San Francisco Symphony after a complete breakdown in relationships during a 10-week strike in 1997.[21] The poisonous atmosphere was so all-consuming that after the conflict was settled, both parties demanded a different approach. Mnookin was engaged to help: both parties' interests merged. His work started by understanding and addressing ways in which the culture had become so divided. He conducted workshops and fact-finding with each side over the next several years, leading to a different approach to bargaining, one built around common interests, for the next contract. And that negotiation was concluded six months ahead of the deadline, without rancor and expeditiously — proof that complete transformation of culture is possible if that is the shared goal of the parties.

It did not last. The parties reverted over time to old adversarial practices, largely because attention to nurturing the new culture waned and due to turnover of individuals involved in the prior process. A culture change was achieved around a crisis, but without continued attention and consistency of leadership, the new culture did not survive.

The pandemic shutdown experience is another example where parties put aside traditional practices to determine together how to maintain relationships with audiences in the absence of live concerts. Finding new ways of producing and delivering music digitally was quick, innovative, localized and the result of the parties coming to-

---

20 Leibowitz, Leonard, "Interest-Based Bargaining: In Whose Interest?" *Senza Sordino*, June 2001.
21 Mnookin, Robert, *Bargaining With the Devil*, Simon & Schuster, 2010.

gether to solve problems, bypassing the constraints of ingrained roles, contracts, traditions and behavior. The results were often remarkable, including experimentation with broader repertoire, programming structures, technology, performance formats and serving communities as never before. Gone were routine and self-interest. This breakthrough achievement around the shutdown demonstrated conclusively that with intense motivation and mutual goals, a constructive alternative to the traditional culture is possible.

It brings to mind Douglas Starr's recent article on "swarm intelligence," about how people can achieve common goals better by instinct than by planning.[22] Based on studies of how animals exhibit inherent ability to work together —birds flocking, ants building hills or fish schooling — the study extrapolated how people collaborate to solve problems in a time of crisis or shock. It postulated five elements that must exist if swarm intelligence is to become a driving force in behavior: unity of purpose, a spirit of generosity, staying in your lane, checking your ego at the door, and interpersonal trust and respect. In the shock of the shutdown, with the necessity of finding new solutions fast, institutional culture adjusted and unified around these five elements to bring about change. That is a lesson to learn from.

It is heartening to see some progress in restructuring labor agreements in a few orchestras, such as the Cincinnati Symphony, which achieved a breakthrough contract based on hours per week rather than services per week, allowing individual musician calls depending on the project. Key will be seeing whether this change permanently blends into the working culture or if the organization allows the status quo to reassert itself.

The orchestra world is in crisis today. The imperative is to build on the energy of collaborative problem-solving and use it to address systemic dysfunction — an effort that has been avoided for too long. This should not be the time to squander the opportunity for real change by sliding back into old culture, treating the shutdown as mere aberration or interruption. Unfortunately, this is already happening. It is discouraging to see union officials reverting to the old call-to-ramparts mentality by urging musicians to "turn back to the kinds of questions that have always been our bread and butter: how to file a grievance because the employer hired out of order or failed to

---

22 Starr, Douglas, "What Should Crisis Leadership Look Like?" *The New Yorker*, October 20, 2020.

pay overtime or suspended a musician; how to support our colleague enduring an artistic dismissal process; what to do when our employer tried to bargain electronic media with our local and committee rather than the Federation; and how to prepare for bargaining our next collective bargaining agreement."[23] How small-minded and petty this sounds in light of orchestras' urgent financial imbalance and the accumulation of critical unaddressed issues, both of which demand unity of purpose across constituencies.

A NEW MODEL

If the goal is to transform our orchestra institutions into the beacons of vitality they claim to be, such unity must replace the bunkered mentality of self-interests and be wholeheartedly embraced by the entire organization. All parties — board, musicians and management — share equal responsibility for both the current culture and the need to transform it. At stake is not contractual change but cultural change — and while change always takes time, cultural change takes longer. It is only possible with commitment to honest dialogue to define mutual goals, strong leadership, a willingness to work hard and take heat, and a commitment to pursue the new approach over time with constant behavioral reinforcement.

In the cold glare of the serious fiscal crisis facing orchestras and the realities of the changing artistic, social and philanthropic environments, finding underlying commonality of interests is not difficult. For example:

- Striving for transcendent musical experiences in each and every thing you do.
- Engendering community relevance in what you do, what you stand for, how you look and who you are.
- Renovating organizational culture to align around values and purpose, with an overarching goal of providing an enriching and satisfying work environment.
- Redefining the meaning of growth as "better, different and perhaps less," not just "more."
- Infusing the organization with the values of being demonstrably nimble, inherently flexible, perpetually adaptable and acceptably messy.

---

23 Skolnik, Rochelle, "Moving Forward in a Post-Pandemic World," *International Musician,* July 2022

- Concentrating on fewer and more varied concerts and events, making each one really matter.
- Embracing risk as essential, allocating sufficient resources to experimentation and innovation, and accepting occasional failure as the tolerable cost of success.

I am not naive as to the difficulties of such an approach. But I also know that continuing the current culture is doomed to failure. The result must be a new contractual structure and relationship. I dream about what possible new structures might look like:

- Musicians, currently untapped artistic resources, would be actively involved in artistic planning in partnership with the artistic director, helping to ensure that the institution is committed to the goal of enhancing artistic satisfaction.
- Orchestra musicians would join boards as full fiduciaries, not as glorified watchdogs as they currently are in so many institutions. As with any board member, musicians would recuse themselves from discussions in which they have a conflict of interest. The implications are far-reaching, as musicians are required to accept formal responsibility for the future of the institution, just as every fiduciary board member does.
- The compensation structure would become all-inclusive, with the base pay covering specified numbers of activities, including rehearsals and concerts, along with non-orchestral services like chamber music and outreach, which currently require extra pay. Also included would be streaming, broadcasting and recording as part of the basic agreement rather than subject to further negotiation with the parent union. Historically, power has shifted from the union and its locals to the orchestra musicians themselves — the ones who now negotiate and ratify the contracts. They have shown themselves capable of handling contractual matters themselves, including issues around electronic media. Simplification is overdue, and the collective with whom the institution deals should be its musicians.
- Weeks of guaranteed employment would be reduced, with a commitment of perhaps only 25 to 30 weeks. The goal would be fewer concerts of more varied types — orchestral, chamber

music, contemporary music, opera, education — to match more accurately the supply of product with demand. The artistic center of the season would be concentrated in these weeks, and musicians would be strongly discouraged from "opting out" with various leaves. The institution could provide the option of additional weeks of work not requiring services of the full orchestra (summer weeks, holiday and outreach events), for which musicians could "opt in" for additional pay.

- Musician job descriptions would be redefined to embrace the changing environment. The current audition system is mired in the mindset of simply playing the best. With the high quality of musicians coming through our excellent conservatories, there is no lack of great players. Finding exactly the right one for the right position in the right orchestra is the challenge, and it requires institutions knowing exactly what they are looking for. Hiring becomes more a *what* than a *who* question. Getting a job must be more than just nailing the traditional orchestral excerpts in an audition.

SOCIAL EQUITY

Orchestras must convince their communities that they matter. Given the perpetual quest for audiences and donors, the community must have authentic ownership of the institution. How does it serve the community's needs and not just its own? How does it diversify and belong to more than just its major donors, most of whom are likely similar in race and economic status? How does it demonstrate that it deserves widespread support? Harping on "excellence" is no longer sufficient to make the case for relevance. More critical will be what the orchestra does and how it looks in the broadest sense.

Though orchestras' gender diversity has improved over the last 50 years, progress in racial diversity has been slow and addressing it must be a priority. Orchestras have long demonstrated little commitment to diversity in the broadest sense in what they play, where they play and how they think. Many have begun to add music by under-represented composers to their programs, a step long overdue. While progress, it is far from adequate to the challenge. It is refreshing to hear unknown works by Florence Price, George Walker and Jessie Montgomery, but I can list hundreds of composers whose music also needs to be heard. Simply adding a few such pieces to a season's repertoire without fundamentally changing the masterworks' dominance of the default program template smacks of disingenuousness and seems like a checking-the-boxes solution. Such improvements, while welcome, are far from the systemic change necessary if these institutions are to make a meaningful case for being more diverse.

Altering the structure of artistic leadership, inviting a diverse range of artists into the central life of an orchestra, broadening and deepening programming and establishing broad community partnerships will amount to real change. Michael Morgan did this for years as music director of the Oakland Symphony. He and the orchestra were genuinely embedded in the community, and his goal of speaking directly to it was palpable in everything the orchestra did. And he began this in 1991, long before addressing social equity became fashionable. Delta David Gier at the South Dakota Symphony Orchestra is another example, fostering real leadership and programmatic partnerships with the Lakota Sioux nation. Teddy Abrams has changed the relationship between the Louisville Orchestra and its community by being an active part of its life far beyond just being the orchestra's music director. These smaller institutions, not strangled by size, tradition and bureaucracy, offer sobering lessons on what can be achieved.

Today, issues of racial and social equity have finally and rightfully become a dominant concern of orchestras, and the current focus has triggered long overdue public debate on hiring processes for musicians. *The New York Times* has advocated for the removal of audition screens and for more intentional hiring practices as a step toward fostering musician diversity, questioning exactly what steps to take to deal with a problem unanimously recognized at last.[24] A compelling idea comes from a group of diverse orchestra musicians who urged going well beyond the current audition process by redesigning hiring practices. The object is to directly recognize the need for enlarging hiring criteria beyond simply playing the best to having interest in continuing learning and development, musical curiosity and ability to engage audiences.[25] This makes total sense not only for addressing diversity but

24 Tommasini, Anthony, "To Make Orchestras More Diverse, End Blind Auditions," *The New York Times*, July 16, 2020.
25 Woolfe, Zachary, and Barone, Joshua, "Musicians on How to Bring Racial Equity to Auditions," *The New York Times*, September 10, 2020.

for identifying musicians with the broader skills needed to deal with a changing future.

Including musicians, staff and board members more racially and ethnically reflective of the community in which they exist gets to the heart of what institutions must be and how they must change. Diversifying boards is a task there is no excuse for avoiding. Diversifying management likewise is in the hands of the CEO. Diversifying orchestra members is more complicated, as it involves rethinking audition procedures and recruitment. But above all is making the issue an intentional priority. There is a long way to go.

THE BOARD

Having strong and consistent artistic leadership, enlivening the artistic product by changing the season structure, rethinking programming, and establishing relevance in the community are prerequisites to creating a vital future, but these cannot be achieved without an overarching commitment to remake the fundamental culture. Prime responsibility for this starts with the board. The primacy of the board in assuring success was drilled into my head during my post-Boston consulting and has been reinforced by everything I have done since. I have never found institutional problems that didn't ultimately originate with the board — a bad music director is a board problem, an ineffective chief executive is a board problem, anemic fundraising is a board problem, continuing financial distress is a board problem.

In the aftermath of Salonen's resignation from the San Francisco Symphony, the orchestra's board, in an unsigned statement,[26] blamed its lack of alignment with him on "serious financial circumstances." But who is responsible for the finances? Who allowed the bad financial results, which the board admitted had been occurring for ten years and well before Salonen arrived, to persist? Who hired Salonen and why didn't they understand what he wanted to do? Who was responsible for ensuring the right executive leadership was in place to support Salonen's innovative vision? Who was responsible for leading the necessary fundraising to make that vision a reality? The answer to all those questions is clear and simple — the board, which instead took the expedient path of blaming Salonen's departure entirely on finances. That is incorrect. The cause is a classic failure of board leadership and governance.

---

26 San Francisco Symphony Board, "Statement on San Francisco Symphony Organizational Context," March 25, 2024.

Squarely facing today's challenges is an essential board responsibility. To create effective change, boards need to step back and take stock, with whatever outside help is needed, to understand that the real crisis is not a financial but a cultural and artistic one. And this comes at a time when boards are facing their own challenges with the changing nature of community leadership. Individuals born, raised and living in single communities, with an innate stake in the quality of community life, have traditionally dominated orchestra boards. But the changing social and business landscape and an increasingly mobile work force have resulted in many community leaders who were not born and raised locally. Rather than traditional corporate chieftains, they are more often entrepreneurs, who are less comfortable with the deliberate and slow-moving processes of board governance. The results are boards that are more diffuse, more impatient and less rooted in the community.

Regardless, it is up to boards to set the tone and instill the drive for change. Hiring the right executive and artistic leaders is essential, but it is possible only for a board with unshaking commitment, coupled with strong continuity in its leadership, to sustain the hard work over time. This requires leadership tenures beyond a succession of revolving three-year-terms, as I found validated in Cleveland. It is up to the board to ensure open and constructive dialogue between artistic director, management, musicians and community, fostering a unity of purpose to face the brutal facts of reality. The way forward can be found only by galvanizing the institution around those unifying characteristics of swarm intelligence — unity of purpose, spirit of generosity, staying in your lane, checking egos, and interpersonal trust and respect.

I do not believe progress will come through coordinated actions across multiple institutions. Orchestras are essentially local businesses, each one in each community different. Given the industry's embedded culture of following the success of others, which I call the "lemming" principle, leading change is an opportunity for an individual orchestra with strong leadership, bold determination, extraordinary persistence, clear vision, sheer guts and total passion for the music to achieve breakthroughs. Their achievements will make them models for others to emulate.

INSTITUTIONS IN THE BROADER VIEW

The underlying challenge of how to overcome institutionalized inertia and to bring about change is not unique to orchestras. Institutions everywhere — governments, colleges, health care organizations — are accused of being out of touch with their basic purposes, strangled in bureaucratic mumbo-jumbo, and trapped in the belief that they exist not for the reasons they were created but for their own preservation. The insidious tendency of institutions' expanding bureaucracies to sap energy and initiative was eloquently foreseen in 1840 by Alexis de Tocqueville in his commentary on the emerging American government.[27] He described a bureaucracy that "does not break wills, but it softens them, bends them and directs them; it rarely forces action, but it constantly opposes your acting; it does not destroy, it prevents birth; it does not tyrannize, it hinders, it represses, it enervates, it extinguishes, it stupefies and finally it reduces each nation to being nothing more than a flock of timid and industrious animals, of which the government is the shepherd." Hardly an appropriate description for institutions that are supposed to be producing sublime musical experiences with visionary artists.

Orchestras today face unprecedented crises around relevance, audiences, money and music. The situation is no one's fault but rather a confluence of natural organizational tendencies, a long history of ingrained habits and a vastly changing environment. There is no alternative to addressing the challenge directly and bravely. History has shown that having the will to make change can work when there is intentional action and leadership. Where orchestras have a powerful advantage over other institutions is being able to unleash the power of music's transcendental magic to galvanize them towards a vital future.

I am energized by today's quantity and vitality of musical creativity, and I want to feel the same about the artistic, organizational and financial state of our institutions. The secret is to conjoin the two by transforming orchestras' very tightly coupled systems, inappropriate to today's world, into loosely coupled institutions that are flexible, innovative and grounded in artistic energy. It can be done. The pandemic shutdown has offered a glorious example of how different thinking, new approaches and brave ideas can work by accepting and

---

27 Tocqueville, Alexis de, *Democracy in America*, English Edition, edited by Eduardo Nolla and translated from the French by James T. Schleifer, Indianapolis: Liberty Fund, 2012.

embracing crisis as a unifying motivator of solutions. The crisis in orchestras today is even bigger and the opportunities far greater. Now is the time to rejuvenate the culture to make orchestras the true crucibles of musical creativity they must always be.

CHAPTER 12
THE ESSENTIAL TRUTH

My career ended up unexpectedly in a place vastly different from where it started. At first, I was driven towards a singular purpose: playing in and then managing the Boston Symphony. By age 34, I had achieved both. When running it lost luster, I was, at 41, in despair and felt my life focus slipping away. Thanks to the influence of key mentors, I discovered I was wrong about what I had thought were sound goals. More than a year of intense consulting provided a base of broader skills and perspectives, enabling me to return to orchestras — this time for all the right reasons, and resulting in a happy and productive period in Cleveland. Yet, years later, increasingly chafing under the rigid rules and negative culture consuming orchestras, I surprised myself by altering direction, embracing more nimble endeavors that finally provided deep satisfaction and clarity.

Today, in the context of a rapidly changing social, economic and musical environment, the future is far from settled as to what orchestras will do and at what scale, how they will be run, and how they will be financed. Much of this evolving context postdates my own time managing them. In many ways, my own disillusionment has mirrored the industry's own struggle for relevance. A key lesson for me was the need to switch gears, thrusting myself into totally new creative challenges. In the process, the artistic stimulation I have experienced since leaving orchestras has provided the key lessons for injecting vitality and relevance back into their world.

While concrete structural and operational steps are necessary to save orchestras from themselves, it is essential to identify and understand a bedrock of strategy to build upon. As such, I see four basic principles that capture the essence of what I have learned.

1. The Power of Creative Partnerships

I never lost my star-struck awe of composers, conductors and performers, but I know they all need producing partners to bring their art to audiences. My journey is a complicated amalgamation of my own aspirations with openness to collaborators, both individually and collectively. They all had significant influence and effect on me, but in different ways, at different times and at different speeds. Some — like Pierre Boulez, Ward Smith and Spring for Music — had immediate impact that led to substantial course correction and new thinking. Some — like Vic Firth, Oliver Knussen and Jim Collins — seeded key thoughts that gradually refined my views over time. Others — like Arthur Fiedler, John Williams, Christoph von Dohnányi and the Ojai Music Festival — were multi-year journeys of creative interaction and evolving learning. All such collaborations magically focused my fundamental need to create musical experiences for others.

Classical music is a curious and somewhat abstract art in which sounds and structure originating in the minds of composers are translated somewhat imperfectly — there is no way to write down the precise intentions of sound, line, balance and color — onto paper through graphic symbols called notation. It takes a performer to retranslate those symbols back into sounds, a process known as interpretation. It is the function of the presenter to translate music into impact by linking sound and listener through performance. And the sound remains without meaning unless listeners are assembled to receive it, a process known as experience.

That impact can be affected by multiple factors under the control of the presenter: artists, pieces, programming, context, venue, setting and production. How audiences respond is driven by the communicative power of the total presentation, not the music's presupposed "accessibility" or "familiarity."

In Ojai, I once asked a prominent member of the community whether he attended the festival. While saying it was really important for the town, he admitted never going because he did not like "that kind of music," launching into a tirade on the unfriendliness of modern music. Upon being pressed, he finally confessed to attending "one wonderful event in Libbey Park in which performers moved about the space while playing, with the audience walking through and around them." He called the experience "energizing." He was talking about the 2012 performance of John Luther Adams' *Inuksuit*. I responded with confusion, since the piece was "that kind of music." He answered that the specifics of the music really didn't matter in this case, saying it was the whole concept and how it was presented that touched him. My point exactly.

Achieving these moments starts with the creative partnership between presenter and artist. My success at this, refined over five decades, has been based on three traits embedded in my DNA which I thank my mentors for nurturing: *curiosity* for and knowledge of music, *imagination* in constructing musical events, and *exuberance* in doing so — enthusiasm is infectious! These characteristics enabled me to establish with artists something essential: trust, the foundation of mutually productive collaborations in which creative energy flows in both directions. Barbara Hannigan describes such interaction as requiring both parties to be "worthy adversaries" in the most positive and respectful sense of the term. Without mutual trust, partnerships cannot survive the necessary sparring.

This book is my first endeavor not built around that kind of collaboration. Working alone on it is not something my experiences had prepared me for, and the process has made me appreciate even more the joy and energy that the incessant back-and-forth of all the creative partnerships that came before had provided.

2. The Meaning of Strong Leadership

Presenting musical events cannot exist in a vacuum: some organizational infrastructure is essential. But the complexity and ponderousness of organizing such events can become real challenges, particularly in relationship to the messy but vibrant world of creativity around them. I have learned that addressing this paradox takes sustained commitment over time, patience, courage and above all strong leadership.

That term is a constant refrain running through this book. Without it, the best intentions and ideas come to naught. Exercising it unwisely neuters its impact. Lack of clarity muzzles its effectiveness. But what does leadership mean?

Strong leadership is so often misunderstood, equated with authoritarian behavior and the raw exercise of power. It is a complicated concept to understand and apply, and I find it helpful to differentiate between its *substance* — the principles embedded in *what* to do — and its *style* — the principles of *how* to exercise it.

The *substance* of leadership is about creating intentional direction, upholding standards and embodying values. Effective leaders make things happen while setting standards for beliefs and behavior, being the final arbiters of when things are not good enough. This is the *sine qua non* of success, and it has never been more necessary than in today's dynamic and complicated environment. In this deadline-driven presenting world, leaders must ensure decisions are made on a timely basis. This means having to finally say yes or no; there is no room for endless procrastination given the inevitability of the next concert.

The *style* of leadership is grounded in persuasion and enthusiasm. A leader must empower followers through inspirational ideas and vision, with clearly stated goals and outcomes to which all can aspire, and then bring them along for the journey. This is hard, as it moves individuals and organizations away from assumed comfort zones and into realms of reasonable vulnerability. In my experience, there is no greater principle in exercising leadership than keeping it simple. The world is complex, and considerations involved in solving problems are daunting. The trick is to strive towards the heart of an issue and strip away the irrelevant and unnecessary complications; this allows framing questions clearly for others by inspiring direction.

Vic Firth understood this principle when playing timpani, and he understood it in his successful drumstick business. His words resonated in an interview upon his retirement from the Boston Symphony:[1] "Either the world is going to end, or it's not. If it's going to end, there's nothing to worry about. If it's not, then we need to focus on seeing opportunities that arise in times of crisis. Without risk, there is a danger of no growth. Without growth, you are taking the ultimate risk of relying solely on luck. The strategy for surviving any downturn is not complicated. You have to make a recommitment to your core product and your branded image."

Simple, clear and inspiring.

3. The Necessity of Outside Perspective

My mindset in Boston, given my lack of experience, was very one-dimensional. It was only after working as a consultant that I was able to

---

1 Interview conducted in 2008 by Pat Hollenbeck, president of the Boston Musicians' Association.

broaden my views on governance, planning and strategies, and that gave me the tools to approach the Cleveland job differently. For my own stimulation and to add context to my work, I vowed to keep one foot firmly anchored outside the city. I believed this was particularly critical when running what was a community icon with national and international brand distinction. It distinctly colored my approach to the job and what I was able to accomplish, forcing me away from the habit of viewing the institution only in the context of its own past and community.

And it was precisely the ever-expanding perspectives I insisted upon that finally disillusioned me with orchestras, leading me to the Ojai Music Festival. To my surprise, those 16 years became in themselves an escalating chain of ever-broader adventures; the different annual music directors with whom I collaborated created a self-reinforcing flywheel of learning. Today, it is precisely the accumulation of all these expanded viewpoints that allows me to see the predicaments of institutions more clearly.

In a 2011 op-ed in *The New York Times*, David Brooks gave advice to college graduates: "Today's graduates are told to find their passion and then pursue their dreams. ... Most people don't form a self and then lead a life. They are called by a problem, and the self is constructed gradually by their calling. ... Life comes to a point only in those moments when the self dissolves into some task. The purpose of life is not to find yourself. It's to lose yourself."[2]

Once I accepted losing myself, my journey after Boston became an ongoing search for what really drove me. I realized it was not power, scale, or fame, but rather working with artists to produce events that, in addition to exciting me, would instill strong reactions in others. My career has been one continual journey towards that goal, with a logical, cumulative process of "losing myself" in opportunities I took. Yet that journey was always narrowing toward a focal point — a progression from power to influence, from span to focus, from doing to inventing, and from surface to substance. Most important, it brought an increasing realization of the absolute need for happiness in my work.

---

2 Brooks, David, "It's Not About You," *The New York Times*, May 30, 2011.

THE ESSENTIAL TRUTH

Music provides me with joy, inspiration, comfort and pure pleasure. I am fortunate to have devoted my life to sharing that passion with others. It has provided me the entry point for successfully leading organizations and presenting events. It is what motivates involvement, it is what inspires support, it is what creates connection and it is what provides nourishment. Having the right marketing, financial plan, pricing and audience engagement strategies are necessary but far from sufficient to spark the magic alchemy, that combustible connection which links content and audience. Whether in painting, music, theater, dance or literature, the art must be at the core of igniting that connection.

My life has revolved around sharing my own infatuation. It has been music that has enthralled and driven me all these years. It is the foundation of everything I have done. But what is it about live music that has such power and meaning?

In 2003, I attended the graduation ceremony of our youngest son from Cleveland's Case Western Reserve Medical School. It was especially meaningful that the event took place at Severance Hall and his diploma was being presented by his older brother, also a Case Medical School graduate. The speaker was Dr. Julie Gerberding, then the head of the Centers for Disease Control and Prevention. In her remarks, Dr. Gerberding outlined what she considered the most meaningful keys to success for a doctor:

> What do people think of when they think of a doctor? The stethoscope. The stethoscope was invented in 1819, and it really represented the first technology of the very first medical instrument. Today, some find the stethoscope archaic. After all you can get an echocardiogram, an abdominal CT, a chest CT or an ultrasound. So why bother with the stethoscope? Because it is the last remaining personal tool that we as physicians have. In order to use the stethoscope, you first of all have to be there — in person. Second, you cannot use the stethoscope if you are not quiet. Third, you have to touch the patient — you cannot use it from across the room. Finally, and most important, you have to listen … The stethoscope is a wonderful metaphor for the most

important message in medicine — the importance of empathy. The patient wants to be touched. The patient wants you to be present. The patient wants you to listen … The stethoscope is not just a tool for listening to the heart, it is a tool for listening to the patient.

This was an "aha" moment for me. The stethoscope is like the live concert. It provides the link between the listener and the music. It is kind of archaic. You have to be there and not in another room to experience it. You have to be still. You must take the necessary time to listen. And you have to concentrate. Why? Because music is alive, it demands that you be present, it requires you to listen, and it wants to touch you.

That is the magic.

And that is why we are thrilled by great live performances. That is why electronic dissemination can never be a totally acceptable substitute. That is why we need these exceptional composers, performers and concert spaces to bring it alive. And that is why I love instilling my own passion for music in others by creating events that are exciting, unpredictable and moving.

This has been a journey of extraordinary challenge and continuous learning. In the simplest terms, I have been joyfully devoted to the music I want to hear, with the artists I love and under the circumstances I create. This makes me the luckiest person alive. I have had the very best seat in the house — whether at Boston's Symphony Hall, Cleveland's Severance Hall, New York's Carnegie Hall, Ojai's Libbey Bowl, sitting with Patricia Kopatchinskaja in her house making programs, playing percussion in the Blossom Festival Band or on the bench in front of my grandfather's player pipe organ so many years ago. It has always been about the music.

ACKNOWLEDGMENTS

This book revolves around what I have learned from extraordinary mentors, collaborators and friends. Deciding on the individuals around whom chapters one through eight are centered (Vic Firth, Arthur Fielder, Oliver Knussen, John Williams, Pierre Boulez, Ward Smith, Christoph von Dohnányi and Jim Collins) was fairly easy because each had such profoundly pivotal and sustained effects on me. What concerned me was creating the impression that these were the only individuals to play significant roles in my life. That is not the case and there are many others, most of whom are mentioned throughout the book. Without them my story would not be what it is.

Growing up in Rochester, my early love of music, nurtured primarily by my grandfather, confounded my parents. However, they were totally supportive, whether in indulging me with drum lessons, sound-proofing my room to ameliorate the deafening sounds emanating from within, buying me countless percussion instruments or attending many concerts. Their continuing curiosity about my passion lasted throughout their lives and I am forever grateful for their genuine, if often perplexed, embrace of my chosen journey.

Thanks to them, I had years of lessons with the masterful William Street at the Eastman School. He whetted my growing appetite for music as I spent hours in his cigar-smoke-drenched studio on Eastman's second floor, being coached on endless snare drum rudiments and marimba exercises and being thoroughly entranced by the colorful stories of his vaudeville beginnings. He was not only a great teacher but showed me the pure joy of being a musician.

At Princeton, while I was clearly out of step with the Schenkerian-analysis mentality of its music department, I am thankful for Robert Freeman, a young professor who was my senior advisor, for his wise counsel that there was a path other than performing – orchestra management – through which I could serve music. Bob's own musicological career took a radical turn soon after I left college when he was appointed director of the Eastman School. In curious symmetry, the job meant living in my grandparents' house, which that they had bequeathed to the school as the director's home. He remained an encouraging cheerleader until his death in 2022.

During my BSO years, I can never forget the early mentoring by James J. Brosnahan ("Mr. B."), my first boss, and BSO horn player and assistant personnel manager Harry Shapiro. They were generous in their perspectives and endless in their stories, and it is through the two of them that I received a serious post-graduate education in orchestra management. Thomas D. "Tod" Perry, Boston's manager who hired me, was always encouraging and I am grateful for his opening up new opportunities for growth within the BSO. Also crucial in my Boston years was Colin Davis, who served as Principal Guest Conductor in the 1970s. It was Colin who took me under his wing and tutored me in programming. He was a tireless advocate for particular composers, such as Michael Tippett and Hector Berlioz. I will never forget a train ride together from Washington to New York on which he literally taught me Beethoven's *Missa Solemnis* bar-by-bar as we followed the score listening on headphones, to the consternation of the other passengers because of Colin's uncontrollable gestures and loud singing. It was his sage advice that proved critical in my accepting the Cleveland offer.

A constant throughout my Boston years, and to this day, has been television producer/director Bill Cosel, with whom I worked on *Evening at Pops*, an astonishing experience that brought me into Arthur Fiedler's sphere and allowed me to have a big impact on the august BSO very early. Bill is incredibly creative, talented, and funny. His impressions of everyone still keep me in stitches, although the one I have never seen him do is me. He was one of the first urging me to write this book, and throughout its gestation has been an invaluable reader of and constant enthusiast for the evolving manuscript.

My years with The Cleveland Orchestra were incredibly happy and productive. Beyond the seminal partnerships I had with Christoph von Dohnányi and Ward Smith, there was of course Pierre Boulez,

ACKNOWLEDGMENTS

who loomed large in those years, having been a critical factor in rejuvenating my enthusiasm for institutions. And I am thankful for the deep friendship of pianist Mitsuko Uchida, a sublime artist who was totally fixated on the purest and highest of musical values and who was always supportive of my most outrageous ideas. Also, Ward Smith's two successors as board chairs, Dick Bogomolny and Jamie Ireland, cannot be overlooked. With Ward, they epitomized what great board leaders should be, and they spoiled me.

And of course, there is Franz Welser-Möst, Dohnányi's successor. Franz and I developed a close relationship during his years as guest conductor, and I consider bringing him to Cleveland one of my finest achievements. While we unfortunately did not work together for long after his appointment, I am eternally grateful for his superb musicianship and ongoing friendship. It has been intensely gratifying to watch his enormous success over what will be the longest tenure of any Cleveland music director. He has kept the orchestra the envy of all.

I always loved building teams and I had great ones in Cleveland. They are all too numerous to mention but I must single out Gary Hanson, my first major hire, who worked closely with me throughout my Cleveland tenure. Also there were orchestra managers NancyBell Coe and Jonathan Martin, chief financial officer Jim Menger, development director Pat Wahlen and artistic administrators Roger Wright and Nancy Chalifour. Hanson was to be my successor. Coe, Martin, Wright and Chalifour went on to stellar careers elsewhere, while Wahlen retired. Menger is still with the orchestra.

In Cleveland, I benefited greatly from the friendship of Bob Bergman, director of the Cleveland Museum of Art, for what was a tragically short period due to his untimely death. It was during those years that I met Daniel R. Lewis, a major benefactor of The Cleveland Orchestra who went on to lead the board and be a major supporter of Spring for Music. Dan remains a close friend and has never stopped being an enthusiastic supporter of my many endeavors. Also, it was during those years that I met Minneapolis lawyer and civic leader Lowell Noteboom. Lowell knows more about governance than anyone I know, and we taught numerous seminars together. It was in Cleveland that I appointed Loras Schissel as conductor of the Blossom Festival Band, in which I have happily played since 2002. Loras is a musical force of nature, who, in addition to being a marvelous conductor, knows more about American music and musicians than anyone I have ever met.

Above all in Cleveland was Rosemary Klena, who served as my assistant throughout my tenure. She served my predecessor and, after my retirement, two of my successors. She was the institutional memory of the orchestra. Her thorough professionalism and good cheer were unbeatable and I simply could not have survived without her. And we laughed together a lot.

Throughout my years in Boston and Cleveland, I was fortunate to work with and be close friends with giants in the field of orchestra management: Deborah Borda of the New York and Los Angeles Philharmonics, Bruce Coppock of the St. Louis Symphony and St. Paul Chamber Orchestra, John Edwards of the Chicago Symphony, Ernest Fleischmann of the Los Angeles Philharmonic and my predecessor in Ojai, Henry Fogel of the Chicago Symphony, Kenneth Haas of Cleveland (my predecessor) and Boston (my successor), David Hyslop of the Minnesota Orchestra, Carlos Moseley of the New York Philharmonic, Peter Pastreich of the St. Louis and San Francisco Symphonies, Seymour Rosen of the Pittsburgh Symphony and Philadelphia Orchestra, Stephen Sell of the Philadelphia Orchestra, Chad Smith of the Los Angeles Philharmonic and now the Boston Symphony (and very briefly my successor in Ojai), and Nick Webster of the New York Philharmonic. I will be forever grateful for their sage counsel and encouragement. Also, I am thankful for Robert Harth of the Aspen Music Festival & School and Carnegie Hall; Ara Guzelimian, also of Aspen, Carnegie and The Juilliard School and now my successor in Ojai; Matias Tarnopolsky of Cal Performances in Berkeley and now The Philadelphia Orchestra; John Drummond of the Edinburgh Festival and BBC; and Roger Wright, who, after working with me in Cleveland, ran Deustche Grammophon, BBC Radio 3 and the Aldeburgh Festival.

As outlined in the book, the Spring for Music festival was revelatory not only in the project itself but in how we managed it virtually. Central were my two partners, Mary Lou Falcone and David Foster, and together we formed a triumvirate that functioned as one because of our personal and professional chemistry around a project we deeply believed in. But there was also the incredible team we put together that demonstrated the power of a virtual organization without hierarchy but based purely on high competencies around a shared vision: Amanda Ameer, Cage Ames, Elaine Martone, Douglas McLennan and Christopher Stager.

Ojai was an astonishing adventure of 16 successive creative partnerships – Kent Nagano, Oliver Knussen, Robert Spano, Pierre-Laurent Aimard, David Robertson, Eighth Blackbird, George Benjamin, Dawn Upshaw, Leif Ove Andsnes, Mark Morris, Jeremy Denk, Steven Schick, Peter Sellars, Vijay Iyer, Patricia Kopatchinskaja and Barbara Hannigan. But whatever success I had was also due to many extraordinary people behind the scenes. They are too numerous to mention but I must single out Elaine Martone, who so superbly served as festival producer for a majority of those years (as well as being involved in Spring for Music), and Gina Gutierrez, who was marketing director when I arrived, serving ably in that role throughout my tenure, and who remains as managing director. Gina has been, and is, the heart and soul of the Ojai Music Festival.

My timing in retiring from Ojai in summer 2019 proved prescient for many reasons; it was time to move on, there were other things I wanted to do and, of course, there was the pandemic. As I figured out what to do next, I am mindful of the counsel I got from many friends that I should write this book. I had always rejected this idea with the excuses that I did not have the time and discipline or that I did not know how to go about it. With the pandemic shutdown, my perspectives changed and here we are. I am mindful of the sage and persistent encouragement for this project I got from beginning from Bill Cosel, Jim Collins, John Williams, Michael Gorfaine (Hollywood music agent and Williams' manager) and Barbara Hannigan. And I must single out a close friend over the years in Ojai, John Russell. A retired businessman, John was not active in the Festival but became a treasured friend. I always benefited from his quiet wisdom and gentle smile at our regular breakfasts at the ever-distinctive Bonnie Lu's Café. John never lost an opportunity to urge me to write something, and he has been an encouraging force over the past four years as the book was born.

Essential in any writing project is having critical readers, friends who are willing to take the time to read the evolving manuscript and provide frank and direct feedback: Barbara Barry, Bruce Coppock,

Robert Duvin, Ara Guzelimian, Sarah Harding, Steven Litt, Elaine Martone, Douglas McLennan, Lowell Noteboom, Barrett Rollins, Michael Sachs, Nikki Scandalios, Loras Schissel, E. B. Smith, Seldy Cramer Speers, Christopher Stager, Mark Swed, Jeremy Turner, Elizabeth Warshawer, John Williams and Zachary Woolfe.

I must thank Bridget Carr, archivist of the Boston Symphony for helping to research several matters relating to my Boston years, and Andria Hoy, archivist of The Cleveland Orchestra. Thanks also to James Oestreich for his amazingly precise editing help early in the process. His attention to detail took my breath away as he gave me the crash course in punctuation and writing style that I desperately needed. Helping out in the final copy editing has been the amazing Matthew Westphal, from whom I have learned tons. I never cease to be amazed that however clean I thought the manuscript was, there were always errors to fix. Bless Jim and Matthew for their patience and persistence.

Christopher Stager, with whom I worked at The Cleveland Orchestra and on Spring for Music, graciously produced the audio version of this book. Chris's incessant enthusiasm for music, his impeccable ability in marketing and his irrepressible sense of humor have always made us soul brothers. He is the only person with whom I can knowledgeably discuss the pros and cons of Eugene Ormandy's multitudinous recordings of Tchaikovsky's "Pathétique" Symphony.

Throughout the whole project, Barbara Hannigan has been a constant cheerleader at every step. Our incredible collaboration in Ojai 2019 has led to a most enduring friendship — we talk incessantly about the state of the music world, programs she is going to conduct and our latest musical fixations. Her deep artistry, unshakable discipline and sense of adventure always inspire me profoundly. I am thrilled and touched by her writing such a generous foreword for this book.

Key in this project has been my agent, Simon Green. Simon worked tirelessly with me over the years, not only in guiding the book to publication but more importantly in helping me shape what was initially a naive and disjointed manuscript into a much more compelling narrative. I could not have done this without him. And heartfelt thanks to the late publisher/author/critic, Stephen Rubin, whom I met during the writing process and who became an early and loud cheerleader. I just wish he had lived long enough to see the book's publication. And to Greg Donley for his beautiful design of the final book.

Finally, immense gratitude to my friend and colleague, Douglas McLennan. I first met Doug when he was covering one of my vision seminars as a journalist in the early 2000s. We became fast friends, and we worked together professionally on both Spring for Music and the Ojai Music Festival. His unceasing friendship and guidance during the last phases of this project have simply been invaluable in bringing it to the light of day.

Above all, I thank my family for putting up with my obsession with music for all these years – Elisa and Christopher; Charles, Tia, Austen and Silas; and Will, Keira, Holden and Haley. They are all the joy of my life and keep me perpetually humble.

And Basil, our cat, who unexpectedly walked into our lives as this project was born, and who provided constant reassurance.

And finally to Jane, my life partner for almost 60 years, who really had to endure the brunt of this journey with me. She was always by my side, always encouraging, always helpful and always with good cheer and a warm smile. Everyone should be so lucky.

IMAGE CREDITS

M. Herbert Eisenhart, aka "Bapop," page 3
Morris Family Archives

At age 3, when it all started, page 4
Morris Family Archives

Performing Milhaud's Percussion Concerto in 1961, page 5
Morris Family Archives

Vic Firth in the Boston Pops in 1957, page 17
Photo by Boris & Milton, courtesy of BSO Archives

BSO percussionists Charlie Smith, Tommy Thompson and Vic Firth in Bruckner's Symphony No. 8 in 1962, page 19
Morris screen shot from television show by WGBH Educational Foundation

Playing with the BSO in Lou Harrison's Canticle No. 3 with Arthur Press and Charlie Smith, page 25
Photographer unknown, courtesy of BSO Archives

Performing Leroy Anderson's The Typewriter *at the Pops in 1979*, page 26
Photographer unknown, courtesy of BSO Archives

In action with the Blossom Festival Band in 2004, page 29
Photo by Roger Mastroianni, courtesy of The Cleveland Orchestra Archives

Me and James J. Brosnahan in 1971, page 32
Photo by Heinz Weissenstein, Whitestone Photo, courtesy of BSO Archives

Arthur Fiedler, page 39
Photographer unknown, courtesy of BSO Archives

Fiedler at Tanglewood with one of the 1812 Overture *cannons — the pose was his idea*, page 49
Photo by Heinz Weissenstein, Whitestone Photo, courtesy of BSO Archives

A collision of musical constellations: Erich Leinsdorf greeting Janis Joplin at Tanglewood in July 1969, page 58
Photo by Heinz Weissenstein, Whitestone Photo, courtesy of BSO Archives

Maurice Sendak with Oliver Knussen in 1984 at Glyndebourne, page 63
Photo by Guy Gravett, ©Glyndebourne Productions ltd/ArenaPAL

Knussen at home demonstrating his toys, including the train clock I gave him, page 66
Morris screen shot from "Sounds from the Big White House," 2001 independent film by Barrie Gavin

The Powers of Two, page 169
Photographer unknown, Morris Family Archives

Random Buzzword Generator, page 173
Morris Family Archives

Jim Collins, page 174
Courtesy of Jim Collins

Cleveland Orchestra Vision Statement, page 177
Morris Family Archives

The Trio: me, Mary Lou Falcone and David Foster, page 191
Morris Family Archives

Waving the scarves at Carnegie Hall, page 198
Photo by Steve Sherman, ©Steve Sherman

Ojai's "new" Libby Bowl, page 220
Photo by Timothy Norris, Courtesy of Ojai Music Festival Archives

Strange and Sacred Noise on a hilltop with John Luther Adams in foreground,
page 223
Photo by Rosie Grimm, courtesy of Ojai Music Festival Archives

Clown noses image, page 224
Photo by Timothy Norris, Courtesy of Ojai Music Festival Archives

The 2017 Concert: George Lewis, Roscoe Mitchell and Muhal Richard Abrams,
page 231
Photo by Tina Tallon, Courtesy of Ojai Music Festival Archives

Ojai Music Festival Flywheel, page 239
Morris Family Archives, Courtesy of Jim Collins

Jacket photo of the author by Michael Weil, PhD

BIBLIOGRAPHY

BOOKS

Bennis, Warren, *On Becoming a Leader*, Addison Wesley Publishing Company, 1989.

Bennis, Warren and Nanus, Burt, *Leaders*, Collins Business Essentials (formerly HarperCollins), 1985, rev 2003.

Collins, Jim, *Good to Great: Why Some Companies Make the Leap...and Others Don't*, HarperBusiness, 2001.

Collins, Jim, *Good to Great for the Social Sector*, Jim Collins, 2005.

Collins, Jim, *Great by Choice*, HarperBusiness, 2011.

Collins, Jim, *Why the Mighty Fall*, HarperCollins, 2009.

Collins, Jim, *Turning the Flywheel*, HarperCollins, 2019.

Collins, Jim and Porras, Jerry I., *Built to Last: Successful Habits of Visionary Companies*, HarperBusiness, 1994.

Fiedler, Johanna, *Papa, the Pops and Me*, Doubleday, 1994.

Flannigan, Robert J., *The Perilous Life of Symphony Orchestras*, Yale University Press, 2012.

Frank, Mortimer, *Arturo Toscanini: The NBC Years*, Amadeus Press, 2002.

Galloway, Scott, *Post Corona: From Crisis to Opportunity*, Portfolio/Penguin, 2020.

Holoman, D. Kern, *Charles Munch*, Oxford University Press, 2015.

Kaiser, Michael, *Curtains? The Future of Arts on America*, Brandeis University Press, 2015.

Kaiser, Michael, *The Art of the Turnaround*, Brandeis University Press, 2008.

Leinsdorf, Erich, *Cadenza: A Musical Career,* Simon and Shuster, 2010.

Lewis, George, *A Power Stronger Than Itself: The AACM and American Experimental Music*, University of Chicago Press, 2008.

Mnookin, Robert *Bargaining with The Devil,* Simon and Shuster, 2010.

Moore, Robin, *Fiedler: The Colorful Mr. Pops - The Man and His Music,* Little, Brown and Company, 1968.

Schuller, Gunther, *Musings,* Oxford University Press, 1986.

Shenk, Joshua Wolf, *Powers of Two: Finding the Essence of Innovation in Creative Pairs,* Houghton Mifflin, 2014.

Tilson Thomas, Michael, *Viva Voce! Conversations with Edward Seckerson*, Faber & Faber, 1994.

Tocqueville, Alexis de, *Democracy in America* English Edition, edited by Eduardo Nolla and translated from the French by James T. Schleifer, Indianapolis: Liberty Fund, 2012.

Waleson, Heidi, *Mad Scenes and Exit Arias,* Metropolitan Books/Harold Holt and Co., 2018.

Zaleznik, Abraham, *The Managerial Mystique*, Harper and Row Publishing Company, 1989.

Various authors, *Symphony Hall: The First 100 Years*, Boston Symphony Orchestra, Inc., 2000.

ARTICLES

Bernheimer, Martin, "Previn Wanted to Run the Philharmonic - So Does Fleischmann," *Los Angeles Times*, April 26, 1989.

Brooks, David, "It's Not About You," *The New York Times*, May 30, 2011.

Chinen, Nate, "50 Years On: Association for Advancement of Creative Musicians Influences Jazz," *The New York Times*, March 16, 2015.

Collins, Jim, "Building Your Company's Vision," *Harvard Business Review*, September/October 1996.

Davidson, Justin, "The New Geffen Hall Is Here: How Does it Sound?," *Vulture,* October 8, 2022.

Dyer, Richard, "Vic is the Ultimate Stick Figure," *The Boston Globe*, June 16, 2002.

Dyer, Richard, "It's Not Happening at the BSO," *The Boston Globe*, May 6, 1979.

Dyer, Richard, "Who'll Lead The Pops?," *The Boston Globe*, October 14, 1979.

Dyer, Richard, "Mix Design and Mystery: You Get a Pops Maestro," *The Boston Globe*, January 17, 1980.

Dyer, Richard, "John Williams Is New Pops Maestro," *The Boston Globe*, January 11, 1980.

Dyer, Richard, "A Thorough Musician," *The Boston Globe*, January 11, 1980.

Dyer, Richard, "Sounds of a New Era: Bravos All Around," *The Boston Globe*, January 22, 1980.

Dyer, Richard, "Williams Passes with Flying Colors," *The Boston Globe*, January 22, 1980.

Fennell, Frederick, "Percussion Procedures," personal files, undated.

Gavin, Barrie, "Oliver Knussen: Sounds from the Big White House," BBC Television film, 2001.

Hernández, Javier, "San Francisco Symphony's Maestro to Step Down, Citing Split with Board," *The New York Times*, March 14, 2024.

Iyer, Vijay, "Our Complicity with Excess," Yale Asian-American Alumni Symposium, May 7, 2014.

Leibowitz, Leonard, "Interest-Based Bargaining: In Whose Interest?," *Senza Sordino*, June 2001.

Mattingly, Rock, "Vic Firth: Beyond the Classical Stereotype," *Modern Drummer*, June 1982.

Morris, Thomas W., "Artistic Vision: True Meaning or Empty Slogan?," *Symphony Magazine*, October/November 2006.

Pareles, John, "Conscience of a Composer," *The New York Times*, December 19, 2014.

Pfeifer, Ellen, "Philly Pops1980's Style: Can Peter Nero Give Boston a Run for its Money?," *Boston Herald American*, November 12, 1979.

Pfeifer, Ellen, "From Star Wars to Boston Pops," *Boston Herald American*, January 5, 1980.

Rockwell, John, "Traditionalist for the Pops," *The New York Times*, January 11, 1980.

Ross, Alex, "Mix and Match: Spring for Music at Carnegie Hall," *The New Yorker*, June 6, 2011.

Ross, Alex, "Outsiders," *The New Yorker*, July 6, 2015.

Rubin, Stephen E., "The Iceberg Conducteth," *The New York Times Magazine*, March 3, 1973.

San Francisco Symphony Board: "Statement on San Francisco Symphony Organizational Context," unsigned public statement, March 25, 2024.

Schuller, Gunther, "Tanglewood Music Center Opening Exercises Speech," BSO Archives, June 24, 1979.

Service, Tom, "I Had to Write It," *The Guardian*, October19, 2006.

Skolnik, Rochelle, "Moving Forward in a Post-Pandemic World," *International Musician*, July 2020.

Starr, Frederick, "Symphony Orchestras: How did we get here?," *Harmony Magazine*, 1997.

Starr, Douglas, "What Should Crisis Leadership Look Like?," *The New Yorker*, October 20, 2020.

Swed, Mark, "How Thomas Morris Brought the Ojai Music Festival to the Big Time," *Los Angeles Times*, May 31, 2019.

Tommasini, Anthony, "Esa-Pekka Salonen Says Tweak the Orchestra, Don't Blow it Up," *The New York Times*, March 19, 2019.

Tommasini, Anthony, "To Make Orchestras More Diverse, End Blind Auditions," *The New York Times*, July 16, 2020.

Walsh, Michael, "The Finest Orchestra? (Surprise?)," *Time Magazine*, January 10, 1994.

Weick, Karl, "Educational Organizations as Loosely Coupled Systems," *Administrative Science Quarterly,* March 1976.

Weick, Karl and Orton, Douglas, "Loosely Coupled Systems: A Reconceptualization," *Academy of Management Review*, April 1990.

Wichterman, Catherine, "The Orchestra Forum: A Discussion of Symphony Orchestras in the U.S.," *The Andrew W. Mellon Foundation*, November 23, 1998.

Woolfe, Zachary, "Ojai Will Never Be The Same, Thanks to His Musical Imagination," *The New York Times*, June 5, 2019.

Woolfe, Zachary and Barone, Joshua, "Musicians on How to Bring Racial Equity to Auditions," *The New York Times*, September 10, 2020.

Zaleznik, Abraham, "Managers and Leaders: Are they Different?," *Harvard Business Review*, May/June, 1977.

INDEX OF NAMES